PLANNING THE FAMILY IN EGYPT

Modern Middle East Series, Number 21
Sponsored by the Center for Middle Eastern Studies
The University of Texas at Austin

Planning the Family in Egypt | *New Bodies, New Selves*

KAMRAN ASDAR ALI

UNIVERSITY OF TEXAS PRESS
Austin

Portions of chapter 7 were published as "Making 'Responsible' Men: Planning the Family in Egypt," in Caroline Bledsoe et al., eds., *Fertility and the Male Life-Cycle in the Era of Fertility Decline* (Oxford: Oxford University Press, 2000). Reprinted by permission of Oxford University Press.

Requests for permission to reproduce material from this work should be sent to Permissions, University of Texas Press, P.O. Box 7819, Austin, TX 78713-7819.

⊗ The paper used in this book meets the minimum requirements of
ANSI/NISO Z39.48-1992 (R1997) (Permanence of Paper).

LIBRARY OF CONGRESS CATALOGING-IN-PUBLICATION DATA

Ali, Kamran Asdar, 1961–
  Planning the family in Egypt : new bodies, new selves / Kamran Asdar Ali.— 1st ed.
      p.   cm. — (Modern Middle East series ; no. 21)
Portions of chapter 7 were published as "Making 'Responsible' Men : planning the Family in Egypt," in Caroline Bledsoe et al., eds., "Fertility and the Male Life-Cycle in the Era of Fertility Decline." Includes bibliographical references and index.
    ISBN 0-292-70513-1 (cloth : alk. paper) — ISBN 0-292-70514-x (pbk. : alk. paper)
    1. Birth control—Egypt.   2. Demographic transition—Egypt.   I. Fertility and the male life-cycle in the era of fertility decline.   II. Title.   III. Modern Middle East series (Austin, Tex.) ; no. 21.
    HQ766.5.E3 A45   2002
    363.9'6'0962—dc21   2002001053

For Bibi, Ehsan, and Raavi

Contents

Acknowledgments

The research for this book was supported by a doctoral-dissertation fellowship granted by the Population Council and by the support of the anthropology department at Johns Hopkins University. In Egypt, I also had institutional affiliation with the Department of Sociology, Anthropology, and Psychology at the American University in Cairo. I wish to thank the staff and faculty members of the department for including me in their professional and personal lives. From among those associated with the AUC I want to specifically thank Asef Bayat, Faryal Ghazoul, Linda Herrera, Nicholas Hopkins, Cynthia Nelson, and Ted Sweedenberg for their intellectual encouragement and continuing friendship. The study could not have been realized without their sustained interest in my work and in my personal life. I thank Barbara Ibrahim and the staff of the Population Council office at Cairo for all they did to ease my stay. My village study was partly arranged in affiliation with the International Islamic Center for Population Studies and Research at the Al-Azhar University in Cairo. I am grateful to the director of the center, Professor Gamal Serour, and to Dr. Ahmed Ragab for all their help in facilitating my work.

From my first day in Cairo I was a part of the Sabea family. I thank Hosni Sabea and his wife for taking me in and accepting me as one of their own. For providing me with a home away from home in Cairo, I thank Sabiha, Tanya, and John Adeylot. Many friends in Cairo helped in different ways during my stay in Egypt. They are too numerous to mention and I thank them all. However, I thank Gamal A, Clarisa Bencomo, Eliot Cola, Aida Seif El-Dawla, and Hania Shukrullah for things big and small that they did for me in Cairo. I would like specifically to acknowledge my dear friends Dalia A, Mustafa AR, Ahmed EB, and Sameh S—this text is as much a product of their concern for my work as it is mine.

I thank my friends in the rural and urban communities and in various government and nongovernment organizations that I visited. I profoundly thank those who opened their homes and shared whatever they had with me. Their incomparable gestures of generosity have created bonds of friendship that exist to this day. I also want to thank those who, despite their job situations and being aware of the political and social risks involved, helped me in securing interviews, visiting clinics, and getting access to data.

Caroline Bledsoe deserves my gratitude for reading most of this text in an earlier draft and for her valuable comments. Similarly I thank Lila Abu-Lughod, Talal Asad, Clarisa Bencomo, Tony Carter, Lisa Cartwright, Ayala Emmet, Bob Foster, Ali Khan, Laura Lewis, Carla Makhlouf, Norma Moruzzi, Connie Nathanson, Martina Rieker, and Shahnaz Rouse for reading and commenting on parts of this study. I also thank my colleagues in the anthropology department at the University of Rochester—Anthony Carter, Ayala Emmet, Robert Foster, and Thomas Gibson, along with Ro Ferrari—for their continuous encouragement and understanding. I could not have asked for a more supportive set of colleagues.

The bulk of this text was rewritten at the School of Social Sciences of the Institute of Advanced Study in 1998–1999. I thank the faculty there for accepting me as member for that year. In particular I thank Joan Scott for reading most of the chapters, despite her busy schedule, and for giving me valuable support and comments. I also would like to thank Clifford Geertz, whose interest in my work was extremely encouraging and whose company was always a source for new ideas and critical reflection. While at the IAS, I was fortunate to have a group of wonderful colleagues who helped me work through many details and also made life ever more pleasant for us as a family. Among them I specifically want to thank my friends Rainer Baubock, Susan Brison, James Brooks, Stephen Caton, Nahum Chandler, Thomas Flynn, Nancy Hirschmann, Jim Mittelman, Michael Mosher, Arvind Rajgopal, and Gordon Schochet.

The study itself was conceptualized in the late 1980s, influenced by the intellectual tradition and critical environment of the anthropology department at Johns Hopkins University. Without being aware of it, my friends and mentors in the department helped me in many big and small ways, for which I will be eternally grateful. Especially among them, I thank my friends Lanfranco Blanchetti, Charles Hirschkind, Samuel Martinez, Felicity Northcott, Monica Schoch Spana, and Hanan Sabea for their friendship, solidarity, and caring. I feel obligated toward Kaveh Ehsani for what I have shared and learned from him; his friendship and political integrity have been invaluable to me.

The faculty members who trained me deserve my utmost gratitude and thanks. I thank Ashraf Ghani, Hy Van Luong, and Katherine Verdery for providing me with an opportunity to study and think about anthropology in insightful and critical ways. No student at Hopkins remained untouched by Sidney Mintz's work and personality. I thank him for his support and for his intellectual legacy that all of us share and have become a part of. I thank Niloofar Haeri, who read many earlier versions of this work when she had so much more on her plate. Finally, among my teachers, I remain perpetually indebted to Gillian Feeley-Harnik, Emily Martin, and Michel-Rolph Trouillot; they taught me to think critically, encouraged my research, bestowed upon me the skills and abilities to conduct my study, and continue to support my scholarship. I am truly grateful to all three of them for their faith in me and for their friendship.

I would like to extend my gratitude to the editor of the series, Professor Robert Fernea, and to Annes McCann-Baker at the Center for Middle Eastern Studies, University of Texas, Austin, for their encouragement and support for this book project. Thanks are also due to my editor, Jim Burr, for seeing merit in this work earlier than I myself was convinced. Thanks also to my "anonymous" reviewers, who patiently went through this text (in one case twice) and gave me critical yet productive advice. I am also grateful to copyeditor Carolyn Russ and manuscript editor Jan McInroy for their careful work on this project.

This journey would not have been complete without my friends and family. My dear friends Iftikhar Ahmed, Shahab Ahmed, Nafiz Aksehirlioglu, Ilene Cohn, Kaveh Ehsani, Julia Elyachar, Iram Haleem, Tanveer Imam, Kaleemullah Lashari, Aamir Mufti, Khalid Nadvi, Salahuddin Qazi, Mujtaba Quadri, Muzaffar Quazilbash, Mansoor Raza, Martina Rieker, Shahnaz Rouse, Manzoor Sheikh, Nadeem Siddiqui, Jeroen Vervliet, and Zafar Zaidi remain a formative influence on what I think, write, and practice today. They have my deepest gratitude.

My siblings, Scheherazade Asdar Ahmed and Adnan Asdar, and their spouses, Fahim Ahmed and Mahboob Khan, have throughout been a source of much love, caring, and unflinching generosity. I do not have words to convey my gratitude to them. My sister, Scheherazade, was an early source of inspiration in my life. Thank you, Baji, for your love and for always being there.

I cannot even begin to adequately thank my mother, who surmounted all odds as a young widow to give all three of us a decent education and a sense of purpose. Although never quite understanding my detour from medicine into something called anthropology, she has, in her own way, reconciled herself to this fact. In addition to profusely thanking her for all she has endured and done for me, I also ask her forgiveness and hope she someday sees some merit in what I do.

This book is just a small token of appreciation for Syema's (bibi) unflinching solidarity and her belief in my capabilities. Her caring, support, and affection are the treasures of my life. With love and gratitude I dedicate this book to her and to our two lovely and energetic young sons, Ehsan and Raavi, who have made life a joy for Syema and me.

Note on Transliteration

The transliterations in this text are primarily of the colloquial Arabic spoken in Cairo and the Delta. This is not a written language. Typically, in pronunciation the Arabic letter "quaf" becomes a "hamza" and the "jeem" becomes "geem," pronounced with a "g" sound as in "goat." This is not universal, as there are variations within the colloquial dialect. Other spoken words simply do not exist in modern standard Arabic.

Note on Transliteration

PLANNING THE FAMILY IN EGYPT

Introduction

I say this frankly. It is very difficult business. You should know that we have increased in only five years by six million people, about as much as [the total population of] one or two countries around us. You see we have increased in six, five years [by] a country or two.

HOSNI MUBARAK, PRESIDENT
OF EGYPT, *Al-Ahram*, 1 MAY 1987[1]

This text discusses how development initiatives in general and family planning in particular help train and produce new bodies and selves in the wider context of capital expansion and accumulation as we enter the twenty-first century.[2] I argue that family planning programs do not just reduce the number of children and regulate reproduction. Rather, they also introduce or foster notions of individual choice and responsibility, risk aversion, and personal independence. In short, they help to construct a new kind of individuality, guided by legal constructs of citizenship rather than by communitarian and familial control.

Taking the Egyptian family planning program as a case study, I also demonstrate how the Egyptian poor, the intended targets of the fertility control program, make fertility decisions informed by their own notions of sexuality, fertility, the body, and the self. My study integrates their responses to the family planning program and to the global and local social processes that shape their lives.

The Egyptian state has, in the last fifteen years, collaborated with international donor agencies on an ambitious population control program.[3] The program operates on the assumption that rapid population growth is a prime obstacle to the realization of development goals set by the Egyptian state.[4] During the period of my stay in Egypt (1992–1994), the Egyptian state argued that the high population growth rate (2.6% annual growth) was the cause of the economic and social crises confronting the country. Governmental agencies and the media maintained that the poor, who have larger families, were responsible for their own plight as well as for the general economic crisis. The obvious solution, they claimed, was to reduce the population to a level that would permit continued economic development.

The arguments surrounding the active population planning program in Egypt echo larger international debates on population control. Ecological degradation, hunger, poverty, and political instability are buzzwords that are used in studies to define the present world population problem (Hartmann 1995).[5] According to demographic estimates, the world's population exceeds 6 billion people, with the greatest population growth occurring in the lesser developed countries. Concurrently, experts predict that an increase in the density of the human population will lead to further erosion of agricultural lands and subsequent decreases in food production worldwide. It also is believed that, despite technological innovations in agriculture and other development projects, the increased population will not be adequately sustained.[6]

Industrialized countries in Europe and North America cite the rise in emigration of people from the southern to the northern hemisphere as a key factor in the "world population problem," while third-world countries identify rural-urban migration as contributing to the creation of economic crises (Sen 1994:62). Analysts contend that millions of inhabitants in most third-world megacities need to adjust to a life with fewer state-sponsored infrastructural resources. Such arguments proclaim that one of the main reasons that most non-Western states are unable to provide adequate investments in housing, education, and other social services is because of their large populations. Keeping these arguments in view, the internationally sponsored development effort in Egypt, exemplified by the population control program, combines the arguments about scarcity of resources, cultivable land, and adequate employment.

It is necessary to look at recent Egyptian economic history in order to situate these arguments. One narrative on this topic is as follows. In the late 1980s, after a decade of growth and rising income,[7] the Egyptian economy started to stagnate under increased international debts, high unemployment rates, and growing budget deficits.[8] The Egyptian government's investment priorities, international borrowing, and accounting policies led to an accumulation of internal and external account imbalances. Egypt became caught in an economic recession because of reduced remittances and an international debt of almost $50 billion, exacerbated by a decline in migration to the Gulf states and a drop, during the mid-1980s, in the price of petroleum on the international market.

As a result of the recession, Egypt was unable to service its debt and paid only half of its $6 billion obligation for the year 1989–1990. The

Gulf War also contributed to the severe economic crisis, leading as it did to a sudden return of many migrants and a reduction in tourism earnings. The year 1990–1991, therefore, saw Egypt with reduced creditworthiness, decreased revenues, double-digit inflation (20%), and 12–14 percent unemployment rates. In response to these factors, in May and November of 1991 the International Monetary Fund (IMF) and the World Bank negotiated a Standby Agreement and a Structural Adjustment Loan with the government of Egypt. This provided the basis for the Economic Reform and Structural Adjustment Program (ERSAP).

Immediately after signing the agreement and because of its role in the Gulf War, Egypt was granted debt reduction by the Paris Club and, independently, by the United States, which cancelled $6.7 billion in U.S. military debt.[9] In July 1991, other creditor nations reduced the net value of Egypt's debt by 15 percent. Additional relief of between 15 and 20 percent was promised upon completion of goals required by the IMF (U.S. Embassy Cairo 1993; Abdel-Khalek 1993). These reductions helped fiscal reformers establish control over national accounts, reduce the deficit (from 17% of GDP in 1990–1991 to 1% in 1997–1998), improve the balance of payments, and increase domestic savings. Whether the impact of the reductions on poverty levels, inflation, and employment was as positive is, however, less clear.

What the narrative given above ignores is that in the 1990s, unemployment levels remained high; notably, university and technical institute graduates constituted 65–75 percent of the openly unemployed.[10] Although official figures reported unemployment at 8–10 percent in the early 1990s, other estimates ranged from 15 to 20 percent of an Egyptian workforce of almost 18 million people (U.S. Embassy Cairo 1993; Pfeifer 1999). Unemployment could rise further with privatization of state-owned enterprises and workforce reductions.[11] Linked to unemployment figures is the rate of inflation, which was officially stated to be under 5 percent in 1996 (Pfeifer 1999); unofficial estimates, though, considered it to be in the double digits, between 12 and 14 percent. The rise in inflation was primarily a result of increases in the cost of food, energy, and transportation (U.S. Embassy Cairo 1993; Korayem 1993).[12]

The 1991 adjustment package has substantially raised the poverty levels in Egypt, at least in the short term. The per head GDP decreased from $640 in the late 1980s to $610 in mid-1995. Poverty is defined by international standards as a total income of $35 per month; by that definition the percentage of Egypt's population living in poverty increased from 20–25 percent in 1990 to almost 33 percent in 1995, and to more than 45 percent by 1997 (EIU 1995; Mitchell 1999).[13] Economists estimate that since

1991 there has been a 680 percent increase in key food and energy prices, items that acutely affect poor families. Such families spend 60 to 75 percent of their monthly budget on food and another third on energy bills (U.S. Embassy Cairo 1992; EIU 1995).

The population program in Egypt needs to be understood in relation to the above-mentioned changes in the Egyptian economy. A USAID report in 1989 recounted how urbanization had caused loss of agricultural land, how the universities could not absorb more students, how the government's capacity to employ graduates had diminished, and how gross domestic savings had declined (Gillespie et al. 1989:3–4). The report argued that a reduction in population size might translate into reduced development expenditures for the state and less pressure to provide for education, health care, and jobs in the future.[14] Social expenditures for Egypt's people remained secondary in this process to the transfer of resources to international financiers of the modern-day economy.

International development agencies have compelled the Egyptian state to rationalize its economy, privatize its assets, and remove social subsidies. These same donor agencies provide the largest subsidies for population control. They argue that a reduction in state support for children would increase the cost of having children and thus persuade families to adopt planning as their own "voluntary and non-coercive" choice. The IMF-sponsored structural adjustment policy is supposed to cut excess in the economy. The family planning program should, presumably, guarantee a correspondingly lean family. Playing on the imagery of surplus and waste, both the structural adjustment program and the population program in Egypt can be viewed as ways to streamline the social and economic corpus of Egypt.

THE ARGUMENT

A key feature of present-day economic globalization is the flexibility of capital. Due to its flexible nature, capital no longer depends on the availability of labor at a fixed site. The world labor market is differentiated according to skills and pricing, which creates competition among developing economies for foreign investment by guaranteeing a disciplined nonunion labor force (Trouillot 2001; Miyoshi 1996).

Along with new labor practices globalization also entails active participation in what has been referred to as the "ideology of consumption" (Jameson 1998:69). The aim is to create wants, desires, and demands that are linked to new notions of individuality and selves, in order to increase consumption among the diverse populations of the world. Consumption by the upper classes is believed essential to the growth and accumulation of capital. In this context, recent global economic restructuring as promulgated by the World Trade Organization (WTO) has provided arguments for free trade and open foreign markets and has acclaimed the emergence of difference, plurality, and tolerant coexistence. Yet the forced integration of national markets into the world system, the disappearance of national subsistence, and the new forms of division of labor present a different aspect to this reality (Jameson 1998:57).

The poor in first- and third-world countries suffer the effects of resource management and the removal of social subsidies (Harvey 1996. 143–144) that the process of economic globalization forces upon individual states. As development initiatives in the service of global capital help curtail social expenditure, they also work to create a more compliant and disciplined citizenry.

To enable this process, I argue, the family planning program in Egypt, through its pedagogical efforts, not only seeks to reduce population size but also introduces notions of individual choice and self-regulation. The target of the family planning program in Egypt, as elsewhere, is primarily the female body, though the male body is not ignored. Egyptian women are invited to participate in family planning through their own conviction and not through coercion. They must be persuaded, which entails the production of desires that help women make the choice of contraception for themselves and, by extension, the good of the nation. Through such means, the family planning program introduces Egyptian women to new ideas and values about home, child welfare, motherhood, and, consequently, the meaning of family, community, and nation.

In this text I will present Egyptian voices that oppose or accept such impositions, but I will also go beyond such an exclusive presentation. I will illustrate how Egypt, as a modernizing state,[15] uses the family planning program as a pedagogical project to manage its population. To understand how people in Egypt enter into modern projects that transform them into self-regulating individuals, it is imperative that we simultaneously understand how new categories of individuals are produced and strategically deployed (Trouillot 1991).

In the following chapters I seek also to account for the tensions and contradictions that exist within the state system while presenting the complex set of factors that impact on population control in Egypt. Therefore, as much as this narrative discusses the Egyptian state's imposition of new categories of self and personhood on its population, I am sensitive to the negotiations, ambiguities, and contradictions that are inherent in these undertakings. I examine, in the following sections of this introductory chapter, two interrelated phenomena: first, the efforts to produce self-regulating, new, and modern individuals of which the family planning program in Egypt is one component; and second, responses and reactions to such interventions.

EVALUATING THE QUESTION

The historian Nikki Keddie suggested in a review article about gender and women in the Middle East, "Problems in the Study of Middle Eastern Women" (1979), that a future research agenda for the Middle East should include the study of sexual habits of the people. She argued that methodological problems posed by such studies should be overcome in order to gain a better understanding of gender relations in the Middle East (Keddie 1979:239). An elucidation of sexual relations would, according to Keddie, aid our comprehension of people's attitudes toward childbirth and their use of contraception. She claimed that researchers would be able to gauge the success of the fertility control policy only after knowing the intimate details of domestic life in the Middle East. Keddie's desire to learn about the private lives of the Arab family may be embedded in the liberal feminist political concerns of the 1970s. But her position may also be linked to a developmentalist agenda that seeks to change the private behavior of couples so that they can successfully use modern contraceptive methods. This concern with the private and sexual lives of the people persists, in many forms, in contemporary debates on health and reproduction in the Middle East.

These debates continue to generate arguments on how new methodological perspectives can be applied to acquire information about people's intimate lives. I became aware of this during my fieldwork months in Cairo (1992–1994), but a more recent example helps to further clarify this point. In early 1998 I attended a seminar in Alexandria, Egypt, sponsored by the Population Council and USAID, on male involvement in reproductive health in Egypt. At this seminar I witnessed a distinct shift in methodological preference for research on reproductive health issues. Demographers and statisticians repeatedly emphasized qualitative methods that had helped them to improve questionnaires or had provided them with better data on household practices as related to family planning. It was clear that qualitative methods for these researchers primarily meant focus groups. At this seminar, though, a consensus evolved that, without long-term ethnographic work within communities, intrahousehold dynamics and methods of communication between husbands and wives could not be ascertained. Focus group techniques, despite their value as research tools, were deemed incapable of uncovering the complexity of familial situations.

This seminar reflected potential changes within the larger field of population studies. Anthropological theory has repeatedly criticized the economistic reasoning inherent in demographic quantitative literature that guides the creation of knowledge about populations and their relationship to resources. Anthropological knowledge has, on the contrary, focused on the multiple ways in which people create meaning and construct symbols to explain their actions in different cultures. Further, ethnographic studies profoundly deepen our understanding of people's lives by being flexible and able to probe sensitive matters in their social, cultural, and economic contexts.

Similarly, anthropologists who work in the field of development research argue that health interventions into communities are bound to fail if they continue to rely on technical solutions and fail to pay attention to the social and cultural characteristics of the target populations. Many anthropologists who work with international health agencies enumerate the ideas and practices of peoples so as to assist health planners in formulating programs. A certain form of medical anthropological input, therefore, provides a local perspective to health policy managers. This knowledge is crucial to the design of international health programs because it assures that the "cultural facet" of the community or target group is considered (Pigg 1997).

This call for understanding the people's perspective also has an antecedent in the history of colonialism. In the early part of the twentieth century, colonial discourse on health in, for example, India and Africa used a specific notion of "culture" that ascribed groups with defined and fixed traits and habits. Megan Vaughan (1991), in her historical work on colonial health intervention in Africa, argues that colonial public health officials attributed ill health among Africans to their traditional culture. Culture, in some cases, was condemned as hindering the progress of scientific modes of treatment. This static and objectified notion of culture was used, at other times, as a pragmatic vehicle to introduce Western ideas into people's lives (Pigg 1997). In the past several decades, international health campaigns have identified this notion of culture, with slight shifts, as one of several factors that influence the health of a given community.

Theoretical changes in the discipline of demography now emphasize the micropractices of individuals as prime determinants of fertility change. Embedded in this new approach, demographic research works with a concept of culture that links an ideational change model to the acceptability of modern birth control (see Handwerker 1986; Caldwell et al. 1987). This argument again consists of a narrowly construed formulation of culture as communication within a household with minimal reference to the social, political, and economic forces of the larger society (Greenhalgh 1995:7). It also encompasses the idea that people in traditional cultures are more fatalistic about their fertility outcomes and are willing to leave reproduction to the will of God (Schneider and Schneider 1995:181). This understanding of culture effectively places households/families and their behavior patterns on a traditional to modern continuum.

As a general critique of demographic literature, social researchers such as Agnes Riedmann (1993) describe demographic surveys and research as an extension of colonial penetration and bureaucratic surveillance of people's lives in postcolonial independent societies. Riedmann asserts that these surveys seek to modernize third-world populations by shifting them toward individualistic values and nucleation of households (Riedmann 1993:3). The international researchers who conduct these surveys are censured for their disregard of indigenous cultural norms such as family size, sense of privacy, and territorial integrity. Riedmann would like the interventionist demographic agenda to shift toward anthropological research that acknowledges the historical, cultural, and social causes of population growth.

Though I am sympathetic to Riedmann's criticism of demographic methodology, I believe that more culturally sensitive research can also present the possibility of intervention. The crucial issue in my perspective is not a comparison between good social science versus bad social science, or anthropological analysis in contrast to demographic research; rather, it is that both these methodologies are embedded in historical forms of social inquiry that create facts and represent reality.

I would advocate caution with regard to the use of anthropology in the service of larger developmental goals.[16] This caution is necessary because the liberal stance within the field of anthropology, linked as it is to the notion of progress (Ferguson 1999:33), continues to play a major role in developmentalist discourse. Anthropologists may need to question the liberal, humanistic, and reformist assumptions of anthropology before embarking on a progressive crusade to change the world. These assumptions have their own historical baggage, which, in the name of understanding diversity, might in fact seek to homogenize the world (Pool 1994:16). There is always the danger that the use of anthropology to understand native categories and to bridge the gap between differing knowledge forms may in fact serve to reduce all forms of knowledge as a variation of a universal (read Western) theme (Pool 1994).

My intent in writing this text is not, therefore, to provide an ethnographic model that overcomes the shortcomings of demographic surveys; neither is it to specifically gauge the success or failure of a particular development project. Nor am I interested in supplying evidence about women's motivations for accepting or rejecting contraceptives. These issues are discussed in the body of the text but do not necessarily form the core of my argument. Rather, the development debate and the family planning program as they are manifested in Egypt provide an opportunity to investigate how these processes aid in the construction of new bodies, new selves, and new notions of individuality.

This approach helps me distance myself from development-oriented remedies and enables me to move away from certain tropes of representation prevalent in the field of Middle Eastern anthropology. More than a decade ago, the anthropologist Lila Abu-Lughod (1989) argued that there are three central zones of theorizing within Middle Eastern anthropology: segmentation, harem, and Islam. By focusing on the construction of new subjects, I would like to push the boundaries of these theoretical zones and seek to place the production of knowledge on the Middle East at the juncture of a more dynamic and interactive globalizing moment.

THE CONSTRUCTION OF THE MODERN SUBJECT

Enumeration and classification historically are products of improvement in statistical sciences in nineteenth-century Europe. Methods of counting population were generally used for the purposes of taxation and army recruitment before the nineteenth century. Statistics became linked in the nineteenth century to emergent social laws designed to regulate populations and create the notion of the "normal." For example, regularities in social life were vigorously studied in Victorian England so as to understand the social deviancies of suicide, crime, prostitution, vagrancy, and madness.[17] Survey methods used currently in demographic research are related to this ongoing history of normalization and progress that is linked to data collection and enumeration of deviances (Hacking 1990).

Statistical language is one of the "strong languages" that is also one of the "discursive interventions by means of which the modes of life of non-European peoples have come to be radically changed by Western power"(Asad 1994a:78). Cast as vital to the concept of progress in developing countries, statistical methods are presumed to represent and to construct people's lived experiences. Techniques used by governments are linked to this language about the control and discipline of the body. A socially pathogenic value, for example, may be attributed to high birth rates. Discourses on personal responsibility and the sacrifice of personal pleasure are then related to procreation. This may motivate a couple toward having fewer children and, therefore, toward a larger social good.[18]

The liberal notion of the self-regulating individual is paramount for these disciplinary techniques. The history of liberal political thought prepares us for the pedagogical exercises of constructing such a self-regulating individual. Harnessing the absence of self-control and the excess of passion is crucial to the construction of the Lockean concept of the self-understanding individual. As the political theorist Uday Mehta (1992) argues, for this to happen individuals need to be embedded in social institutions, especially the institution of education. Education, Mehta stresses, reins in the natural untutored imagination so that it submits to conventional authority and social norms. Liberalism, from this perspective, does not consider individuality to be a foundational given that can be regulated by political institutions; rather, it is a process of coming-to-be, a constructive agenda through which the individual is fashioned. A picture of liberalism that incorporates the ethical individual with collective rights and governmental restraint may be proper, but we need also to pay attention to liberalism's underlying fear of libertine excesses and human passions. The control of desires, self-denial, responsibility, and reason are taught and learned so as to curb natural instincts and to become self-disciplined and disciplining individuals (Mehta 1992).[19]

Nineteenth-century debates on poverty and its reform in Britain give us empirical evidence of the processes that created self-governing individuals. By midcentury, social knowledge produced by scientifically gathered empirical facts on people's lives created opportunities in urban centers for public health campaigns, poor laws, sanitary reports, and scientific studies of social evils like prostitution to contribute to development of a normalized individual self. Mary Poovey (1995) shows how

the charisma of the early-nineteenth-century social reformers and the social investigative and reformative laws passed by government bureaucrats
should be seen as two faces of modern administration. Both these methods were used to organize the poor in England. They combined tutelage/
education of the poor by the reformers with production of rationalized
knowledge and information about the lower classes by the government
bureaucrats. These interventions were intended to produce disciplined
individualism, which would help people express their freedom through
voluntary compliance with the law (Poovey 1995).

The task of reconstructing practices of body and health was not limited to Europe. The colonial enterprise, linked as it was to the extraction
of surplus and the exploitation of resources and labor, also was involved
in reshaping and redefining indigenous beliefs and practices. The history
of colonization might be understood, in part, as the institutionalization
of new practices to rationalize and control colonized populations. As
David Scott (1995) shows, colonial reforms in nineteenth-century Ceylon
sought to create desires in which individual agency and free will took
precedence over the natural rights of the sovereign or the landlord. The
reorganization of market and labor was planned in such a way as to
covertly lead individuals to regulate themselves into responding to the
pressures of want and self-interest. The market was meant to inculcate a
"desire for industry, regularity and individual accomplishment" (Scott
1995:211). The political problem was not only to contain resistance or
accommodate local grievances but also to assure that these could be
defined only in modern political and social categories (Scott 1995:214).[20]

Historians of the postcolonial era have argued that in the last two
hundred years "Europe" has remained a silent referent to all histories
including those that are non-Western.[21] The subjects of these Eurocen-
tric histories, the colonized societies, are never credited with reaching
their objective and, as a consequence, are characterized by a lack. Dipesh
Chakrabarty (1992) argues that British rule in India was about creating
subjects that were always caught between the categories of traditional/
modern, feudal/capitalist, and despotic/constitutional. The colonial "subject," Chakrabarty stresses, had not yet evolved enough to be the rational civilized person with industrial habits, a sense of responsibility, and the
strength of character to become a citizen for the British imperialist liberal theory. The colonized nationalist elite in India resisted this imposition of inadequacy and engaged in political struggle for a nation-state and
citizenship (Chakrabarty 1992; Chatterjee 1993:6).

The changing nature of Egyptian society in the late-nineteenth century, after a period of colonialism and almost a century of continuous European presence, was made manifest through the introduction of ideas of equality and justice and regulations that reordered Egyptian society. This was backed by the political ideology of European liberalism. Timothy Mitchell (1988) systematically shows how European influence and colonialism in Egypt ordered and disciplined the body and minds of the Egyptian people by introducing modern education and modern methods of policing through the discourse of law and order, periodic census, registration of births and deaths, and new ideas about health and hygiene.[22]

In a manner similar to that of Indian nationalists during the colonial period, the emerging Egyptian nationalists politically challenged the British, not so much as a mechanism for change, but to determine who would be responsible for these changes and forge the people into a unitary nation. Colonial Egypt too lacked capital development and the presence of an independent bourgeoisie, as well as the modern notion of the "private" and "public" spheres that are regulated through laws embodied in the structure of the state. The privilege of citizenship was not available to the Egyptian elite until much later in this historical narrative of progress and nation building. Hence histories, whether nationalist or colonial, were written as one of arrival and becoming. Though the modern indigenous elite may have "arrived" and become part of a universalizing history, millions of poor, the disenfranchised and, in the case of Egypt, the peasantry were still placed outside this narrative.[23] Similar to what Deniz Kandiyoti described in the case of Turkish modernity, the rural hinterland became the repository of immobility, tradition, and backwardness (Kandiyoti 1997:117). The postindependence nation-state, much like that of the colonial regime, has attempted to incorporate the populace into this civilizing project through violence, pedagogy, consciousness raising, or the market.

In this text I argue that the educated and the elite Egyptians who represent the Egyptian state today possess the particular subjectivity for them to play the roles of protector, educator, and the champion of justice for others and consequently to act as gatekeepers to modernity (Colla 1994). Late-nineteenth-century Egyptian reformers primarily concentrated on the improvement of their own class yet saw themselves as representing the future of the entire Egyptian nation. Today, as non-Western states like Egypt aspire to integrate into the global market, they increasingly regulate the lives of their populations with the help of modernizing developmental agendas prescribed by Western donor agencies. The modern Egyptian state, in alliance with international capital, seeks to admit others into the realm of citizenship through the process of public health campaigns and rural uplift programs or through the rhetoric of equality and justice.[24]

Development in the postcolonial era is linked to a teleological narrative modeled on histories that have already been experienced in the West. It becomes the self-representation of modernity for third-world states that aspire to bring the fruits of progress and innovation into the lives of their citizens (Gupta 1997). National governments in Egypt or in India, armed with an anticolonial rhetoric, did seek to create a debate on a path of development that was critical of Western impositions. Yet increasingly in the late twentieth century, development initiatives linked to economic globalization led to the rationalizing and naturalizing of capitalism's power in progressivist terms "as the engine that brings those on the bottom 'up' toward those who are already there" (Cooper and Packard 1997).

In this scenario, modern states[25] become guarantors of progress; they function as referees that mediate individual obligations to moderate the burden of risk that a person imposes on society. A language of individual choice and freedom is propagated by the state seeking to displace the traditional forms of control on the individual (in the case of women, the family patriarch). At the same time, this freedom of choice is socialized as the state decides the parameters in which these choices may be made. The problems of the state are, further, rebounded on the people so that society itself is implicated in the task of resolving them. Health, for example, becomes an issue of civic responsibility. As a list of unhealthy behaviors that adversely affect the economy is prepared, public health campaigns seek to target irresponsible social groups that are "defined in terms of greater pathological risks they present to and the cost they impose on the collectivity" (Donzelot 1991b:273).

These regulatory powers have already been established in Western industrial societies; thus, countries like Egypt emulate their example by constructing the legal and social institutions that are a necessary prerequisite for exercise of these powers (Asad 1992a:336). I argue that international development programs, such as the family planning program in Egypt, are precisely meant to advance the construction of modern subjectivities linked to the process of creating more socially controlling institutions similar to those that are present in industrialized democracies.[26]

Modernizing developmental states also employ these governmental technologies to deliver social goods to their populace at a low cost. The task before such states is not merely one of constructing rights for their citizens but also of managing the population. Partha Chatterjee (1998) ar-

gues that the emergence of the modern state in the West in the twentieth century is marked by the distinction between the domain of theory
linked to citizenship and the domain of policy inhabited by populations.
Following Michel Foucault's now familiar argument on governmentality,
Chatterjee asserts that populations are identifiable, describable, and classi-
fiable through statistical techniques. The concept of population, unlike
citizenship, which carries an "ethical connotation of participation in the
sovereignty of the state" (Chatterjee 1998:279), allows governments to
intervene politically and administratively in the lives of the populace who
become the targets of its policies (279). Governments such as that of
Egypt may seek legitimacy not only by encouraging liberal notions of
participatory democracy but by "claiming to provide for the well-being
of the population" as well (279).

Playing on similar themes of social costs and well-being, the Egyptian
family planning program seeks to persuade women to shed their ideas of
their bodies and selves and convert to scientific ideas of fertility management. This process emphasizes the construction of a modern individual
associated with notions of rights, rationality, responsibility, and sexuality,
embedded in a new order of morality and law. Through the systematic
deployment of different apparatuses of institutional discipline and control, it also creates arenas to change and govern bodies, and manage man-
nerisms and behaviors (Lukes 1985).

Such interventions, however, do not remain uncontested. For example, there are other factors besides that of the family planning program's language and policy that shape the responses of the people to
contraceptive methods and to other developmental strategies. Religious
groups, political parties, feminists, and popular media help condition attitudes toward fertility issues. Further, unstable socioeconomic conditions,
increased rural–urban migration as a result of diminished opportunities
to own arable land coupled with an increasingly wage-based rural economy, high levels of urban unemployment, housing shortages, and a lack
of modern educational opportunities influence decisions about household size. The increased disparity of income levels, which is independent
of family size, also allows for a critique of the state's emphasis on family
planning over issues of equity of distribution and social justice.

The process of managing populations, hence, is invariably connected
to and influenced by the responses of people themselves. The Egyptian state's desire to change and modernize its masses inadvertently confronts inherent gaps and contradictions. This text attempts to portray the
relationship between impositions of the state and the way people respond
to the development agenda. As the state, linked to international capital,

seeks to change the behavior and practice of its populace to produce self-regulating and modern desiring subjects, it faces a population that conceives and constitutes its selves, bodies, and communities in different and diverse forms.[27]

I emphasize that people, through their practices, transform the meaning and intention of developmental impositions[28] and give us a sense of leading modern lives that do not completely comply with the homogenous and teleological model posited by the history of the West. These "resistances" and transformations are conducted in a terrain constituted by the modern state. It is in the modern state that we find struggles over issues of individual rights, gender politics, procreation, or sexuality.[29] Those who do not conform to the new social categories, those who adhere to other notions of the individual, the community, or the nation are particularly sought out by the state to be educated out of their beliefs so that they can also participate in the predetermined history of progress, freedom, and modernity, linked as it is to the forward march of capital (Chatterjee 1993).

This being so, it is important to investigate the differences that hinder this forward march. The task before me is to represent bodies and selves that continuously disrupt modern government's desire to subjugate and to civilize; lives that from within the narrative of capital and coexistent with it remind us of different ways of being human (Chakrabarty 2000:94). This investigative emphasis compels us to "take the vernacular voices of the popular and their modes of self fashioning seriously" (Scott 1999: 215). This is not to simply resurrect the figure of the subaltern as a subject of modern democracies linked to a desire to make society more representative as a whole (Chakrabarty 2000:94), which is a laudable goal in itself and is often championed by progressivist historical narratives. Yet what gets elided in these emancipatory narratives, Dipesh Chakrabarty reminds us (2000), is how the secular-modern middle classes, the authors of these narratives in their liberal or socialist versions, have historically excluded the popular. Following David Scott (1999) I argue that to take the vernacular voices and practices seriously is to recognize their popular refusal to integrate into the available forms of middle-class identifications and moral truths provided by the postcolonial state (Scott 1999:215).

MY INTERVENTION

I conducted my fieldwork in multiple sites rather than doing intensive research at one field site as is still customary in anthropology. The questions

that I sought to investigate partly determined my choice of this methodology. Following the development population agenda as it was manifest
in Egypt meant not only a multisited ethnography but also one that was
analytically multileveled.[30] I had initially planned to spend an extended
period (eight to twelve months) in one village (preferably in the south of
the country) to acquire a situated knowledge of a given community's response to the fertility control program. This was not to be, however. I did
get access to a Delta village and even poor urban neighborhoods, but only
after much apprehension and creative maneuvering as a result of problems with Egyptian security services.

My credentials as a medical doctor, an anthropology graduate student
from Johns Hopkins University with a fellowship from the Population
Council, and my local affiliation with the American University in Cairo
did not change the fact that I was a Pakistani national. Whatever that may
mean in other parts of the world, for the Egyptian state intelligence services in 1992–1994 it meant that I was a man who could be in league with
the Islamists. Mine was a case in which national identities became enmeshed in political struggles and stereotypic constructions.

The years 1992–1994, during which I did my fieldwork, were the worst
in the violent conflict between the state authorities and the Egyptian
Islamist political groups. Pakistan, my native country, was one of the
frontline states used by the United States against the Soviet invasion of
Afghanistan. It was primarily in Pakistan that U.S.-sponsored experts gave
training and resources to Muslim "freedom fighters" to fight the "Red
Devil." They trained an international group of religiously motivated
young men to resist the invading Soviet army. The Egyptian state apparatus now feared that Egyptian nationals returning from that *jihad* had
entered another one against the secular authorities at home. I may have
been viewed as suspicious because of these complicated circumstances.

I was regularly asked by police and military officials, with whom I
needed to meet periodically for security clearance prior to the start of my
research, why I, as a Pakistani, was not conducting research in my own
country. They would say that they could comprehend Euro-Americans,
Egyptians, and other Arab Middle Easterners conducting research in
Egypt, but a Pakistani? This in itself was suspicious. The understanding
of the paths by which middle-class and privileged third-world nationals
acquire access to first-world education and sources of funding, allowing
them to be competitive in the same spheres as their first-world colleagues,
was still alien to these officials. These encounters also raised questions of
how research in this globalizing world is contingent on an individual's

passport and the sense of security, power, and prestige it provides. As a result, I could not obtain the necessary permission to do fieldwork in the village of my choice. Thus, the change of locales was also partly imposed.

A multi-sited ethnographic fieldwork, however, offered a broad understanding of social phenomena from different and varied perspectives. These perspectives helped me to link macrolevel arguments on population control and middle-level implementation by state bureaucracies to the effect of these policies on the people on the ground. I also used a variety of sources: archives, literary works, official reports, my interviews, and observations and questionnaires. In addition my ethnographic encounters included interviews with bureaucrats who worked in international agencies and the health ministry in Cairo, with doctors and nurses involved in family planning clinics, and with the women and men in the rural and urban localities in which I did my community fieldwork.

I asked government bureaucrats at the Ministry of Health (MOH) and the National Population Council (NPC) questions about the family planning program, the problems they faced in its implementation, their successes, and their vision of the future. I visited the offices of USAID, the World Bank, the Ford Foundation, the Population Council, the United Nations Development Programme (UNDP), and other nongovernmental organizations (NGOs) (e.g., the Egyptian Family Planning Association) in Cairo. I attended seminars offered by these institutions on population issues and interviewed those responsible in their offices for the health and population sector. I asked them general questions on their short- and long-term priorities with regard to the population program in Egypt and visited specific projects that they conducted. I also systematically visited family planning clinics in Cairo and, when possible, in villages in the Delta and in southern Egypt. There I spoke to the doctors, nurses, and patients about various aspects of the program. For example, I was interested in popular forms of contraceptives prescribed in the clinic and also why a specific method was so widely used. I periodically asked patients about the benefits of contraceptive use and about the side effects and problems of these methods. In the communities where I lived and worked, I was interested not only in the specific responses on family planning methods but also in how people lived, what they earned, and how they related to each other. In addition, through discussions with the people in those communities, I sought to learn how they conceived of their own bodies and what their ideas were about health, procreation, and sexuality.

I was introduced to a Delta village community through doctors who ran a clinic there for a major medical university in Cairo. As I spent time within the village, which I call Qaramoos, I put myself in a configuration of power where others also had control over my life. This is pertinent because, as alluded to earlier, the Egyptian state's security apparatus can make extensive fieldwork virtually impossible without the protection and support of the local population itself.

As I started visiting Qaramoos I became acquainted with people from many households. I initially hesitated to ask women questions that I thought were too intrusive. As a non-Egyptian yet Muslim male, albeit with a medical degree, I was unsure as to how women would react to my questions about personal relations, birthing, menstruation, and sexual practices. The issue was partially resolved as women started sharing with me some of their ideas about self, body, and health.

During the course of my stay, my host family's relatives and friends sought advice from me on minor ailments. While I remained sensitive to local notions of respectability and gender relations, I used these exchanges to converse with women visitors about issues that pertained to my research, but my queries were not always welcome and were, at times, ignored. I spent considerable time with men; however, during the midday or evening meals I had opportunities to speak with the older women. They were interested in my personal life (how people lived in rural Pakistan or the United States), and I would attempt to speak to them about their lives. I also talked with traditional midwives (*daya*s) whom I had met earlier in focus group sessions. These women were extremely important because they helped me to understand how women thought of their bodies and health. The *daya*s were comfortable speaking with me on topics that would be considered impolite among other women because they were much older in age and thought of themselves as professional healers.

I would stay in Qaramoos for two or three nights and then return to Cairo due to security reasons. In Cairo, I worked in the northern urban neighborhood of Behteem. Cairene friends who knew male industrial workers in the area facilitated my introduction into Behteem. I would spend most of the weekends speaking to men and visiting various households accompanied by my fellow female researcher, who would speak to women about our research issues. Over time, we became a common fixture in the area, and we were invited to gatherings and celebrations. The women of the area, especially from the homes of men who had now become my friends, would now speak to me directly about their ailments and about the problems they had with their contraceptives. These encounters, in the framework of the larger realities of their social experiences, helped me to understand priorities in the women's lives and put into perspective their ambivalent relationship with the state and its family planning agenda.

Finally, my fieldwork experiences need to be looked at as a reminder of how the "field" is a place where the authority to define, to report on, and to assemble facts on one's informants is continuously challenged. In the narrative that follows this introductory chapter, I hope the reader, like my friends in the village and other locations in Egypt, will critically engage with the text and continually questions its assumptions and representations. The important issue is not only the presentation of "data" but also the production of a narrative that is situated in a field of power relations and in the subject positions that the ethnographer inhabits.[31]

OUTLINE OF CHAPTERS

Moving through different levels of society exposed me to the underlying social and economic changes in people's lives that, to some extent, determined their acceptance and use of family planning methods. The organization of chapters conceptually represents this movement through societal levels. The text is divided into three parts: Part 1 has two chapters that describe and analyze the various facets of the family planning program in Egypt. Chapter 1 gives a detailed history of the population issue in Egypt. It recalls early-twentieth-century debates on population pressures and presents the changing nature of the impact of international demographic theories on family planning policy in Egypt. It also gives an account of the various actors and agencies that participate in the family planning program in Egypt.

Recent emphasis in family planning circles in Egypt is on the quality of care and treating the client with respect, as the overall approach toward family planning service delivery is being reoriented toward "client satisfaction." The client needs are posited as primary, and the provider plays the role of a helper who guides the client toward solving her problem and choosing the most appropriate contraceptive. This engagement leads to the construction of consent and individual choice. To emphasize this encounter, in the second chapter, through ethnographic examples, I briefly evaluate a public health campaign that was created to motivate contraceptive use among rural Egyptians. I demonstrate how the need for individual counseling leads to training sessions for doctors. Finally, I describe counseling and service delivery in an urban family health clinic.

Part 2 of the book is based on ethnography from the rural and urban communities in which I worked. Chapter 3 presents data on social life within those communities. It spatially and socially situates the ethnography presented in the remainder of the text. Chapter 4 examines how the family planning program in Egypt may falter in its attempt to convince women of its goals and benefits. I focus, in this chapter, on how rural and urban poor women construct their own notions of birthing and fertility. This suggests an implicit critique of the family planning program's model of the individualized self by highlighting the experiences of women themselves. Based on my ethnographic findings I demonstrate how some women continuously experience their bodies as linked and situated in a larger social world. Continuing on the theme of the fourth chapter, chapter 5 guides us toward a greater understanding of the many ways women reach their contraceptive decisions. Chapter 6 is a larger discussion of how the family planning program cannot be understood solely through the construction of individual choice for women. I introduce, as an example, the emphasis by international family planning programs on the male point of view. This chapter discusses how men are implicated in the population discourse, illustrating male notions of health, fertility, infertility, potency, and virility.

Part 3 has two chapters that illustrate the expanded discursive and political context within which people make decisions on fertility control in Egypt. In chapter 7 I present the argument on reproductive rights and give some examples of secular women's groups that criticize the state for not fulfilling its social role as a provider of safe and affordable health services for women. The last chapter discusses how Islamists challenge the morality of the Egyptian state in propagating family planning and how, in the process, they present an alternative view of domestic life and the larger nation.

Part One

History of Family Planning | *Chapter 1*

In a work of fiction from late-nineteenth-century Egypt, the main pro-
tagonist is a writer who goes to the tombs outside Cairo for inspiration.
One day he encounters an elderly noble who steps out from one of the
graves. After a brief introduction the grave dweller asks the writer to go
to his house and fetch him his horse and some clothes. The author re-
spectfully replies that he does not know where the nobleman lives. The
infuriated elder curses and says:

"Tell me which country you are from, for heavens sake? It's clear that
you are not an Egyptian. There is no one in the whole country who does
not know where my house is. I'm Ahmad Pasha al-Manikali, the Minis-
ter of War in Egypt."

The author replies:

"Pasha, believe me, I'm from pure Egyptian stock. The only reason
why I do not know where you live is that houses in Egypt are no longer
known by the names of their owners, but by the names of their street,
lane and number. If you would be so kind to tell me the street, lane and
number of your house, I will go there and bring you the things you ask
for." [1]

I present this exchange from Muhammad al-Muwaylihi's book to emphasize the changing nature of Egyptian society in the late nineteenth
century, after almost a century of continuous European presence in Egypt.
This ordering of Egyptian society through regulations and numbering,
irrespective of personal rank and status, was due to the introduction of
modern notions of equality and justice backed by the political ideology
of European liberalism.

Modernizing changes occurred contemporaneously with a growing
understanding of the population problem. By the late nineteenth century,
census data "scientifically" represented the "reality" of the alarming population increase and its impact on future food distribution in Egypt. Use

of numerical and statistical analysis brought to life the relationship between overpopulation and the narrow strip of agricultural land along the Nile that constitutes the fertile yet restricted cultivatable land in Egypt (Owen 1996).

This chapter historically situates the population debate in Egypt. It recalls the colonial administration's insistence on a negative correlation between population growth and available Egyptian land, elucidating the research, periodic censuses, and arguments behind that correlation. It links these arguments to theories of demographic change then fashionable in Europe and the United States. Further, it sketches the changing assumptions behind these theories to show their historical and present-day relationship to the population control policy in Egypt. The chapter describes the primarily USAID-sponsored contemporary Egyptian family planning program and discusses how international recommendations—and internationally spread theories—about fertility control continue to influence and define the parameters of population policy in Egypt.

THE POPULATION QUESTION IN EGYPT

The population of Egypt steadily grew in the nineteenth century[2] despite periodic plague and smallpox epidemics in the earlier part of the century and subsequent cholera outbreaks. One of the prime reasons historians give for the population growth is the civil stability that Muhammad Ali's (1805–1848) long rule afforded to the population. Despite forced recruitment, war, and pestilence, the pasha's army did not treat the territories as conquered land, and the argument has been made that peasant families had enough peace in their lives to bear children (McCarthy 1976).[3]

Until the mid-nineteenth century a large population was considered a source of strength for the state apparatus. As the population increased, numbers of peasants moved to the cities and, by the end of the nineteenth century, older towns began to grow. This growth was deemed responsible for what the Egyptian élite perceived as disorderly crowds and the unhygienic conditions in the cities (Mitchell 1988). The visual impact of urban crowds, the unemployed mob, aimlessly roaming youth, and people selling valueless objects was continuously substantiated through the census and statistical data of the colonial and formally independent Egyptian state[4] in the early decades of the twentieth century (Owen 1996).

The first official census in Egypt was conducted in 1882.[5] This was a time of upheaval as a result of the revolt by Egyptian officers against the slow and steady usurpation of power by European governments. Considerable administrative effort was put into sending census takers to towns and villages to accumulate data to be sent back to Cairo. However, the population estimates were vigorously contested and are regarded generally as undercounts. The second formal census was conducted under British rule in 1897, and other censuses followed every ten years.

Roger Owen (1996), a historian who specializes in the economic history of the modern Middle East, argues in an essay on censuses in the Middle East that these censuses, organized under formal and informal British rule, were used to produce facts in order to manage territories on a more scientific basis. The presentations of data in tables and graphs with their multiple correlations helped the colonial government to set priorities, allocate resources, and distribute wealth according to its interpretation of the census data. It allowed Egyptian readers of this data to think of their country as being populated by various kinds of people and made them sensitive to the relative density of one area over another. Moreover, the data established a sense of geography and space for the people, helping them to imagine and fix Egypt's boundaries with a people called Egyptians living within it. It is not that earlier regimes did not have systems of enumeration. The cadastral surveys and statistical regimes created during the reign of Muhammad Ali served as a basis for tax collection, recruitment, and public health campaigns. British-inspired counting mechanisms, however, were not merely used for utilitarian purposes. They became a part of the illusion of bureaucratic control that relied on countable abstractions of people and resources to implement policy. At the same time, the information encouraged new forms of social practices and self-representation by the people themselves (Appadurai 1996:116).

The historian and anthropologist Bernard Cohn (1987), writing on late-nineteenth-century colonial India, asserts that for the British in India the censuses were meant to objectify the country to its own population. He shows how the categories of inquiry introduced by colonial modernization made processes embedded in religious rituals, custom, and traditional symbols into something that could be "selected, polished and reformulated for conscious ends" (Cohn 1987:229). Through the census, what was considered unconscious practice could be examined, understood, and debated. The census touched on each and every aspect of Indian life; questions were asked about family, caste, religion, literacy, and infirmity. This information was then compiled in categories that would help the British to govern. Yet, it also provided Indians an arena in which to ask questions about themselves as they began to see themselves at a distance, objectified and represented in columns of different categories (Cohn 1987:230).[6]

In Egypt, from 1897 onward, the censuses similarly reflected the colonial desire to gain knowledge about the populace. From the very beginning, classification of data followed an established international pattern that allowed comparisons on a cross-country basis. The questionnaire started with the usual questions—number of people in a household, name of the head of household—then moved on to sex, age, civil status, religion, language, literacy, place of birth, racial composition, national identity, and so on. The colonial state made an exceptional effort to record every dwelling and note essential details of each person. The power of the state was evident in its ability to force people to answer questions that defined them according to categories the state had devised (Craig 1917:215–216; Owen 1996).

The colonial state was skeptical of the historical enumeration procedures practiced by earlier Egyptian regimes. Early-nineteenth-century state-sponsored enumerations, as mentioned above, were primarily for conscription or tax purposes. Colonial authorities argued that the *fellah*, ever vigilant and fearful of such an enterprise, would underreport earnings or be unavailable on designated days.[7] Before 70,000 census takers went out to conduct the survey on 6 and 7 March 1917, authorities arranged meetings in the main towns so as to explain the modalities of the census. Mosque *imams* were expected to talk about the census in Friday prayers, and "every scholar in Egypt whether belonging to a Government school or otherwise was presented with a two page leaflet setting forth the objects of the census and its utility" (Craig 1917:231). The public relations campaign was meant to allay fears that the census was intended to measure a system of new taxes or that it was in preparation for a general conscription (Craig 1917; Owen 1996).

We can look at that campaign as an early pedagogical effort by the Egyptian colonial state to convince the population of the desirability of the census. It was maintained that the census was for the benefit of the people, and their participation in the process would be in the national interest. Indeed, it was argued that the demographic evaluation would assist the state to devise programs and policies that would hasten Egypt's progress.

According to J. I. Craig (1917), controller of Egypt's Statistical Department and Census Office in the early part of the twentieth century, statistics and censuses were important because they gave information about the relative population growth and the diminishing size of agricultural land in Egypt. Craig argued that if the high fertility rates of 1917 were maintained, then the population would more than double from 13 million to approximately 29 million in fifty years. He questioned whether the projected 8.7 million feddans[8] under cultivation in fifty years' time (1967) would be sufficient to feed the increased population, because 4.4 million feddans barely supported the then-current population of 13 million (210–211).[9]

By the early-twentieth century, the view of an over-populated Nile Valley supplanted the earlier precolonial assumption of people as the strength of the nation. Reflecting this position, Wendell Cleland, a professor at the American University in Cairo in the 1930s, emphatically argued for a comprehensive birth control policy. Wendell claimed Egypt was primarily a rural country, and since most of the agricultural land was under the control of a few owners, it was already difficult for Egypt to maintain a population of 16 million in the mid-1930s. He asserted that the high fertility rate in Egypt would double the population in fifty-two years. He argued that the population should be reduced to 12 million inhabitants until resources could be generated to sustain further growth, in order to attain a higher standard of living. He gave three solutions that would secure this reduction: economic growth, emigration, and birth control. He called on the state to increase its national wealth, to encourage almost 4 million people to emigrate to Anglo-Sudan or Iraq, and to establish a birth control program. Cleland was an advocate for universal education and for raising the legal age for marriages. He also supported eugenic solutions for those who were "unfit and a social burden due primarily to hereditary mental defects" (Cleland 1939:480).

There were dissenting views that countered Cleland's prescriptions, notably that of A. E. Crouchley, an Englishman who taught at the Fuad I University in Cairo in the 1930s. Crouchley (1939) argued that the assumption of overpopulation was based on incorrect inferences from the available data. He contended that the land problem of Egypt was not due to overpopulation but to maldistribution. Where Cleland had failed to see any hope of change in landholding patterns, Crouchley saw opportunities for bringing more land under cultivation and a future in industrial development. He believed modern industrial development would increase the productivity of the country, which would help to support a larger population.

A proponent of a similar argument, Hamed El-Sayed Azmi, worked in the Statistical Department of the Egyptian government. In a published lecture (Azmi 1937) given at the American University in Cairo, Azmi stated that even though Egypt had a very high population growth rate, an industrialization scheme could productively employ the growing population, and the distribution of cultivable land could improve the miserable living conditions of the peasantry.

Such differing views were representative of early-twentieth-century debates on birth control and demography in Europe and in the United States. The first two decades of the twentieth century saw the rise of the eugenics movement in the United States as a bona fide academic and scientific endeavor supported by wealthy foundations with names like Carnegie, Harriman, and Kellogg. In the 1920s, Margaret Sanger, who led the birth control movement, also moved closer to the goals of the eugenicists by demanding birth control and sterilization for the unfit, the undesirable, and the poor (Hartman 1995:99; Hodgson 1983:15). Cleland's interventionist social-engineering agenda of keeping population down through forced migration, birth control, and eugenics was evidently influenced by these debates.

Crouchley's and Azmi's contrary analysis also had a respectable lineage, which would gain visibility soon after the Second World War. Early-twentieth-century demographers discussed population trends in Western societies where fertility declines had been linked to industrialization. There were generally two assertions made on the relationship between socioeconomic change and demographic change. First, agrarian societies with high mortality and high fertility rates would change to lower indices as society moved toward industrialization, and second, this shift would decrease the mortality rates more rapidly with the subsequent possibility of an initial period of population growth (Hodgson 1983:7). In his 1929 article "Population," Warren Thompson outlined a similar schema for societies, predicting that they would go from high to low fertility as they moved from an agrarian economy to a transitional phase and finally into an industrialized society. These works became the basis of the demographic transition theory developed at Princeton in the mid-1940s.

The population question as a policy issue has a long history in Egypt. Early-twentieth-century censuses in Egypt found general correlations between land availability and population growth. Its analysis also provides us with unique insights into how demographic theory developed in the West.

DEVELOPMENT OF DEMOGRAPHIC THEORIES

In the 1940s a number of demographers such as Kingsley Davis, Ansley Cole, and Dudley Kirk worked at Princeton's Office of Population Research under Frank Nostestein's direction. A major aim was to develop a demographic explanatory theory that could work beyond the industrialized world.

The classical demographic transition theory predicted that all countries would follow the European demographic path once societies moved from agriculture-based economies to industrialization. This concept was linked with the general modernization process.[10] Nostestein and others argued, based upon historical trends, that the demographic change in Europe and North America had occurred mostly without the use of contraceptives. It was asserted that fertility declined when men and women became motivated to have fewer children. Motivation changed as a result of structural changes in the social system (Hodgson 1988:542).

By the late 1940s, however, Nostestein and his colleagues started to view population growth in nonindustrialized societies as an impediment to modernization. They contended that waiting for the demographic transition to run its course would be catastrophic to the standard of living in the developing countries. There was, as a result, a major shift in the analysis of world population. This shift represents the orthodox version of the demographic transition theory. Demographic change was previously believed to be a consequence of socioeconomic change, but the focus shifted to high fertility rates, which were deemed to be a cause of underdevelopment that needed to be countered with aggressive interventions by the state (Hodgson 1983:12−13). This focus on population control in the nonindustrialized world took on added importance during the Cold War. Rapid population growth was held responsible for economic and political instability that could benefit the spread of Communism. There was a sense of political urgency among some North American researchers to stop population growth by providing family planning information and methods.[11]

The single most important change in classical demographic theory to its present-day orthodox version was the emphasis given to the individual in contrast to societal changes (Khan 1994). In this new model individuals were viewed as isolated atoms that would act rationally in their own interest if given contraceptives. Kingsley Davis argued that peasants would be encouraged to accept birth control as living conditions became more difficult. "After all," Davis and Nostestein stated, the peasants were not "stupid" (quoted in Hodgson 1983:22−23; Khan 1994:7).

The new orthodox demographic theory has been widely criticized in the last several decades for its lack of emphasis on social structural development. The theory's stress on family planning has, however, survived as a component of the larger development efforts of international agencies in the 1980s and 1990s. International institutions have renewed their emphasis on the security aspect of population growth. Just as it was once thought with alarm that expanding populations were contributing to the spread of Communism, they are now held responsible for violent conflicts around the world, in places as varied as Rwanda, Haiti, or the Zapatistas' Mexico (Hartman 1995:150).

Population experts at the United Nations, the World Bank, USAID, and other international agencies continue to correlate low living standards in poorer countries to their high birth rates.[12] In the last two decades, though, some economists and demographers affiliated with the National Academy of Sciences have challenged the dominant position among population experts that population increase has a negative effect on the economy and leads to resource exhaustion (National Academy of Sciences 1986 as quoted in Hartmann 1995). In 1988, a group meeting of UN experts supported this argument by asserting that population growth may not have played a major role in enhancing or retarding the economic progress of developing countries (McNicoll 1995).

Trends in population policy have ignored these revisionist rationales. Major global players in population policy, such as the Population Council in New York, the United Nations Population Fund (UNFPA), the World Bank, and USAID (organizations that are sometimes referred to as the "population establishment" by some feminist and libertarian scholars, see Hartmann 1995) are prone to shift the argument on population in order to retain fertility control as a major component of the program. For example, when the argument linking environmental degradation to demographic projections was academically challenged, these organizations switched to an argument based on a defense of women's autonomy and reproductive health (McNicoll 1995).

In line with this latter rationale, the 1994 International Conference on Population and Development (ICPD), held in Cairo, focused on gender equality, equity, and the empowerment of women. Pronouncements from the conference were, however, still closely associated with strengthening of family planning programs. The shift also paralleled a change from an earlier service delivery model based primarily on a strategy of targets and incentives to one that integrated *i*nformation, *e*ducation, and *c*ommunication, the "IEC" approach (Hartman 1995:155).

Current Egyptian policies follow the above-discussed trends. Policy advocates have invested in rhetoric on women's equality and reproductive health and on expanded family planning delivery services in conjunction with the IEC programs.[13] The Egyptian family planning program also retains two basic assumptions of the orthodox theory: (1) that rapid population growth is a major social problem in Egypt that justifies, prior to full industrialization, providing people (especially the poor and peasants) with contraceptives to lower fertility; and (2) that lowering the fertility rate will enhance the rate of structural change and improve the standard of living for the entire population.

THE EGYPTIAN FAMILY PLANNING PROGRAM: THE EARLY YEARS

The Egyptian state's acceptance of the orthodox demographic theory was not straightforward. The state had resisted the pure service delivery approach until the 1980s. The Egyptian government had been sensitive to the developmentalist argument of the earlier classical theory since the 1950s, yet dependency on international support increasingly forced a shift in focus.

A National Committee for Population Affairs was formed to address population issues after 1952 when the Free Officers, under the leadership of Gamal Abdel Nasser, took control of the government. The committee emphasized socioeconomic development rather than provision of family planning services. A growing number of administrators were, however, wary of the negative impact of population on development (Ibrahim 1995). A Supreme National Council for Family Planning was established in 1965 as the pressure mounted from within the state bureaucracy for a more directed family planning agenda. The Egyptian state adopted a new policy aimed at reducing the crude birth rate[14] by one per thousand per annum, which stemmed from the council's recommendations in the mid-1960s. This policy provided for a National Family Planning Program that relied on Ministry of Health clinics and health centers to distribute contraceptives. The Sadat (1970–1981) government articulated a similar national population policy after the 1973 war. However, family planning delivery services remained part of a development process that included better living standards, expanded education opportunities, improvement in the status of women, mechanization of agriculture, industrialization in rural areas, lower infant mortality, improved social security coverage, and better informational and communication facilities (Ibrahim 1995).

The "National Strategy Framework of Population, Human Resource Development and the Family Planning Program" issued by the government in 1980 emphasized a similar comprehensive development program.

Following the guidelines set up in the 1970s, the 1980 policy argued for an increase in contraceptive use among married women, which would result in a reduction in the crude birth rate by twenty percentage points by the year 2000. The guidelines also promoted lower infant mortality, improved health status, and higher education levels. They further recommended a reduction in urban concentration and rural-urban migration through the construction of new cities in the desert along with the integrated development of rural areas (Ministry of Health 1981).

USAID AND FAMILY PLANNING

International donor agencies, primarily USAID,[15] criticized the integrated development approach to population policy as being ineffective. They found the agenda and mandate too broad. To effect change with regard to this policy, in the late 1970s and the early 1980s USAID exerted considerable pressure on the Egyptian government to change its focus toward a more directed fertility control program. Bilateral U.S. assistance to Egypt's population program through USAID commenced in 1977 and far exceeded any other source of international funding.[16] The timing of the funding was linked to the Carter administration's peace initiative and the signing of the peace accord between Egypt and Israel. USAID allocated $87 million in funds between 1977 and 1983 to the state-run program, with a promise of an additional $20 million in 1985 (World Bank 1984).[17]

When a comprehensive peace was achieved and Egypt was thought to be securely in the American sphere of influence, USAID consultants argued for a change in the population policy. USAID threatened to stop funding on the eve of the 1983 contract renewal if the government of Egypt did not accept its views (USAID 1982a:38). The carrot-and-stick ploy was successful and an extension was granted in 1983. An additional $102 million was allocated to the population sector for the years 1983 – 1988 (to a total of $117 million by 1992).

USAID proposed changes in the areas of policy, information, services, and research to strengthen the family planning program.[18] The current policy relied on the donor-funded Contraceptive Prevalence Survey and the Egyptian Fertility Survey of the early 1980s. These surveys showed lower-than-expected levels of contraceptive use and a high rate of population growth. Based on this information, the primary emphasis was on expanding and strengthening the Egyptian family planning service delivery in the public and private sectors (USAID 1987).

In 1985 international donors such as USAID recommended the establishment of a National Population Council,[19] through which the donors introduced a new National Population Plan that focused on family planning with an emphasis on service delivery. The plan emphasized the "free choice" of citizens to control their family size and the right of people to migrate internally or externally. It also addressed specific developmental concerns linked to population control, such as grass roots participation, empowerment of women, mass education, environmental protection, and the role of the NGOs (Ibrahim 1995).

In 1988, the National Population Council (NPC) coordinated a drive to decrease the rate of population growth from 2.8 percent annually to 2.1 percent by the year 2001. The NPC estimated that, in order to meet this goal, 51 percent of couples would have to use contraceptives as opposed to the 35.4 percent currently using modern methods (USAID 1994). Although demographic surveys showed that the contraceptive prevalence rate[20] was 47 percent among married women, and the total fertility rate (TFR)[21] had declined from 6.6 in the late 1960s to 3.9 in the early 1990s (DHS 1996), the population donor agencies continued to expand their effort in the public and private sectors. Hypothetical population projections made by the donor agencies indicated that the TFR was too high. They claimed that the rate of increase would raise unemployment rates, accelerate the loss of agricultural land, speed up urbanization, and reduce the per capita investment on education. In short, all the indices of development and standard of living would be adversely affected (Futures Group 1992).

Based on survey data,[22] international analysts argued that, although the prevalence rate had increased, there was still an unmet need for contraceptives. Simply put, unmet need was described as those women who said that they wanted no more children or wanted to space their pregnancies but were not using contraception (Cochrane and Massiah 1995). Analysts contended that there was an estimated 15 to 20 percent unmet need for contraceptives by married fecund/fertile women in Egypt, which could be improved with family planning services that gave women more contraceptive choice (Cochrane and Massiah 1995:15–16).

THE FOCUS ON FEMALE BODIES AND SELVES

Until the mid-1980s, the contraceptive pill was the contraceptive most widely used by Egyptian women. With USAID's direct involvement in family planning policy, IUDs became increasingly available in the public sector with a concomitant rise in their use. However, as a high percentage of women have discontinued use of both these methods, policy planners have further introduced injectables and Norplant in the public and private sector. All these methods are distributed in most of the approximately 3,500 Ministry of Health (MOH) facilities, which include general and district hospitals and maternal and child health centers.

During the 1980s, research by NGOs under USAID contracts regularly monitored women's use of oral contraceptives. Their reports demonstrated that women used the pill according to their own health beliefs and disregarded family planning program recommendations with regard to proper use. These reports claimed that women did not follow the prescribed 21- or 28-day cycle and instead disrupted the pill sequence primarily because of "perceived side effects" (SPACC 1990). Pill skipping resulted in breakthrough bleeding, which was sometimes understood as menses by women and in turn further delayed the continuity of the pill cycle. Women also discontinued the pill if they were not sexually active or their husbands were away for a few days. Researchers found that women taking oral contraceptives for some months would "take a rest" from the pill without changing to any other method of contraception. Women also were believed to be easily influenced by family and friends with respect to knowledge about contraceptive use (SPACC 1990; DHS 1992).[23]

The studies of oral contraceptive use mentioned above may have convinced policymakers that Egyptian women were not "responsible" enough to use them properly. They devised ways to bypass that difficulty as a result. By the late 1980s, government health clinics expanded IUD availability and aggressively introduced the highly subsidized IUD CuT380,[24] a long-acting contraceptive. Medically trained staff inserts the IUD, and women are counseled to come for regular checkups. The clinic staff uses these visits to check on whether the IUD is in place and also to counsel and reinforce the woman's acceptance of the method.[25] Once the IUD is inserted it cannot be removed by the user without some health risk. It can be effective for eight years, which gives the family planning program more control over women and their bodies, as well as the outcome of contraceptive use. The effectiveness of this method, therefore, depends much less on the women's behavior and ideas.

Providers have encouraged the use of other long-term methods, some of which are not reversible, such as injectables. Depo-Provera injections and Norplant were introduced into mainstream family planning services in the early 1990s. Both these methods were heavily subsidized by USAID and targeted rural and poor women. Irrespective of the uproar in the U.S. media created by women's organizations on the use of Nor-plant on poor, indigent, and minority women, in Egypt USAID pro-moted the widespread availability of Norplant under the rhetoric of ex-panded choice.[26]

These new "choices" are provider-dependent and have taken away decision-making power from Egyptian women. Under the argument of "unmet need," I believe, there has been an effort to expand control of women's contraceptive use by international providers. Long-term IUDs, injectables, and Norplant guarantee that Egyptian women, who cannot be trusted to take the pill regularly, can be regulated for many years. In this process, the potential hazards and risks that such "reliable" contra-ceptives pose to women's health remains secondary.

While the program aims to control women's bodies, it puts very little emphasis on condoms and voluntary vasectomy, the only internationally available male contraceptive methods. Family planning officials purport that condom use is a cultural barrier that they are unable to overcome. In my conversations with USAID and NGO officials, it was regularly stated that women view condom use within the family suspiciously; it is inter-preted to be indicative of men seeking sexual pleasure outside the family unit.[27] Men were not targeted for condom use by the media; rather, fam-ily planning advertisements primarily sought to influence male behavior, that is, to make men more accepting of the use of contraceptives by their female partners.

The international donor agencies would have liked male methods to be more popular, but they sensed resistance from their Egyptian coun-terparts. This has not meant a complete cessation of voluntary steriliza-tion / tubal ligation as a method for women.[28] The issue was one of power. International agencies, ever mindful of local cultural politics, adhere to codes of power differentials in the communities they serve including that of gender. Women are politically and socially weaker in Egypt, and, as such, they are manipulated to accept a range of contraceptive methods with only a rhetorical gesture toward the health risks.

It should be mentioned that USAID in Egypt contributes to a range of health-related development initiatives beyond family planning ser-vices. Its activities include child survival programs, diarrheal disease con-trol, breast-feeding training initiatives, and maternal mortality research. Most of these health programs, however, incorporate counseling sessions that urge women to have fewer children and to use contraceptives, which helps in further shaping of "new" women selves and making women more open to acceptance of contraception.

NONGOVERNMENTAL ORGANIZATIONS
AND FAMILY PLANNING

President Hosni Mubarak of Egypt has frequently used his position to blame people for overpopulating and overconsuming and, thus, straining the infrastructure of the country (Wahba 1993). In an address he asserted that

> the over-population stands in the way of development. It affects the standard of living for millions of Egyptian families, and it limits the government's abilities to increase the services for the citizens. It causes budget deficits that lead to inflation and the taking of loans from other countries. Also, a large family prevents parents from taking care of their children. Some people have 10–12 children and their income does not cover the needs of their children, so they remain illiterate or become thieves and unhealthy members of society.
>
> *Al-Ahram,* 2 MAY 1991

This language from the highest office in the country places blame for overpopulation and the debt crisis on the Egyptian masses. Such speeches rhetorically link social problems such as illiteracy, theft, and other vices to the presence of too many people within the country. The National Population Council has responded to such diatribes against uneducated people with a movement to eradicate female illiteracy and to support the social and economic development of women—two indicators linked to smaller family size.[29] The program emphasized the integration of arguments about population growth into the education curriculum. It organized female adult literacy classes that targeted poor women and girls who drop out of school. Poor women, both rural and urban, were targeted because they were considered outside the self-regulatory structures guaranteed by formal education. The curriculum for women focused on issues of family size, good motherhood, and child care (Mahran 1993).

Further, as I shall elaborate in greater detail later, in the early 1990s policy shifted toward creating a relationship between the individual and the state, mediated through the constitution of new kinds of families where the notion of individual choice within the nuclear family became paramount. This idea of free choice was linked also to the universalized language of rights and laws. During my stay in Egypt, this universal standard was emphasized in multiple forums sponsored by the international development agencies in Egypt. In a policy paper prepared for the Population Council's Middle East office in Cairo, for example, Nahid Toubia, a Sudanese physician and a leading voice on women's health in the Middle East, and Abdullah An-Na'im, an eminent Sudanese jurist, reflected on the legal dimensions of the health of Arab women. The authors advocated the implementation of international standards of treatment toward women in the national life of Middle Eastern states. They acknowledged the presence of overlapping sets of legal practices in the social life of people in the Middle East. The customary laws, the *Shari'a* (Islamic law), and the guarantees in the state constitution, according to the authors, guide the personal and family life of women in the region. They suggested some sensitivity toward these legal traditions in formulating linkages to international human rights proclamations. However, they argued that the constitutional guarantees should override all other provisions and practices especially with regard to protection of freedom from discrimination on the grounds of sex and gender (Toubia and An-Na'im n.d.:15). The authors cautioned that this possibility was diminished in Middle Eastern countries for two main reasons: (1) The governments are authoritarian and oppressive, and (2) civil society organizations are weak. States that were signatory to international treaties opposing discrimination against women and other relevant international human rights law, the authors charged, should be made accountable by international pressure. In this they asked for the assistance of international nongovernmental human rights organizations to generate adverse publicity. They also advocated enhanced diplomatic pressure and sought to link aid provisions with treaty compliance (18–24). The role of the NGOs was, therefore, presented as crucial to applying pressure to governments to be held accountable for noncompliance with international treaties and to acts of discrimination that affect the status of women (Cook 1993:83). Such arguments clearly call into question the sovereignty of the Egyptian state by advocating the supremacy of international standards. They inevitably become sites of tension between the Egyptian state bureaucracy and international donor agencies.

Despite these frictions many NGOs participate along with government agencies in family planning and other development projects. Liberal-minded Egyptian scholars have argued that civil society in Egypt may have a pivotal role in achieving the goals of the population program. Scholars such as Saad Eddin Ibrahim (1995), an Egyptian sociologist, have asserted that rivalries among government ministries and the resultant bureaucratic inertia make the state unable to fulfill its role in implementing the program. He claims that the undemocratic nature of the state has harmed the potential of civil society. Civil society, therefore, needs to be strengthened for substantial improvement to occur in development goals, which include family planning.

According to Ibrahim, another major reason for the lack of success of the family planning program is the staffing of government clinics by medical doctors sympathetic to the Islamic groups. These doctors, he asserts, are hostile to fertility control policies and may subvert the programs. The NGOs that represent civil society are presented as "uneasy allies" of the state against the hostile Islamic groups "in the specific battle of family planning" (Ibrahim 1995:74–77).[30]

Although Ibrahim's position called for democratic freedoms and transparency in government functions, the donor agencies, especially USAID, have themselves been exclusionary in their funding choices. Nongovernmental organizations that use explicitly structural developmental or other approaches to population reduction have not received much funding. On the contrary, USAID has largely supported NGOs that echo its priorities. Transfer of technology, training of competent local staff, family planning research, family planning service provision, and private sector distribution of contraceptives are some of the fields in which these Egyptian NGOs have worked under USAID supervision. They have become the conduits through which the internationally sponsored family planning program has sought to establish itself outside the realm of governmental control.

The Contraceptive Social Marketing Project (previously Family of the Future), for example, was allocated $12 million between 1988 and 1993 to market contraceptives through the private sector to lower- and middle-income Egyptian couples (USAID 1992). Another NGO, the Clinical Services Improvement Project, was budgeted for $13 million for the same period to establish 112 upgraded fee-for-service family planning clinics in various governorates (USAID 1992). Similarly, the Egyptian Young Medical Doctors Association was given $2 million for a five-year period to recruit doctors in private practice for family planning training and to establish private clinics as extensions of the family planning services. These NGOs were supervised by U.S.-based consultants, such as Family Health International, Futures Group, Pathfinder, Johns Hopkins University Population Communication Services, and John Snow Inc.[31] USAID-funded NGOs follow the rhetoric of fertility control embedded in policies of expanded contraceptive choice and behavior change. They were also projected to receive almost 50 percent of USAID's population budget by 1993 (Gillespie et al. 1989), hence becoming the major players in disseminating family planning information, in training physicians in counseling techniques, and in holding workshops and outreach programs to educate women and men on the benefits of contraceptive use.

Most such NGOs remain ideologically committed to family planning and to the related structural adjustment program. In an interview with a senior member of the Egyptian Fertility Care Society, an NGO that works primarily in the area of research and evaluation of contraception, I was told that contraceptive use should precede focus on economic growth if a rapid fall in fertility rates is desired. My informant stated that structural adjustment policies and removal of social subsidies would benefit the program because they would force people to realize the costs of having a large family. While talking to a clinical staff member of the Cairo Family Planning Association (a pioneer NGO in the family planning field),[32] I was similarly told that, along with cultural concerns and the low social status of women, a major reason parents did not desire a small family was due to some of the existing social subsidies guaranteed by the state.[33] Only a removal of this support would make families aware of the real costs of raising children. These arguments are comparable to views on welfare reform that have been prevalent in the last decade in the United States. They are also clearly influenced by the emphasis placed by international donor agencies on the removal of social subsidies and their link to fertility control. In short, the positions of many NGO members on family planning tend to be a part of a worldview that they share with the international donors.

I end this chapter by emphasizing that international donors have effectively changed Egyptian family planning policy. The earlier emphasis on structural development and social equity has been replaced by one on behavior modification and expanded contraceptive choice. Behavior modification requires some consent on the part of the population; therefore, local NGOs have had a role in assisting donors to shape people's ideas and behavior. Under the international donors' influence there have been two other noticeable shifts in the program. There is one toward the construction of an individualized notion of self. The second shift is the inclusion of men in programmatic priorities. I will discuss these issues in the next and in later chapters in more detail.

A promotional video on counseling techniques that is shown in Egyptian family planning clinics tells the story of Fatima. Fatima lives in a working-class neighborhood in a large city. She is shown to be frustrated by her daily chores and by the burden of caring for her children alone while her husband is away at work. One day a neighbor explains to her the benefits of family planning. The neighbor then accompanies Fatima to the clinic where she is received with extreme courtesy and is counseled on the pros and cons of a range of contraceptive choices. The neighbor, although the facilitator of this process, makes it clear that her personal experience with contraceptives does not make her eligible to give Fatima advice. It is only the trained staff of the clinic that can help Fatima with clear and precise instructions because every individual is different and each body has particular needs.

Advertisements like these carry two major themes. First, women should not listen to anyone but the family planning program specialists for proper contraceptive instructions. Second, queries about contraceptives should be made in the personal context of the session, and each woman has to be counseled separately. Indeed, during the time of my research, the overall approach of family planning service delivery in Egypt was being reoriented toward "client satisfaction." The emphasis was on quality of care and treating the client with respect. As well, an initiative was under way to train family planning providers to become more sensitive to client needs. Client/provider language posited the client as primary, with the provider playing the role of a helper who could guide the client toward solving her problem of choosing the most appropriate contraceptive.

The Information, Education, and Communication (IEC) project in Egypt has been successful in making population one of the major issues that people think about when considering Egypt's future development. Data collection through biennial contraceptive prevalence surveys, attitudinal surveys, anthropological research, and focus groups is used concurrently to evaluate and technically strengthen the program. This information helps to produce directed media messages to dispel rumors and provide focused communication regarding the benefits of family planning (Gillespie et al. 1989).

This chapter focuses on specific interventions through which the Egyptian family planning program seeks to create knowledge and consensus regarding its policies. To show the breadth of the program and its implementation at various levels and sites, I will begin by presenting a textual analysis of survey reports on the roles men play in fertility decisions within the changing milieu of family and gender relations in Egypt. Following this I will briefly evaluate a public health campaign organized to create motivation for contraceptive use among rural Egyptians. Through ethnographic examples I shall further show how the need for individual counseling leads to training sessions for doctors. Then, I will describe actual occurrences of counseling and service delivery in an urban family health clinic. Through these examples the chapter will, therefore, present instances of how the family planning program gathers information on family life and gender roles and uses this knowledge to influence behavior patterns at the community and individual levels.

MALE ROLES AND FAMILY PLANNING

The historical invisibility of men in the debates on fertility control and contraceptive methods has been partially due to the persistent structuring of population control debates around female/male, reproduction/production, and domestic/public dichotomies.[1] Recently attention in international family planning circles has been given to the multiple forms in which cultures organize fertility decisions; this has moved planners to consider the views of male partners regarding fertility control. Surveys conducted in developing countries to study male beliefs and practices related to family planning have helped in comprehending male behavior in fertility regulation and in identifying trends for future family planning policy initiatives (Mustafa 1982; Mbizvo and Adamchak 1991; Jejeebhoy and Kulkarni 1989; Khalifa 1988; Abdel-Aziz, El-Zanaty, and Cross 1992). International family planning efforts have successfully integrated male methods, such as condoms and vasectomy, into their various programs. In Egypt, however, the user rates for these methods, as mentioned earlier, are extremely low. Policymakers explain this failure partly by evoking traditional culture, patriarchal norms, native notions of maleness, the "backwardness" of the peasant population, and "Islamic doctrine." Planners then seek to overcome these perceived threats to the family planning program through a concerted media campaign to educate and inform men on the importance of family planning.[2] I will use an extended example to illustrate some of the ways these culturalist perspectives are used to gather information on and to influence Egyptian fertility behavior patterns.

In 1991, the Egypt Male Survey was conducted by Macro International and Cairo Demographic Center, under contract from USAID (EMS 1992) to investigate male attitudes and behavior in Upper Egypt and Cairo with respect to family planning. The study sought to explain differences in family planning use between the two areas and to assist planners in increasing contraceptive use, especially in rural Upper Egyptian households (EMS 1992:1).

Development experts consider Upper Egypt to be a more "traditional" region in contrast to Lower Egypt (the Delta region) and Cairo. Upper Egypt's representation in ethnographic and development literature is generally more conservative, its men are shown to be more resistant to change, and its households are seen as more entrenched in a culture that subordinates women. Keeping this distinction in mind, the survey used variables of education and place of residence to understand the influence married men have on their spouses' fertility decisions. The rationale for the 1992 survey was that available data from the 1988 Egyptian Demographic and Health Survey (EDHS 1988) indicated that the percentage of currently married women who had ever used contraception in rural Upper Egypt was less than half (26%) that of rural Lower Egypt (58%). Similarly, the current contraceptive use among women was three times higher in rural Lower Egypt (36%) than in rural Upper Egypt (12%) (EMS 1992:2). The 1988 survey also showed that a higher percentage of women in rural Upper Egypt believed that their husbands disapproved of family planning. Reflecting these attitudes toward acceptance and use of modern family planning methods, the EDHS data further demonstrated that only 38 percent of married women in rural Upper Egypt said that they had ever talked about family planning with their husbands, compared to almost 70 percent of women in rural Lower Egypt (3). It was argued that the current low use of family planning methods in Upper Egypt was due to persistence of traditional norms and the dominance of the males in decision making within the household. Hence, the survey was set up to provide a comparison between the knowledge, practices, and attitudes of men from Cairo, considered more modern, and those of Upper Egypt, especially in the rural areas, the more traditional.

The first report of the survey showed that the percentage of men in Cairo who had ever used or were currently using any modern contraceptives with their spouses (81%) was twice as high as that for men in rural

Upper Egypt (11%) (EMS 1992:22). A significant reason for a low user rate in rural Upper Egypt was shown to be a desire for larger families among rural Upper Egyptian men.

The survey went on to report that men in Upper Egypt were more "likely than men in Cairo to cite fatalistic reasons (e.g., 'there is nothing one can do,' 'I accept what God gives me') for not intending to use" contraceptives (EMS 1992:32). These responses regarding nonuse of contraception fit, according to the survey, "with a view of more traditional men in Upper Egypt" (32). Urban residence and men's education levels were positively linked, as predicted, with family planning approval, higher user rates, and higher autonomy for their spouses.[3]

In Cairo, where husbands and wives were said to have more equitable roles in decision making, there was found to be higher approval, knowledge, and adoption of modern family planning methods. This conclusion was further "confirmed by the reported level of equal influence of both husband and wife in such a decision. The highest level [was] observed in Cairo (34%), gradually declining to 27% in urban Upper Egypt and 19% of men in rural Upper Egypt" (EMS 1992:59). Similarly men in Cairo (56%) were less likely than men in Upper Egypt (66%) to say that they had more influence than women in household family planning decisions. In sum, the lower level of contraceptive use in Upper Egypt could be at least partially attributed to the persistence of traditional ways of rural Upper Egyptian men who, among other traditional practices, did not allow as much freedom of movement and opinion to their wives as did men in Cairo (53).

Yet other findings did not always follow prediction. A higher percentage of Upper Egyptian men (47.3%) than in Cairo (40.3%) had discussed fertility desires with their wives (EMS 1992:45). Again contrary to belief in family planning circles that Islam is a major hindrance to contraception, religion did not seem to stop the respondents from using family planning methods. In fact, rural Upper Egyptian men were less likely (8.9%) than men in Cairo (14.3%) to cite "religion as the main reason for not intending to use" contraception (32). The survey analysts implied surprise at this finding, as the text suggests: "Contrary to the theories that men in rural Upper Egypt do not use [contraceptives] because they are opposed to family planning on religious grounds the data showed no evidence of this" (32).

Results frequently challenged the predictions of the analysts, showing that the overall percentage of men in Upper Egypt who reported that using family planning methods for the first time was mainly their wife's idea was higher in Upper Egypt (39%) (43% for rural Upper Egypt) compared to those for men in Cairo (31%) (EMS 1992:63). The survey analysts, though they effectively acknowledged that the results seemed to undermine the conservatism thesis—"contrary to expectations" (63)—interpreted the findings in a way that made this connection obscure: the "wife's role was negatively related to the level of modernization" (63).

The core of the matter is that although this USAID-sponsored survey did uncover some differences in knowledge, use, attitudes, and decision-making practices between men in Cairo and men in Upper Egypt, the differences were not sufficient to account for the difference in contraceptive use. The findings often contradicted conventional culturalist expectations. However, and most important, the report concluded that the prevailing conservative and traditional social norms in rural Upper Egypt influenced men's decision-making role in family planning in the area and might be responsible for the differences in contraceptive use (EMS 1992:70). Anomalies were forced to fit the culturalist paradigm.

The survey analysts perhaps found it difficult to understand that people could simultaneously hold different views that undermine neatly laid-out schemes of behavior prediction. In that sense the above-mentioned concluding statement may be analyzed not only for the answers received but especially for the terms and categories through which the problem was defined and articulated. Survey questions on discussion within the household, who makes decisions on fertility control, compatibility of responses among husband and wife, and freedom of opinion and movement of women, are queries that are influenced by a modernist paradigm. The anthropologist Susan Greenhalgh (1995, 1996) critically evaluates this thrust in survey design by emphasizing the embeddedness of demographic research in modernization theory. She argues that the classic transition theory linked fertility decline historically to Western-style socioeconomic modernization, industrialization, modern education, Western behavior patterns, and political liberalization. Recent shifts in this theory, Greenhalgh maintains, still retain the evolutionary impetus of modernization and Westernization. Modernization of behavior may, therefore, lead to the constitution of modern families that are more open to the use of modern contraceptives.

Demographic research further shows that the level of education, autonomy of women, and consensual companionate marriage are demonstrably linked to higher acceptance of contraception. In this process the notion of the free-choosing individual who as a consenting adult creates the bond of conjugal marriage is crucial. Dipesh Chakrabarty (1994a) outlines social processes in colonial India in which the construction of a modern domestic sphere relied on promoting the idea of "friendship" between spouses. Husbands and wives were supposed to be friends/companions reflecting the well-known Victorian ideal of companionate marriage (Chakrabarty 1994a:51). The construction of this domestic/private sphere in embodying within itself the modern private/public dichotomy sought[4] to isolate the "couple" from the local familial and community contexts and exposed it to the controlling gaze of the statal laws and regulations. Hence, the notion of social good and responsibility within the "private," which casts the individual into the role of the citizen, enhances the ability of the modernizing state to regulate the reproductive sexual relations of the conjugal couple without hindrance or competition from other kin, affine, and community members (52). I suggest that the population-planning program sponsored by the Egyptian state and the international agencies attempts to socialize the domestic sphere in precisely these terms; it seeks to create modern notions of subjectivity, individuality, and bodies linked to an inclusive notion of responsible citizenship.[5]

I assert that, although not explicitly stated, the Egypt Male Survey assumes the nuclear household as a normative decision-making unit and the sole locus of social respectability. The contrast made with rural Upper Egyptian men through representative sampling is drawn precisely to study their departure from this norm. Historically, by the early twentieth century, marriage patterns based on choice and "love," reflecting changing social and economic structures, were becoming common among the élite of Egypt (Baron 1991). The insistence on a nineteenth-century version of the liberal European family that is currently being imposed on Egyptian households through media campaigns and developmental efforts seeks to "normalize" the vast majority of the Egyptian poor who, although statistically living in nuclearized households, are not "behaving" as modern families (as the Egyptian élite themselves had chosen to live), especially in their nonuse of fertility control methods.

In the process there is also, of course, a construction of a community described as Upper Egypt, whose complexities and internal hierarchies are flattened by the classificatory criteria to make it a suitable target for administrative policy (Chatterjee 1998). Moreover, as indicated, the survey was not primarily conducted to encourage men to use contraceptives. The data were generated to ascertain male influence on female decision making, so that if it was negative, the men could be motivated through information and communication campaigns. Based on these assumptions the family planning program set itself the task of changing people's behavior where these behaviors patterns seem to deviate from the norm defined by the program.[6]

CHANGING BEHAVIOR

In Egypt the task of changing people's behavior is carried out by many actors serving the larger social goal of fertility reduction. Specifically, as suggested earlier, USAID-funded NGOs follow the rhetoric of fertility control embedded in policies of expanded contraceptive choice and behavior change. They are major players in disseminating family planning information, in training physicians in counseling techniques, and educating women and men through workshops and outreach programs on the benefits of contraceptive use.

I attended a workshop called the Family Health Week. This week-long workshop was organized in Minya, an Upper Egyptian governorate,[7] through the collaboration of Johns Hopkins University Population Communication Services (funded by USAID) with the National Population Council, the Ministry of Health, and sixteen local family planning and IEC organizations. Components of the program included outreach activities, seminars, evening mass meetings, church and mosque meetings, and small community meetings aimed at promoting general awareness about family planning.

As mentioned above, in developmental rhetoric Upper Egyptians are thought to be culturally and politically more conservative. Although most of the country's development projects are based in this region, development experts argue that traditional behavior patterns in the region are difficult to change. The Health Week was designed to motivate Upper Egyptians to modify their negative attitudes toward family planning. Minya was chosen as a test site for this program.

In one of the outreach visits I accompanied a senior woman doctor from the regional directorate of health services to a village health center a few kilometers outside the city of Minya. When we arrived there were about thirty women sitting in the clinic's small reception area. The whole episode had a staged appearance to it. It was obvious to me that the women, some of whom were well past child-bearing age, had been asked to show up by the clinic's staff, who themselves had been under orders from the regional health directorate to ensure that our visit was a "success." These measures were taken to guarantee that the program's objective of reaching a certain target population was met. The doctor gave a lecture to the assembled women on the benefits of IUD use. Her talk included a discussion about women's health and how giving birth to three children within the space of three years was against natural and scientific norms. She then argued that spacing childbirth gives women time to recover their health and also helps the mother to breast-feed a child without competing demands from other children. Before asking for volunteers who would be counseled on the benefits of using contraception, she told the women that IUDs were better than pills because pills could be excreted in the mother's milk and harm the breast-fed child. The doctor primarily used ideas about the well-being of the women and their children to influence their attitudes toward childbirth and fertility control. The women were mostly silent during the whole seminar and eventually, out of the thirty, three volunteered to stay on to relate their health needs.

During the same week I also accompanied religious leaders and doctors to a nearby village where a lecture was arranged for men on the benefits of fertility control and the conformity of family planning to Islam. When we arrived after sunset there were about twenty men present at the primary school building. The *shaykh,* an important person among local leaders of Minya, started speaking in the glow of kerosene lanterns. Using Egyptian Arabic (i.e., nonclassical Arabic), he argued that Islam is not against having children, "but the children should be healthy and educated." He continued to assert that a physically, morally, and intellectually unhealthy nation would be undesirable in Islam. He added that the present deteriorating economic circumstances would force large families into dire social conditions, hence, family planning was necessary to avoid a bleak future. He gave graphic examples of how too many children could affect the health and welfare of the mother. "We could imagine," he continued, showing his theatrical skills, "how a mother may have two babies suckling on her two breasts while she is already pregnant with another child."

If this was supposed to amuse or shock the men, they did not show it, or it may have been too dark for me to notice. However, during the question-and-answer session, one of them asked why, since women had started taking pills, they now had more twins and even triplets and thus were endangering their lives. The *shaykh* responded with annoyance and admonished the crowd that these rumors were spread by the uneducated and the idle. Raising his voice, he said, "The people should only trust the doctor while discussing birth control and its effect on the body, for they have the scientific knowledge."

These two episodes reflect how local-level NGOs, in collaboration with the Ministry of Health and international donors, work to create consent and argue for the legitimacy of scientific methods for family planning. State planners and international donors also have shared concerns for the success of their program. For example, using the *shaykh* to deliver the message to men aided in deflecting arguments against family planning from religious leaders belonging to the Islamist movement. During the period of my stay in Egypt (1992–1994), the governorate of Minya was a hotbed of Islamist resistance to state authorities. At the time of my research there were daily armed attacks on police convoys by Islamists. In exchange the security services would be involved in search-and-destroy missions in the countryside. This political situation itself had an effect on the outcome of this Health Week.

The organizers had produced a play aimed at male participation in family planning that was scheduled to be performed at several sites during the course of the week. The script of the play had been preapproved by the government censors and the security apparatus as having no politically objectionable material. The actors were also considered politically trustworthy, meaning they were not sympathetic to the Islamists. Yet on the day of the first performance the governor of Minya, an army general, canceled the play.

It should be kept in mind that the Health Week activities were part of the government-sponsored development program for the region. However, assembling a large audience, given the prevalence of violent skirmishes between the state forces and the Islamists in the area, was considered a security risk by the governor's office. The international sponsors of the program protested to the higher authorities in Cairo but were politely told to follow the regional government's orders. Hence, the political system with its heightened concerns for maintaining law and order became a hindrance to the propagation of the state's own policy initiatives, leaving the foreign donors and their locally supported NGOs frustrated and incapable of completing their goals.

The above examples also reflect other predicaments that the international donors may have with the program. Earlier in the text I mentioned that the family planning program targets rural and urban poor women in part because such women are outside the self-regulatory structures guaranteed through the process of formal education. States like Egypt have yet to fully develop the administrative and ideological structures found in Western democracies that lead to creating "free subjects" (Asad 1992). Therefore, force and coercion still take precedence over techniques of persuasion and pedagogy as methods of managing populations. Moreover, the desire to produce a self-motivated populace that voluntarily uses contraceptives is based on liberal notions of egalitarian social relationships; that goal may thus fail at times in societies like Egypt where social hierarchies may still be rigidly maintained.

As if to underline this point, the international agencies blame the hierarchical nature and the bureaucratic inertia of the state structures for the nonimplementation of the program. They also maintain that the doctors who work in the government clinics are supportive of the Islamist political groups and are active in sabotaging the family planning project (Ibrahim 1995).[8] Irrespective of the prevalent fear of Islamists, the doctors whom I accompanied on outreach visits in Minya agreed to participate in the program because they were ordered to do so by their superiors, who in turn faced pressures from the international donors. For some, like the female doctor I accompanied to the village clinic, the reason to participate was the monetary compensation she received. Similarly, as I found out later, most of the men and women gathered at these events were promised either a small fee or a generous snack. Self-motivation in this regard, for doctors and "clients," was intrinsically linked to material incentives.

Sensitive to this process and at the risk of becoming ineffective, international donors pay particular attention to individual behavior change along with large media and health campaigns. Social awareness toward family planning is consolidated by family planning service providers at the individual level. Techniques for incorporating the patient's point of view are thought to be efficient ways of increasing "user rates" and are used as a strategy to deal with the ongoing problem of noncompliance. International donors also seek to actively change the nonenthusiastic and hierarchical behavior of the health professionals themselves. Keeping this in mind, programs concentrate not only on fundamentally changing patient behavior but also changing that of the physicians themselves.

Arjun Appadurai (1996a), in an article on British colonialism and its statistical enterprise in India, argues that new techniques of numbering and counting were not only meant to measure land or create social facts. They were also pedagogical exercises that sought to train low-level Indian functionaries in the culture of numbers in which statistics became the authorizing discourse of rule. As a consequence the census-taking enterprise also produced new kinds of selves that served as statal agents (126–127). Similarly in Egypt, in the late twentieth century, the task of training physicians was linked to the task of producing family planning workers as agents whose views are consistent with those of the international donor agencies.

TRAINING OF TRAINERS

At the time of my fieldwork (1992–1994), there were several training programs in Egypt for family planning workers in counseling techniques. One of these was located at the Regional Center for Training at the Ain Shams University in Cairo. Like the one in Minya, this program was sponsored by Johns Hopkins University and funded by USAID. The center conducted a number of short and long courses for doctors, nurses, and other family planning service providers. I attended a week-long course for doctors, concentrating primarily on the sessions that dealt with counseling techniques within the larger TOT (training of trainers) program.[9]

I attended sessions with twenty physicians, both male and female, from different parts of the country. Counseling lectures were scheduled for the third and fourth day of the workshop after the group had been given an overview of female reproductive physiology and had undergone training on the risks and advantages of various contraceptive methods.

The instructor was not a medical doctor but had received training in counseling methodology from Johns Hopkins University at Baltimore.[10] The instructor started the counseling session by proposing steps doctors should take when a female client enters the family planning clinic. Prior to this the designation of doctors as providers and women visiting the clinic as clients was understood, acknowledged, and agreed upon by all present. The instructor mentioned five basic steps for counseling: listening, dealing with the feelings of the client, giving clear information, questioning, and using visual aids. Then she asked rhetorically: "Why should we do counseling?" She provided the answer herself: "Because we need to help a woman decide the correct method for herself." All present nodded their heads showing agreement with this conclusion.

The lecturer then initiated a discussion by asking the assembled group what was the best form to interact with clients. Some doctors were interested in how they should approach the initial questioning of their clients. The instructor asserted that doctors should strive to use a good tone of voice, to be friendly, and to avoid medical terminology. This behavior would, according to her, relax most women and generate a level of trust in the client-provider relationship. The group was also told to avoid leading questions as the client might feel apprehensive about answering them. In all circumstances the client needed to feel comfortable and able to provide information with a minimum of coercion. The woman was to be encouraged to ask questions, and the providers were supposed to listen carefully. This was necessary, the instructor emphasized, because the client's questions would reveal her misinformation, ignorance, and apprehension along with her degree of knowledge, level of motivation, and attitude toward family planning.

These behavioral models of self-improvement imported from Western management techniques sought to resocialize and acculturate the doctors to be more efficient and client friendly. In the process, I would argue, new norms of "correct" behavior for enhanced productivity and client satisfaction were being introduced into Egyptian social life.[11] By improving their interpersonal skills through learning techniques for better communication and for presenting oneself as caring and trusting individuals, the instructor argued, the doctors could give better advice and help women make decisions on the most suitable kind of contraceptive for them. Counseling was, hence, meant to be a mutual exchange of ideas between the provider and the client, not a session in which the providers tell women what to do.

The next theme that was discussed was how counseling could help combat rumors about family planning. Some doctors raised the point that many Egyptian women believe that an IUD can rise to the heart. A general discussion followed among the participants on how best to counter this rumor in a clinic setting. One of the suggestions was to explain carefully that there was no connection between the uterus, where the IUD is placed, and the heart. "Tell them that the IUD is in a closed box," said one participant. Another person remarked that women should reassure themselves by continuously feeling the IUD thread. Then the instructor showed us a model of the uterus. She said that such a model should be present in every clinic, and women should be instructed by showing them this model about how the IUD is inserted and retained within the uterus. Scientific information in lay terms was, according to her, supposed to have worked elsewhere in countering this rumor.

The discussion moved to the rumor that contraceptive pills cause cancer. The instructor argued that first the credibility of the source of this information was to be attacked. If a neighbor had told a woman that pills caused cancer, then it needed to be emphasized that the neighbor did not know as much as the doctor. In the ensuing discussion one of the doctors said that she convinced her patients by giving them simple analogies. "I tell them," she said, "that everything is according to a person. As you cannot fit into any shoe or skirt, there is also a specific pill for you."

Religious ideas that interfered with the family planning message were supposed to be answered by quoting from the Qur'an while emphasizing the compatibility of religion with family planning. Similarly the instructor emphasized that uneducated people should be given examples of educated and important people in the community who use contraceptives. These examples would impress upon women the widespread use and safety of the methods.

One of the participants raised the issue of side effects due to different methods. There was a discussion about when not to prescribe certain methods depending on the history of the client. Yet there also was a consensus that some side effects should be treated as normal. For example, everyone agreed that women should be told that not having or having a menstrual cycle while on Depo-Provera (injectable) was normal. Similarly, headaches or swelling of breasts were to be taken as the norm when on pills. It was deemed preferable to tell a woman beforehand about these side effects so that she would not discontinue taking the pills when she experienced these symptoms.

Finally, the group was given the acronym GATHER to memorize.

G = Greet. We were told how we should greet the clients and how we needed to be courteous and pleasant. The instructor insisted that even if the client was dirty and had a bad odor, we should ask her to sit near us in a private part of the clinic and warmly ask about her well-being and employ small talk to relax her.

A = Ask. The next step was to ask the client about her personal history, number of pregnancies, number of children, past use of family planning, medical history, and sexual history. We should encourage her to ask questions and answer them.

T = Tell. We were asked to tell the client about her family planning choices and inform her of all the methods available. We should explain how the methods work and their advantages and side effects.

H = Help. Considering the information available to us, we were then supposed to help the client choose the best method for her.

E = Explain. The client was to be told how to use the methods correctly. For example, it was deemed necessary to remind clients that pills should not be skipped. Clients were to be told to look out for the warning signs for side effects.

R = Return. We were supposed to ask clients to return for regular checkups. For IUD users the first return visit was after one month, then six months, then a year, and then yearly. Similarly, women using the injectable method needed to come back for their next injection, just as pills users were supposed to return for their next batch of pills.

These sessions, as observed above, were meant to educate doctors to behave less authoritatively toward their family planning clients. These training sessions were based on literature that has developed in health communication studies regarding problems of noncompliance. This literature emphasizes that an authoritative doctor can have a negative impact on the long-term drug compliance of patients; that restoring the patient's trust in her physician necessitates a relationship-centered medicine that takes the patient's perspective into account (Roter 1995); and that while mass media campaigns, subsidized prices, and social marketing are important, face-to-face personal communication is extremely significant for effectively delivering the family planning message (Population Reports 1987a).

In this regard, the training sessions in Cairo advocated that doctors appear more caring in order to encourage women to use contraceptives. In addition, improved communication by the counseling staff was thought to lead to an enhanced understanding of the health risks associated with the contraceptive methods. Medical literature on compliance emphasizes the importance of continuing treatment even when the patient feels symptom free, and despite side effects (Leventhal and Cameron 1987). Similarly, women were supposed to be told to continue taking oral contraceptives even if their husbands were away, and regardless of side effects such as headaches, breast tenderness, or spotting of blood.

The training sessions need to be seen as conduits through which models of patient compliance are imported into the Egyptian family planning context by the international donor agencies. These models are intrinsically connected to evolving health practices in the West. They are built on the notion of a speaking patient who gives the doctor a history of subjective complaints. The histories are treated as those aspects of the patient's life that are not visible to the doctor. The physicians need to listen not only to obtain information but also to understand the person. Through this process the patient and doctor are supposedly bound in a relationship of mutual assistance, situated within the realm of the same kind of medical knowledge (Armstrong 1984). Indeed, counseling techniques embedded in models of "listening to the patient," as the training instructor put it, are concrete forms through which medical science seeks to make inroads into the private aspects of people's lives. With the new emphasis on and sensitivity to the client's voice, what once remained unsaid in patient-doctor encounters is now brought forward under the rubric of helping women help themselves and the rhetoric of facilitating decisions.

Further, family planning counseling procedures in Egypt as elsewhere tend to develop particular forms of self-awareness among women through a language of rights. The procedures are intended to develop a contractual relationship between women and providers where women have a right to information and choice of different contraceptive methods. In return, women accept counseling on contraceptive use. The language of informed consent is used to show the equal nature of the encounter. Women are given options from which to choose out of their "free will." [12] This supposedly egalitarian language of the client-provider relationship obscures the fact that the provider is the one with the biomedical knowledge and the client is only to be guided into this knowledge. When coming to the clinic the client is assumed to be reasonably aware of family planning methods, either from her friends or through the mass media. The task of the counselor is to further enhance the possibility that the women leave the clinic only after having made a choice from among the contraceptives available there. [13]

It is important to bear in mind that the donor-assisted family planning program seeks not only to enhance the range of individual choice available to women but also to create conditions in which only certain choices may be made. The program forecloses discussion of any other viewpoint or practice and, within the discursive terrain set up by the program, leaves no space to maneuver except within a tightly constricted arena. However liberatory the language of individual choice may be, it nonetheless precludes not choosing contraception.

The choice and autonomy that these counseling sessions advocate is, hence, illusory. The terms of the contract are not freely chosen by all. Rather they are preset by the clinical staff and the family planning program. The constant invocation of individual risks related to multiple childbirth and the social risks of having too many children is made to make women feel responsible for the social and economic problems facing the entire nation. In the name of individual choice they are guided into accepting contraception as part of being responsible citizens who may have to suffer "minor" health problems for the larger social good.

In counseling sessions that I attended, doctors would routinely go beyond telling women of the health risks involved in multiple pregnancies. "Why do you want to have so many children, are you going to feed them grass?" one counselor admonished a mother in a clinic I visited. Another staff member at a Cairo-based NGO told me that in their information campaign they emphasize that women who have many children should understand the social impact of their decisions. Women were told that if the population does not decrease, people will have to start living in the desert. Similarly, at another family planning training session for doctors and nurses, the trainer told us, "You should tell women that, if they can endure pregnancy for nine months, is it not better to use pills or IUDs and just endure discomfort for three months." This message, according to the trainer, would impress on women that temporary symptoms related to contraceptive use are far preferable to the agony of being pregnant.[14]

The rhetoric and aspirations of policymakers do not always translate into corresponding practices on the ground. In the following section I will briefly describe how counseling occurred in a family planning clinic in a popular neighborhood of Cairo. The women who came to this clinic belonged to the lower socioeconomic strata. The young doctors who worked in the clinic themselves felt the pinch of the social and economic crisis in Egypt, finding it difficult to maintain their living standard on the regular pay they received. Hence, as in most other places the doctors experienced some of the same social and cultural conditions of life as their patients.

A FAMILY PLANNING CLINIC

I regularly visited a clinic located in a public hospital in Shubra, a lower-middle-class neighborhood of Cairo. I was introduced to the clinic staff by a senior female doctor who worked for a family planning development project at the Ministry of Health. Over the course of a year, I went to the clinic once a week and had the opportunity to observe the treatment and counseling of women away from the policy assertions of higher-level bureaucrats.

The clinic was a small room in a hospital and was open from nine in the morning until about two in the afternoon.[15] The furniture in the clinic consisted of a large desk with a number of chairs behind it for the doctors. The patient area included a couple of chairs in front of the desk and a bench in the passage outside. The room was divided by a movable curtain partition into the "consultation" section with the desk and the chairs and the "examination" section with an examination table.

I normally attended the clinic with three female doctors who would occasionally be joined by a male doctor who was also the manager of the clinic. There was a senior nurse present along with some younger trainee nurses. They would assist the doctors with injections and IUD insertions. In their conversations with me, the doctors stated that life was economically very difficult for people of the area and most men worked two or three jobs. According to them family planning gave people some hope of reducing their household expenditures.

IUDs were the most popular method prescribed, and the doctors maintained that women preferred them to injections or the pill. However, the high frequency of IUD use may also be attributed to the monetary in-centives available to the clinic staff from the Ministry of Health. The doc-tors stated that women complained of weakness and headaches with pill use. These complaints were shrugged off by the clinic staff as exaggera-tions, or as excuses made to let them take time off from their daily chores.

The doctors were generally sympathetic in interacting with women patients/clients, addressing them with common terms of endearment and politeness. This, it seemed, was how people generally spoke to one an-other rather than the result of a conscious effort due to training.

The clinic was not very busy, since it was situated near other hospitals and mother-and-child Centers. During a normal working day the doc-tors would see ten or twelve women. Women would normally come ac-companied by a female relative or a friend. At times they would come with their children and occasionally on their own. Most women who vis-ited already had children. On one of my visits, four women came with complaints concerning their IUDs. The first woman had displaced her IUD string and had been continuously spotting blood. One of the doc-tors removed the IUD. The woman was then told to refrain from inter-course and come back in ten days after her normal menstrual cycle, at which time she would be given another IUD. She was counseled that if she wanted to have sexual relations during this time she needed to use foam tablets, while her husband should use condoms. The woman seemed ambivalent about these suggestions and left saying that she would speak to her husband.[16]

On another occasion a woman who had had an IUD inserted a few months previously came to the clinic complaining of heavy bleeding dur-ing her menstruation (menorrhagia). She was in her late twenties and had three children. A doctor removed her IUD and tried to persuade her to accept monthly injections as an alternative. The woman refused the offer and left without accepting any other form of contraceptive. After the woman left, there was a discussion among the doctors about whether the proposal to give her injections was a wise one. One doctor, somewhat older than the others, argued that injections should not be given to younger women, especially those who had not completed their family. A much younger doctor, who had advised the use of injections and had re-cently completed a three-week family planning training course, much like the one I had participated in, argued that there was no contraindica-tion based on age in the medical literature. The older doctor insisted that it was not only a matter of age, arguing that since "the injections also cause cancer and we do not know their long-term effect on the uterus, giving it to younger clients may risk their future fertility."

This discussion suggested that, regardless of guidelines on available contraceptives in family planning manuals and the very strong emphasis on the noncarcinogenic nature of injections in these guidelines, the doctors still created their own reasons to prescribe various contraceptives. Not only did the doctors differ in their understanding of medical literature but their personal life histories and political views played a role as well in their attitudes towards family planning. The older doctor who had opposed the suggestion of the injection was more religious in her general outlook on life. While working in the family planning clinic she was also an articulate critic of the family planning program and would argue that recommendations on contraceptive use were not made with the cultural and social conditions of poor Egyptian women in mind. She believed that injections were always harmful for younger women and should not be prescribed to women who had not completed their family. Similarly she was against the use of Norplant and also thought that women should not be exposed to long-term pill use. She saw her role as a judicious mediator between the harmful effects of some contraceptives and her unknowing female patients.

By and large the doctors agreed, however, when prescribing contraceptive methods. The counseling techniques mentioned above were seldom used to persuade women. Although polite in their demeanor, the doctors were aware of their social power and prestige in the eyes of their poor urban clients. They would suggest a contraceptive and sometimes firmly order the women to act accordingly. When this would fail, the nurse, who was closer to the patients in social class, would try to join the conversation and admonish the women for not thinking about their health and their family's future. This pressure invariably would have an effect on women who were initially reluctant to continue with the IUD or were thinking of postponing taking contraceptive pills.

The clientele at the clinic was quite varied. There were women in their forties who came regularly to get Depo-Provera injections. Other women came to initiate contraceptive use because their husbands were coming back from abroad. I do not have data from the clinic to suggest a pattern of how contraceptive use differed between those with many children and those with one or two. Based on my observation, however, most of the younger clients (in their twenties) were deciding to use contraceptives in order to space their pregnancies and had not yet completed their families.

Sometimes women would come and argue that they would like to have their IUDs removed because they thought it was *haram* (forbidden) in Islam. Many, however, came with problems of bleeding and infections while on IUDs. This population may not be a large enough group from which to generalize about the prevalence of IUD-related problems in the entire community, but almost every fourth client at the clinic came to have her IUD removed for a specific complication.

Once, when a woman came in experiencing extreme pain in her pelvic area, she was taken behind the curtain to be examined. I was sitting on the other side of the partition and could hear her scream with pain as the doctors tried to manipulate her uterus to extract her IUD. The woman's pain was most likely due to infection caused by the IUD. Lack of resources compels some doctors in government clinics in Egypt to work in circumstances where cold specula and unsterilized equipment are the norm. These procedures are mostly the lot of poor Egyptian women who have little say on what kinds of contraceptives they use yet bear the health-related consequences of their "choices." Unhygienic IUD insertion techniques result in high rates of infection and increase these women's general misery.

When I asked the head of the clinic about the level of care offered to these women by the Ministry of Health, he replied: "The MOH treats us like stepchildren. Look at our pay, why should we care?" He went on to state that since the government does not pay them enough, they are more interested in their private practices than in providing services to the people who come to the public clinic. "Anyway," he continued, "these are poor [women] who come here. When we see infections it is mostly with those patients who have not come for their follow-up due to financial reasons. The issue is poverty, not our skills." As these doctors strive on their meager pay to provide inadequate services to the poor women of the area, the poor, as I show in later chapters, may themselves seek out different solutions to their own predicament.

CONCLUSION

During the nineteenth century, as discussed in the introductory chapter, the improvement in gathering and analyzing numerical data led to determinism giving way to indeterminism, chance, and probability in the study of natural, social, and biological sciences (Hacking 1990). By studying deviations the state could intervene to improve social conditions. Normal people would conform to the central tendency of laws, while those at extremes were deemed pathological (as families with high birth rates are deemed to be in Egypt). Hence, the construction of categories, like those in the male survey, helped in shaping and defining how men and women would behave. Indeterminism determined classifications through which people could think on the actions open to them.

This assumption about a self-conscious subject may underlie some of the ways in which the modern state constructs its notion of a citizen with entitlement to rights and a legal status. Modern personhood is constructed in this discussion of rights with a substantive "core," which has a capacity to reason and exercise moral judgment (Poovey 1992; Butler 1990). This understanding of Western political and legal thought situates the substantive core of the human being within the construction of the autonomous individual that can act freely of its own choice.

For the Egyptian family program the acceptance and use of contraceptives by women depends on their systematic, regular, and responsible use. This also entails an autonomous self that can act as a "free agent." Through counseling, media advertisements, and adult education classes, Egyptian women are given an explanation of the medical construction of their bodies. In this chapter I show how women are not required to completely comprehend how different contraceptives prevent pregnancy, as long as they accept the efficacy of these contraceptives over other methods and use them continuously according to the physician's instructions, without listening to or agreeing with any other source. In this they need to understand their own bodies as unique and private, unrelated to others, the maintenance of their own health being prior and exclusive to other concerns (Correa and Petchesky 1994; Petchesky 1995). Women are encouraged to subjugate their particular interests for the social good as advocated by state representatives. They are required to set aside familial and domestic concerns and enter as individuals into the realm of the universal and the civil—the domain of citizenship. The family, then, as shown in the discussion of the male survey, is sought to be reconstituted as nuclear. Within this family, men are supposed to positively help women in their decisions on family planning and work as a spokesperson for the state policy. Thus, not only female behavior needs to be changed but male behavior as well, since men too have to comply with new forms of social expectations (see chapter 6).

I would argue that this intervention, embedded in the liberal narrative of managing populations with their own consent, is not always intended to produce full-fledged, right-bearing citizens. Rather, the motive is to construct, particularly in women, an individualized sensibility that would diligently follow the advice of a benevolent state. The crucial aspect to bear in mind in this mechanism of inclusion is the production of consent.

Liberal political theory itself raises the question: Why should a free and equal individual be governed by anyone else? The question is answered by citing an acceptable justification for people to enter into authority relationships (as poor urban and rural women in Egypt are supposed to do with the family planning physicians). That justification is the voluntary act of commitment individuals make, reshaping the relationship of authority and obligation (Pateman 1989).[17]

Further, the notion of the individual in classical political philosophy constructs the female as the site of unreasonableness, of passion, of affection, and of the body. In contrast, the notion of the male is imbued with qualities of detachment, of control, and of the impersonal (Ruddick 1989). To enter into a politics of contracts, which some feminist arguments also favor, is evidently to participate in a debate where women can struggle for civil equality and make claims to their personhood. Yet it also means an aspiration to acquire acknowledgement as reasonable, rational, and responsible individuals. In this sense, some scholars would argue that the modern "individual" belongs to the patriarchal category of Western thought (Chakrabarty 1992; Pateman 1988)

Egyptian women are persuaded to emulate this ideal of a self-regulating, autonomous, and contract-making self before they can be properly trusted by the family planning program. The family planning program provides counseling and guidance to ensure that they make the appropriate contraceptive decision. In so doing it seeks to change who they are. As family planning counselors in Egypt grant women choices, it becomes evident that these choices are determined by a medical discourse and practice linked to the development agenda. While women are counseled into accepting contraceptives, they are also channeled into being socially responsible according to criteria of social responsibility defined by the state and by universalist ideals. The discrepancy, however, between rhetoric of counseling and its implementation in practice, as shown in the example of the family planning clinic, informs us that the social implementation of pedagogical projects sometimes confronts its own limitations. In Egypt, women may yet have other constructions of the self, of the body, and of social responsibility and may, therefore, undermine the developmental agenda's efforts. I elaborate on these issues in following chapters.

Part Two

Spatial Context

As I discussed in my analysis of the Egypt Male Survey in the preceding chapter, demographic studies on Egypt tend to be constructed in terms of the rural-urban divide. In this formulation the rural is defined as the traditional space, and the urban pertains to the modern and the progressive. Egyptian health- and population-related surveys are generally designed to capture the negative impact of rural living and peasant behavior on contraceptive prevalence and acceptance. Arguably there are social distinctions that need to be recognized within a population group on the basis of where people live. In this chapter I use this dichotomy primarily to help readers understand the social and spatial context of my fieldwork. However, I will also seek to highlight some of the problems such generalized dichotomies entail. For example, migration to oil-producing Arab states in the 1970s and the longer history of rural-urban migration within Egypt undermine the sharp distinctions between rural and urban space and social life. In recent years the high cost of living in Cairo, to give another example, has compelled many to continue living in villages while working in Cairo, a process that emphasizes economic and social continuity rather than separation. Similarly, boundaries between rural and urban space are continuously blurred as agricultural lands at the outskirts of Cairo and other towns are encroached upon by informal housing schemes.

This chapter has two aims. I first present an ethnographic analysis of my fieldwork village, Qaramoos. Second, while providing a description of my urban research site, Behteem, I will initially provide a brief background of Cairo's population growth and housing crisis. These descriptions will spatially and socially situate people's experiences for the remainder of the text. They will, in the process, help the reader to ascertain how the rapidly changing social and economic situation in Egypt has impacted upon people's lives.

THE RURAL CONTEXT

The Free Officers revolution in July of 1952 led to Gamal Abdul Nasser's ascendancy to the presidency of Egypt.[1] This was a major turning point in Egyptian rural relationships as the coup, nationalist in nature, had a social welfare ideology based on developmentalism. The army officers were committed to increasing national production and promoting redistribution of national wealth accompanied by social and economic reforms. To consolidate its constituency the first measure taken by the regime was the announcement of land reforms.[2]

Almost 12.5 percent of cultivable land was distributed in the reform process that continued into the 1960s. Approximately 1.7 million people benefited from the redistribution of the plots, which were generally given to the former tenants of the land, who were presumed to have the necessary farming skills (Radwan and Lee, 1986). However, almost 40 percent of the rural families were left landless even after the reform. Although the land reforms had a distributive impact on peasant access to land, the landless families sustained lower wages due to the ability of larger landholders to manipulate the labor market (Radwan and Lee 1986).

By the mid-1970s, President Sadat's open-door economic policies[3] had increased land speculation, and landholdings had returned to their earlier bimodal forms of large and very small holdings (Springborg 1990b). During this period a large percentage of peasants owning less than three feddans[4] lost almost 10 percent of their holdings. The share of cultivable land owned by mid-size or large landholders[5] went up from 33 percent of the agricultural area in the mid-1970s to 47.5 percent by the early 1980s (Mitchell 1995:137). This redistribution further aggravated landlessness and rural impoverishment.[6] Decreasing access to farmland, increasing population, and structural inequality forced the small landholding families to look for subsistence work outside their plots. Urban migration and emigration to the neighboring oil-rich Arab states became a survival option for some among the rural workforce.[7]

The image of an over-populated Egypt living beyond its means was one of the primary arguments presented by international donor agencies for the IMF-sponsored structural adjustment program. In the 1980s agencies such as USAID and the World Bank further directed the Egyptian government to decrease government subsidies to agricultural land and to open up agricultural produce to market forces so that farmers might benefit from increased prices for their crops.[8] In line with this free-market approach, the People's Assembly in the summer of 1992 enacted a new agricultural policy.[9]

The rationale behind the new policy can be summed up by a speech given by Marshall G. Brown, director of USAID for Egypt in the late 1980s. In 1989, addressing a conference on agricultural policy reform in Egypt, Brown argued that Egypt was living beyond its means and not earning enough foreign exchange to satisfy its import needs and to pay its foreign debts. The government revenues were also not enough to finance its expenditures. He predicted that with population increasing to approximately 75 million by the year 2000, Egypt was racing against time to feed, educate, and provide the social needs of its population. The only solution, according to him, was to restructure the economy by privatization and by reduction in government expenditures (Government of Egypt and USAID 1989:7).

Similarly, another USAID report on policy reform from the same period states that food self-sufficiency and food security, although valuable goals, should be modified as policy requirements, because they could only be attained at a high cost of income and growth. There was comparative advantage, according to the report, in focusing on cultivation of high-value crops. The earnings from these crops would then contribute to food security by providing the foreign exchange to import needed food and feed grains (USAID Benchmark 3.2 1989:100).

These directions basically show a commitment to a privatized free-market economy, and the measures undertaken in the agricultural sector provide evidence of this thinking. In the last ten years international lending agencies have encouraged Egyptian farmers to grow fruits and vegetables and to raise cattle for domestic consumption. The process leaves Egypt invariably vulnerable to food security issues. The international agencies, although aware of these concerns, never raise the question of additional land reform to resolve the "economic crisis" of the Egyptian state and people.[10] The policy insistence on larger landholdings and export-oriented agricultural production by international consultants also helps to generate foreign exchange that services the debt owed to international lenders, a situation very similar to that of the colonial era.[11]

The recent changes in agrarian policy have started to affect life in Qaramoos. The crucial issue is how the free-market process will affect future landholdings and income distribution. It is too early to predict, but the concentration of land in larger holdings at the expense of smaller ones will most likely increase. With all the problems of corruption, power plays, and mismanagement, the agricultural reform cooperatives nevertheless safeguarded the peasantry from some of the vagaries of the market and provided them with cheap credit and subsidized inputs (Radwan and Lee 1986; Saab 1967). The new system may make the small holders dependent on credit with high interest rates and force them to compete in an uneven market system favoring those with more resources.

QARAMOOS

Qaramoos is approximately one hundred kilometers northeast of Cairo and a short distance from the town of Abu Kabir in the Sharqiya governorate. Zagazig, the capital of the governorate, was founded by Muhammad Ali Pasha in 1836–1837 as a market town for the region's cash crops. By the 1860s, with the development of the agricultural infrastructure, deepened canals, barrages, a railway connection, cotton gins, and workshops and the settlement of foreigners, Zagazig along with the province of Sharqiya had become the center of cotton trade in the region (Baer 1982; Wilson 1934).[12]

At the time of the revolution in 1952, the land around Qaramoos belonged to Crown Prince Muhammad Ali Tawfiq. During the turbulent period preceding the revolution the peasantry participated in anti-landlord revolts and action all through the Delta region. Gharbiyya governorate, adjacent to Sharqiya, was the site of major peasant disturbances and attacks on the mansions of the estate owners (*Egyptian Gazette,* 25 June 1952). Similarly, villages around Qaramoos revolted against the managers of the crown prince's estate. A large portion of the land in the area was confiscated after the revolution and redistributed as land reform parcels to the peasantry.

In the last five decades the village has grown from a hamlet dependent on the *izba* owners into one with 10,000 inhabitants.[13] It is administratively linked to the district of Abu Kabir, which is a major market and commercial center of the region. Today Qaramoos can be approached by service taxi, bus, and the railway from Cairo. A two-to-three-hour journey through the Delta brings you to Abu Kabir, and from there a commuter truck takes you to the village. The village itself is divided by the central main road into two distinct parts, both surrounded by agricultural land. As in most Delta villages, the most noticeable sight is the mushrooming new construction resulting from the inflow of remittances and the investment in housing by returning migrants. Informants told me of the rapid expansion of concrete housing replacing the older adobes or mud brick family compounds. Elders in the community described the growth since the 1970s as extremely brisk and attested that a quarter or a third of the village had been built on agricultural land during the last two decades.

The majority of landholdings surrounding the village in 1992–1994 were still incorporated in the land reform cooperative and organized around the crop rotation patterns of the system. Qaramoos was historically the mother village of the larger estate, and a number of *kafoor* (plural of *kafr;* hamlets) surround it. The major crops grown were cotton, corn, and rice in the summer and wheat and fodder (*berseem*) in the winter. Vegetables and fruits were grown interspersed with these crops and some beans were also produced on excess land.

Most of the landholdings were two to five feddans in size. The holdings were divided among family members, especially if there were adult sons in the household. This division fragmented the holdings into smaller plots. To avoid this fragmentation, families sometimes let one member take care of the land and draw most of the profit from it. This member might then supply the others with fodder for their cattle, allow them to grow vegetables, and also share some basic staples that were not sold in the market. The scarcity of land and the small size of holdings had led most landowning farmers to obtain government or other jobs to supplement their earnings from farming.

Those who had emigrated to the city or the Gulf Arab states rented out the little land that they owned,[14] in order to guarantee a family income in their absence. Others who were gainfully employed with the government or in the private sector and possessed very small holdings of a few quirat[15] also frequently tended to rent out their share of land. Similarly, women whose husbands were not at home or who were widowed often participated in this practice.

Farmers who rented land sometimes had access to additional income from adult members of their families who had nonfarm incomes. These farmers controlled sizable amounts of land due to their access to finance through their relatives. For example, a farmer who tilled eight feddans of reform land, comparatively a large holding in the village, had three sons in Cairo as midlevel government servants and two in Kuwait. He rented four feddans of land and also managed a poultry farm of 250 chickens. His dependency on the state or private sources for credit was minimal because he had access to money directly from his sons, who were compensated by him through the agricultural earnings.[16]

Off-farm employment in recent years had become a major source of income for the young men in the village. Some who had access to land stayed in the village and worked on the family farm. Those who were somewhat educated or had learned a trade, for example as masons or electricians, got jobs in the construction sector in nearby towns like Zagazig or even Cairo. In the last two decades many also emigrated to the Gulf Arab states and to Jordan, Saudi Arabia, and Iraq.

Since the Gulf War in the early 1990s there has been a generalized return migration. The decrease in remittances due to declining emigration stagnated the construction sector, the one area where jobs had been plentiful in the past several years. My friends with college degrees who had gone to Jordan or Iraq came back to a somewhat changed world partly created by the inflationary tendencies set up by remittances of people like themselves. Some returning migrants, educated but landless, now worked as low-level government servants. They may have saved enough perhaps to build a house, pay off their loans, or accumulate luxury goods like a television or a VCR. But they still felt trapped in their salaried position without access to land.[17]

For example, Idris, a forty-year-old university graduate, had spent most of the 1980s in Jordan. The son of a peasant, he had sent money home so that his younger siblings could be educated and their house could be better constructed. Coming back after the Gulf War in the early 1990s meant living on his savings, as he was without a job for almost six months. During my stay in Egypt, he was working for the agricultural cooperative office as a low-level employee. "I have friends who are university graduates who are (working as) *ummals* (workers)," he said one day, frustrated at his inability to earn a decent living and also not having enough resources to get married. "I do not have enough land to support the whole family," he continued, "and I am the only breadwinner now. My younger brother is learning the electrician trade, and after military service we will try to send him to Kuwait, but it is getting difficult as the visa papers are very expensive."

Migration remains the only hope for a number of young men, both educated and uneducated, who seek to create a better future for themselves and their families. I occasionally heard of men who were even trying to migrate illegally to European countries like Spain or Germany. These tendencies point toward a sense of anxiety, especially among those without resources like land or a well-paid job. Although some men were still lucky to indeed have a job, inflationary tendencies and changing expectations for better living were major challenges for the future. It could be said that those who had not migrated were biding their time, waiting to leave. Unfair distribution of income is an important incentive for many of the most productive Egyptians to contemplate leaving their country (Ajami 1983).

Men's anxieties over employment opportunities were reflected in the nature of the marriage arrangements they faced. My unmarried friends blamed their inability to marry even into their thirties on the inflationary economy and the changing nature of society. Whereas older male informants would tell me that when they were married they presented only a silver bangle to their brides, the recent shift was toward gold bangles and jewelry along with other household items such as washing machines and televisions. Although these practices are somewhat favorable to women, they also mean a delay in marriage for a high percentage of couples. Such high expenditures partly explain why a man like Idris, who was educated and did not consider himself *fellah,* had not been able to get married; he simply could not afford the marriage expenditure in light of all the other responsibilities toward his family.

Marriage patterns were generally changing for women, too. Women in Qaramoos would tell me that the tradition of parents arranging matches was giving way to men and women choosing each other. They insisted that all this was done within the parameters of modesty and not like in the city, where men and women were without any shame. Even this discreetness was criticized by the older generation as an older woman complained about the situation in the following terms: "We are *fellahīn,* and should marry within ourselves, but now these girls go to school and want an educated *muwazzaf* (government employee), they are now all choosing for themselves, *wallahi,* I was married for just thirty pounds."

Increased male migration from rural Egypt has also increased the number of females in the rural labor force.[18] Historically, women in rural Egypt have always worked along with their family members in the agricultural sector. Yet at times of shortage of male labor their presence becomes more obvious to policymakers because it leads to essentially a feminization of agriculture in most areas (Springborg 1990a; Toth 1991; Dethier 1989).[19]

Studies on women left behind by male migration in Egypt rarely emphasize the increased responsibilities and labor that overwhelm women in the absence of their male partners. Literature has looked at how the migration of male labor in Egypt has broken down the authority of the extended family and the senior female member of the family (mother-in-law). Hind Khattab et al. (1982) have argued that the migrants' wives, due to remittances they receive, have gained an enhanced status in rural communities. Khafagy (1984) presents a similar argument by showing that women gain power in the public sphere by being responsible for negotiating terms with the cooperatives and making other decisions for the household in the absence of their male partners. Mona Abaza (1987) partially agrees with this analysis but contends that as women get more access to decision making in the agricultural sphere, their work becomes socially devalued by men as peasant work. According to Abaza, as women seemingly become more independent, their work is denigrated as being of lower status than when done by men.

Further, Lynn Freedman (n.d.) analyzes the consequences of structural adjustment on the rural labor of third-world women. She shows that as cash crop production with better wages is introduced into local economies, women are forced into subsistence agriculture. Comparably, mechanization in Egyptian agriculture has resulted in men taking the more highly paid jobs of transport and machine operating while women have been pushed into the lower-paid mundane chores (Hopkins 1983).

In Qaramoos, although men would deny at times that their women folk were involved in agricultural labor, it was common for peasant women to be looking after the cattle, working on vegetable patches, cutting *berseem* for the market, and effectively being employed along with their children during the cotton-picking month. The denial may reflect a rhetoric of masculinity and self-sufficiency that is perpetuated by men in economically unstable times.

This said, Egyptian rural statistics show that the number of family members employed in farm labor is lowest for the smallest and largest landowning groups. This indicates that those with very small landholdings need to find off-farm work, while those with large landholdings can employ others to do their work (Springborg 1990b:38). Hence, women in the village whose husbands were educated and had well-paying jobs, or were landowners with better incomes, or were rich migrants had opted out of the rural job market.[20]

THE URBAN SETTING

In addition to agricultural reform, Nasser undertook industrialization reform in the 1950s. His industrialization policy manifested itself in the construction of iron and steel works in Helwan at the southern edge of the city, which was balanced by the expansion of an industrial park in

Shubra al-Kheima in the north of Cairo. Peasants streamed into Cairo searching for employment and thus creating pressures on the housing market that could not keep up with the population growth, especially at the lower end of the real estate market. To ease this pressure, the state directly intervened in the management of housing stock and constructed rows of popular housing at very reasonable rates in Cairo and other cities for low-income government servants and industrial laborers.

From the early part of the twentieth century until recent years when Cairo's population stabilized, the city's population grew at a faster pace than the rest of Egypt. With increasing employment opportunities during and after the First World War, Cairo went through a massive increase in population size. By the late 1920s Cairo's population had surpassed the million mark (Abu-Lughod 1971:125).[21] The city's population grew at an annual rate of more than 4 percent in the 1960s, and by the mid-1970s the population size was approximately 8 million, up from 5 million inhabitants in 1960. This growth rate rapidly fell as rural Egyptians emigrated to oil-rich Arab states to seek employment in the mid-1970s.[22]

In the 1970s Sadat's open-door economic policies created a boom in privately owned luxury housing largely concentrated in the upscale neighborhoods of Cairo and along the Nile Corniche. Increased prosperity due to emigration to the oil-rich countries, coupled with high interest rates, inflation, skyrocketing real estate prices, and increasing building costs made it difficult for low- and middle-income households to afford home ownership. At the same time, because of Sadat's removal of substantial government subsidies for renters, new owners charged rents based on what the market could bear. This created a discrepancy between the earning level of a majority of Cairenes and their capacity even to rent a house.

In the last twenty years the real estate market has grown beyond state control, both for rentals and for purchase. Since the economic opening of the early 1970s, land speculation linked to housing construction has given rise to new methods for gaining access to housing in Cairo. The differentiated real estate market can consist of invaded or squatted land used for self-help housing, private plots, apartment buildings for rental, small-scale apartments for renting, subdivision of existing housing for rental, or shacks on empty public land (El Kadi 1988). Multiple players profit from what is one of the most serious social issues that Cairenes face, shortage of domestic housing.[23]

Planners have responded to population growth by proposing that new communities be built in the desert areas not far from Cairo. These self-sufficient towns are meant to provide employment and housing, decreasing the spatial and social pressures on Cairo. The Ministry of Housing and New Communities issued legislation in 1979 to work toward a master plan for new cities connected to the regional development of cities like Cairo, Port Said, and Ismailia. These satellite cities are estimated to have one-half to one million inhabitants. Further, schemes are being developed to encourage people to leave the Nile Valley and construct desert communities. The Aswan Dam in the south of the country and the eastern and western deserts are promoted as areas where people could earn a living through agriculture, fishing, small industries, or craft production (*Egyptian Gazette,* 17 July 1993).

These schemes notwithstanding, owning a house in Cairo still remains difficult for most low-income households. With credit and house financing on easy installments hard to acquire and with the rising cost of land and construction, renting remains the main solution for most families' housing needs. Families that already have apartments with frozen rents fare better in this market. Young couples that try to get into the rental market now pay more than 25 percent of their salaries, the common standard in a free-market economy, to acquire a rental dwelling. This skewed accessibility to shelter has forced most poor families to pool their resources and create what are commonly known as informal housing areas (Hanna 1985; The Greater Cairo Region Master Scheme 1991).

The growth of these housing areas has progressively expanded the city's boundaries. Cairo has spread outward by incorporating agricultural land and the surrounding desert. In densely populated areas the building spaces have been increased by adding additional floors to the already existing residential or commercial structures. Area surveys indicate that the inner city of Cairo is losing population due to changes in land use. The widening of existing roads, the reorganizing of sewerage facilities, the removal of illegal encroachments, and the collapse of old buildings have led to the evacuation of people from the more crowded neighborhoods of the city. In contrast the outlying northern, southern, and western edges of the city have a very high growth rate, and communities have doubled or tripled in size in the last twenty years.[24]

BEHTEEM

My urban fieldwork was primarily conducted in the low-income industrial area of Behteem, situated in the governorate of Qualubiya, north of the city of Cairo. Behteem is an extension of the industrial sector of Shubra al-Kheima, where numerous textile factories and public housing estates were established in the post–World War Two period. As land prices remained low, Behteem became a highly desirable area for housing expansion for middle- and low-income families in the 1960s. Initially, the area was farmland, traversed by irrigation canals. Farmers anticipating profit subdivided their land and started selling as Behteem started becoming populated in the 1970s and 1980s. While I was there, the edges of the area were still agricultural land, but they were rapidly being sold to build new housing.[25]

Behteem is reached from the center of the city by taking public transport to the northern bus terminal of Musturud, a travel time of thirty to forty-five minutes. This terminal serves the larger industrial area of Shubra al-Kheima and was historically the last stop on the tram lines developed in the earlier part of the twentieth century. From the bus stop, private pickup trucks run at frequent intervals to Behteem, a four-mile distance that can take an additional twenty minutes. The whole journey may cost half a pound. For daily commuters this means an expense of almost twenty to thirty pounds a month, about a third of their monthly earnings. Moreover, the overwhelming crowding in the pickup truck and the ride on poorly paved roads make the journey extremely uncomfortable. Most city planners do not have to go through this experience every day of their lives and hence are unaware of how people manage the hardship of the transport system to live in affordable housing at the very edge of the city.

The population of Behteem consists primarily of industrial laborers, craftsmen, and low-level public servants. The area is divided by a main road with public-sector apartment blocks on one side and privately owned housing on the other. Buildings on the nongovernment side of the road are built along narrow lanes that are just about wide enough for pedestrians to walk on. On the edge of this community there is an open sewage drain that divides the area into older and newer sections. This drain is the drainage area for effluvia from the area's factories and is a major public health menace for the people.

A large number of the people I spoke to were industrial laborers who had moved into the area in the last ten to twelve years. Most were men who had come to Cairo in the 1960s to seek jobs and started settling down in the 1970s and 1980s. Being at the northern edge of the greater Cairo Region, in the governorate of Qualubiya, several of my informants were from the Delta and retained relatives and families in villages there.[26]

Interestingly, families that I knew traveled more often to their ancestral villages than to the center of Cairo. Men's lives revolved around going to work at a factory in Shubra al-Kheima and then returning to their neighborhood. The center of Cairo was an alien and inhospitable place for them. Once when I invited a number of them to share a meal in the city's center (*wust al-balad*), all but one had difficulty managing the trip by themselves. I gave them the bus number, waited for them at the city bus terminal, and navigated them through the touristic central districts to the restaurant where we would eat. The trip to the larger city with its shopping districts and fancy hotels was alienating and difficult for most of my guests.

This feeling of strangeness to their surroundings was not only due to their being recent migrants from rural Egypt. The state and the ruling elite have historically reflected ambivalence toward the rural and urban poor. The city elite has always perceived the peasant as an intrusion into modern space. These hierarchical distinctions are ever present in Cairo where certain upper-class housing areas, like the island of Zamalek or Garden City near the center of the city with its clean streets and well-cared-for parks, are in stark contrast to the unpaved roads and piles of garbage that mark areas like Behteem. The rhetoric of city planners aside, my friends from Behteem argued that they were the neglected and forgotten part of the state. "Our problem is rising prices, transportation, housing, and poverty," one of them said to me, "and the state is only interested in buying Mercedes for its ministers."

In Behteem houses are mostly built on sixty square yards of land. These multistory buildings are cramped next to each other with the main door opening onto the street. Multiple families may share the same house. Families live in rooms and share the common area consisting of the landing and the bathroom. Many families I knew lived in this condition. Abduh, a friend of mine who worked in a nearby textile factory, had six children and lived in two rooms. The other three floors of his building were occupied by other tenants. However, all shared the same bathroom. While talking to Abduh one day on family planning, he interrupted me and said:

> The social and economic factors are more important. See us living in close quarters—we are five families sharing the same bathroom. We have children living in the same room while I want to be with my wife. Our whole lives are open. Do you think family planning is important to us or getting a better apartment?

Abduh is a labor activist who had been denied government-subsidized housing due to his political affiliations. His seniority in the factory he works in, he claimed, entitled him to an apartment on easy installments. His answer to my question may have reflected his political viewpoint and his sense of victimization. It also indicated how cramped living conditions forced people to suspend their notions of privacy and modesty. Abduh would argue that it was difficult for him to have a sense of respectability in situations in which his whole life was exposed as if he were living on the street. Abduh continued:

> We want to live decently, but when we share a bathroom with five other families, what do you expect? My sixteen-year-old daughter comes out after a bath and at the door is the twenty-year-old son of my upstairs neighbor, who sees her with her hair loose and arranging her clothes. How can this not be if we are living in such miserable conditions?

Women also shared this sense of lack of space. They felt vulnerable to touches and glances of men from the same building. For them, living in such close quarters was a constant negotiation of space and boundaries. Sana'a, a twenty-four-year-old mother of four, related this to me:

> I was born here and was married here. We moved into this apartment when I got married about five years ago. It was easy to find this apartment then. It may still be easy, but apartments are extremely expensive now. We have only two rooms and we are six. If we have more money we will try to move, but it is not possible now. The situation is bad, sometimes there is no water for three days, other days there is no electricity for the whole day.

Like Sana'a's living arrangement, most households contain nuclear families. Because most residents had moved into the area within the last twenty years, the average age in the community was still young with a high number of young children among them. Some households may have had a shared family with two or three generations living in the same house. People who owned their own homes initially built a room on the ground floor, and as their economic conditions improved they added further floors. If sons got married another apartment or a room or two would be added to the top floor.

Most women did not work for wages, and their lives revolved around taking care of the house. They did all the washing, cooking, and taking care of the children and the elderly, managed the budget, and on occasion visited neighbors and relatives, not venturing far from their respective streets.

Neighbors could be trusted to look after homes, yet women I spoke to would argue that if they worked, who would look after their children? In this regard these women were different from the image of the *baladi* women from the older inner-city neighborhoods of Cairo, who work as domestic servants or as market women and are famous for their self-confidence in dealing with city life (Rugh 1984).

Women got together in many forms within the community to resolve their personal and financial problems. Housewives I knew were involved in saving schemes or *gamaya,* collectively putting in a few pounds every month for a rainy day. Some women also joined religious groups that met every week to hear sermons on the life of the Prophet and moral questions. In addition to their religious motivations women would tell me that these meetings would give them some time to get out of the house and meet women from other parts of the area.

In the years 1992–1994, while I was there, marriages among neighbors were just beginning to provide a basis for people to start associating with each other as relatives. Men and women of marriageable ages in Behteem preferred partners from the community itself. Younger women who had been married in the last few years were reluctant to move away from the area because they would lose contact with family members who lived nearby. For example, Abduh's wife had arranged her brother's wedding to the daughter of one of their upper-floor neighbors. The major problem the groom's family faced was obtaining an apartment either by renting, by key money[27] or by purchase. Many young men postpone wedding plans until they can accumulate enough money at least to rent an apartment. In the case of Abduh's brother-in-law, the solution was found shortly before I returned to the United States. Abduh finally was granted an apartment by the factory he worked in. His tiny two bedrooms became available at a discounted price. Hence the marriage took place with the couple moving into Abduh's old apartment. In this case the bride just moved one floor below her parents' residence.

At the time of my fieldwork land was priced between LE 100 and LE 200 per square meter, depending on the location and the availability of sewerage and water lines. Newer areas that were still agricultural fields were approximately LE 100 per square meter on installments and LE 75 if there was full payment. Rental rates for small two-room apartments ranged from LE 20 to LE 60, depending on the key money invested by the renter. The rates are low by the standards of other Cairo localities yet were high for a majority of my friends, who were earning an average of LE 100 to LE 150 a month.

Rather than pay rent in Behteem, Ahmed, another friend of mine, who worked as a driver for a nearby sugar factory, decided to move his family to a new area almost twenty kilometers northeast of Behteem at the edge of the eastern desert. Ahmed had purchased sixty square meters of land for LE 12 per square meter there. The construction of a room cost him an extra LE 1,000. He sold his key money apartment for LE 2,000 so that he could avoid paying LE 25 every month to the landlord. His decision was made on the basis that in Behteem he could not buy land below LE 75 to LE 100 per square meter.

I along with other friends helped Ahmed move and assisted in building his house. It was located in a semiarid area with no civic facilities, such as water connection, electricity, or sewerage line, and was a mile from the nearest main road. We were not alone, however. While we were working on Ahmed's house, several other crews were busy constructing houses in the vicinity. The government is spending millions to develop new townships in the desert area to settle what it calls its "surplus population." In the meantime poor households like Ahmed's seek permanent shelter far away from their workplace even if it means living without water, sewerage connection, and direct transportation facilities.

CONCLUSION

The economic pressures people face in neighborhoods like Behteem make them compare themselves negatively with the villagers. They did understand that in the villages unemployment was also creeping up due to returning emigrants. Yet they always asserted that at least in the rural areas people grow their own food, while in the city families are totally dependent on the market. As discussed earlier, with the decrease in food subsidies, food expenditure within households has substantially increased in the last ten years. This has led many households that were spending more than 75 percent of their money on food to substantially cut their food consumption. People in poor urban neighborhoods where I worked have stopped consuming meat, and their food consists primarily of staples like bread and beans. Although it is estimated that per capita daily caloric intake in Egypt increased from 2,660 calories in 1969 to 3,501 in 1986, the poorest 10 percent of the urban population consume only 26 percent of this increase compared to the wealthier 10 percent who consume 255 percent. Despite the general increase in per capita income in the 1970s and 1980s, income disparities have become more prevalent since the mid-

1980s. Based on estimates of market prices for minimum food intake in the early 1990s, almost 51 percent of the urban and 47 percent of the rural population lived under the poverty line, and 35 percent of the total Egyptian population consumed fewer than 2,000 calories a day (Nassar 1992).

Moreover, even after adjusting for inflation, real wages by 1990 had gone down by 5 to 7 percent since the mid-1980s (Handoussa 1991; Ferghany 1991). With unemployment and rising poverty, places like Behteem were considered politically volatile areas by the state. The state was threatened by the possibility of urban opposition movements related to recruitment by Islamist groups in these communities. This was the reason given for the heavy policing of these areas by the local police and by security details of the intelligence services. In day-to-day encounters with the state security system, the inhabitants of such communities related to a very oppressive police force that mistreated them. On an occasion when I spent the night in Behteem at a friend's apartment, there was a knock on the door at about three in the morning. Several policemen came in and went up to the second floor to arrest a man suspected of embezzling LE 100 from the factory he worked in. The whole neighborhood watched as the man was humiliated and taken to the police station in chains. People were furious. They attested to the honesty of the person and said that, even if he were guilty, why did the police have to come at three in the morning?[28]

On yet another occasion, arriving at the home of a friend in another low-income neighborhood, I was told to leave immediately because many unknown people (meaning security police) were around, and it could be dangerous for me and also for my friend's family. A couple of weeks later, I was informed that two preachers from the local mosque had been picked up by the state security on charges of being allied with the Islamists. They had not returned even after two weeks, and the families did not know their whereabouts. The situation had an ominous air to it. In a community where people spent most of their time greeting neighbors, visiting each other, and generally participating together in joyous and sad occasions, no one had gone to console the families for their missing sons for fear of being harassed and questioned by the security police.

Such occurrences alienate the inhabitants of popular neighborhoods from the state. As people continuously experienced hardships of housing, transportation, unemployment, and lack of civic amenities, these violent intrusions into their lives further reminded them of their marginal existence. The more politicized among them would openly attack the state in their conversations. When a police inspector was killed in an area near

Behteem in an encounter with Islamists, one of my informants made the remark: "Why should we not rejoice at this killing? After all this is the man who was continuously harassing us in our workplace and wanted us to spy on our neighbors."

The social unrest unleashed by changes in the agricultural system, the removal of subsidies, and the rise in unemployment rates continuously created problems of law and order and civic management for the Egyptian state. During my stay in Egypt, the state-sponsored news media was full of reports of the state's violent engagement with the Islamist groups, portraying it as attacks on "terrorist violence." Seldom was there an analysis of the social and economic violence of poverty and the lack of amenities suffered by the Egyptian rural and urban poor.

In the last few decades, the state has also been made acutely aware of the volatility of the urban population by food riots in 1977 and again in 1986, when its own rurally recruited police force participated in the rampage as bread prices went up. The more recent skirmishes with the Islamist groups in poor urban localities and in Upper Egyptian villages have also sensitized the government to the "breeding ground" imagery that the popular media uses to describe these events. Not surprisingly, the government's solution is focused on security and order rather than on distribution of resources and social justice.

The poor are accused of ruralizing the city and making Cairo a city of peasants. This image of disorder and chaos is not dissimilar to the late-nineteenth-century descriptions of unruly *fellahīn* in Cairo. These are old differences that the elite have managed to their advantage numerous times before. However, the Egyptian state, under pressure from international debtors and pursuing a free-market policy, is not prepared to follow Nasser's example by using housing and civic reform to incorporate those left out at the margins. The government's answer is to apply continued economic pressure and the heavy hand of the security system, forcing people like Ahmed to leave the city altogether.

Chapter 4

‖ # Women's Bodies

My introduction into Qaramoos, the Delta village community in which I did part of my fieldwork,[1] was through a local family health center, staffed primarily by doctors from a medical research university in Cairo. The doctors provided services and conducted research in the area for their postgraduate degrees. At this stage of my research, I was interested in becoming familiar with the people who used the clinic.

One of the doctors, a senior gynecologist and obstetrician attending to the clinic, suggested that conducting focus groups would aid in the process of my introduction. To broaden the research agenda, the focus groups were organized with selective groups that consisted of men of all ages and professions (for example, peasants, local school teachers, public servants); community leaders (*shaykh*s of local mosques, members of cooperative councils, people deemed important due to their wealth or connections to the state structure); *daya*s (traditional midwives); religious leaders (instructors in religious schools); and two groups of peasant women who lived in nearby villages. The doctor moderated the sessions and I participated as his assistant.[2] We discussed the questions before the start of the sessions, and he then conducted the focus groups by asking a range of questions on family planning, domestic relationships, economic and social processes, and so on.

I was introduced as a visiting medical researcher to the participants of the focus groups, a valid representation because of my medical degree. In a session with young men, the doctor with whom I was associated probed the participants on their wives' use of contraceptives. Most men admitted preferring the IUD (intrauterine device) for their wives as they thought it had fewer medical complications. When asked how the problem of breakthrough bleeding associated with IUDs was handled in their private lives, some men whose spouses were using IUDs responded that they treated it like menstrual blood, and they did not have sex with their wives on such days. When we asked whether they engaged in foreplay on such occasions, a primary school teacher shot back: "Do you have foreplay be-

fore having sex or on days she (your partner) menstruates?" This reply reminded us of the boundaries between acceptable questions and those that
would be resisted. In reality, we did not expect questions to be addressed
to us. We were defensive because we were the researchers and needed to
know their ideas; our personal lives, we thought, were not an issue of discussion. From our position of relative authority we might have crossed
certain boundaries; we sought to elicit information that was "crucial" to
our project, but it perhaps was not seen that way by our respondents.

The primary school teacher who had raised the question kept quiet
during the rest of the session while the other men answered in general
terms, though this episode and others like it did not stop us from continuing along similar lines of questioning with other groups. Normally
we would meet in the clinic with various groups of men and, on occasion, the midwives. It was difficult, however, to arrange for women other
than midwives to come to the focus group sessions.

We met with a group of peasant women in a villager's house near the
clinic, in order to demonstrate our sensitivity to local norms. Our respondents were all married women between the ages of twenty-five and fifty;
only one had a high school diploma. The questions turned to body perceptions after asking about their birthing history and questions about gender relations.

Q. What is the ovary and where is it?
One woman replied, "It is what carries the baby inside the mother."
Another woman who had remained silent and was visibly uncomfortable
with the questions, angrily replied, "You are the doctor and should know
more than us."

We replied by explaining that what we knew was present in health
manuals and scientific literature, but we were interested in their perceptions of their bodies. The women, as we continued our questioning, generally gave evasive replies when asked about who teaches young women
about sexual relationships before marriage.

Q. Do you think the girl should know something and not get married
as a blind person (meaning uninformed)?
One woman replied, "We should tell them so that they do not get ill."
Another argued, "They know everything as the rate of education now
is high."
The third replied, "The mother should tell her everything."
And a fourth said, "The mother or a friend should tell her."
Q. Do you think we should tell the men more or the woman?

The woman who had replied third answered, "The men, as they know more."

Q. If there were lessons arranged about how to sleep with men and how to get more pleasure, would you be willing to attend such classes?

Now the second woman said, "No, because all that is known here."

Q. Do you agree or not that women should be taught how to have pleasure with their husbands?

Again the second respondent answered, "The girl is shy and may not like to attend."

Q. Most women say that they do not get pleasure with their husbands, so can we help them get more pleasure?

The woman who spoke second continued to answer: "The woman will not say whether she is pleased or not."

Q. So if she gets pleasure or not it is not important?

The same woman responded, "She is free at home but she will not tell whether she gets pleasure or not."

Q. If we teach women that there are sensitive places that if touched give pleasure, will the woman tell her husband to touch her in these places or not?

The woman who had replied third answered, showing some irritation, "No, they will not."

And the second woman said, "It is impossible that women will go to these schools because people will talk."

Q. From your experience if he touches you some place and you feel pleasure will you ask him to touch again?

The third woman answered, "The man knows what makes his wife happy and comfortable."

Q. But you would not ask him?

The third woman: "No!"

The arrangements for these women to come to the focus groups were made through the networks of social hierarchy present in the village. Our democratic posturing of a dialogue evidently was also not entirely dialogic. We were asking the questions, and the women responded to the issues we raised. The parameters of discussion were not of their choosing. To initiate a conversation about where the ovary was or how women related to their husbands was to draw them into arguments that were, in this specific instance, our concerns and not theirs (Comaroff and Comaroff 1992).

Questions about pleasure exposed our own stereotypes about Egyptian rural and poor women and their passive role in sexual relationships.

On reflection, we were making an explicit argument that their sexual life could be more fulfilling if they asserted their individual desires to their husbands. Our hypothetical idea of arranging lessons and classes fit into a pedagogical agenda designed to encourage these women into a greater consciousness of their bodies and sexuality.

We were assuming, according to our own constructions of selves, that these women possessed a certain universal core self; they only needed to be reminded of it. We were involved in an attempted form of conversion; a conversion into modern sensibilities of self-consciousness and of agency. It is not that these women were not actors or agents in their own right; they were, but we believed that they were not choosing as individuals, not taking responsibility for their own improvement, and, therefore, they were hindered by "tradition."[3]

We were critically unaware, despite our pretensions of cultural sensitivity and my training in anthropology, that the constitution of their individuality was embedded in a multiplicity of social and communitarian relationships. We believed that the information received from them would help us develop policies through which we could teach them about scientifically proven sexual pleasure and the statistically analyzed normative human body. We could, perhaps, only see their lives as an accident of "natural inequality" that social welfare policy, equal opportunity, or pedagogy might resolve (Chatterjee 1993:232).

The problem of sex, which was at the center of our discussion, can also be related to Foucault's discussion on sex in nineteenth-century Europe (Foucault 1980). Women in the village did indeed speak among themselves on the subject, but our intervention was to redefine their personal lives as a subject of study. In our questioning, we tried to create a new notion of sexual discourse and sought to discuss it openly. Questions about levels of fertility, marriage, health, hygiene, or interspousal relationships fed into a knowledge base on the characteristics of a population that needed to be regulated through governmental technologies (Kandiyoti 1998).

Later, in Cairo, I observed several focus sessions conducted by middle-class women's groups. The participants were poor urban women and the questions were very similar to those we had posed. Encounters such as these, in which the urban educated élite benevolently ask questions and the poor answer, are embedded in the schema of traditional/modern dichotomy that is used by family planning research in Egypt. This need to "understand" is associated with an ambition to transform. A summary of my involvement in the focus groups serves to emphasize how my own research was situated within a larger agenda that was beyond my own control. Therefore, male insensitivity, however real, is not the central issue here. The focus groups that we conducted were effectively part of a larger script of research on female reproductive and sexual habits conducted in Egypt under the agenda of family planning research. The detailed discussion of our encounter with rural women is to show how ours was similar to sessions held all over Egypt during the period of my research.

It may be clear by now to the reader that the Egyptian family planning program emphasizes individual decision making by women, the localized action of IUDs, and the somewhat benign health risks of oral contraceptives. Like most of its international counterparts, it also propagates the construction of a modern and medically normalized body. Moreover, there is an emphasis on seeking help only from medically trained doctors for health purposes. How women conceive of their own bodies, and whether they seek other healers or go to local midwives for childbirth, form challenges to the medical model of the body.

Through quantitative surveys and qualitative research the Egyptian family planning program tracks women's and men's ideas and beliefs. Based on this data campaigns are organized to change and counter what are seen as Egyptian women's false conceptions of their own anatomy and physiology. The desire is not to convey every detail of how and why a given method works. It is enough that a commonsensical notion is advertised so that women start accepting IUDs or other contraceptives without delay for their own good and for the social good of the population (Krieger et al. 1990:30).

This focus echoes the recent literature on women and development that cross-culturally gauges women's status linked to the concepts of free choice and autonomous decision-making ability. These culturally neutral and seemingly universal concepts of free choice and autonomy thus become indicators for women's emancipation from more "traditional" sets of constraints (Gita Sen et al. 1994; Dixon-Mueller and Germain 1993).

In this and the following two chapters I will examine how people respond to the Egyptian family planning program's efforts to convince them of the merits of its goals and benefits. I will focus on how some rural and urban women construct their own notions of birthing and fertility influenced by a set of competing ideas. For example, folk constructions of the body in Egypt emphasize illness and abnormal states as caused by multiple sources. These constructions of the body are different yet also influenced by modern medical science. Anger, witchcraft, improper humoral balance, curses, and *microbat* (germs, bacteria) all might play a part in causing ill health. The cure is also at multiple levels. People I knew went to *shaykhs* (spiritual healers) to ward off evil spirits and to *amils* (folk healers) to take care of magic and curses, as well as to doctors for symptomatic treatment.

Women with whom I spoke were quite aware of the efficacy of modern medicine, especially in the case of infections and more serious diseases like diabetes and cancer. However, even when they defined infections as being caused by "microbes," they used household or folk cures (*wasafat baladiya*) to balance what they referred to as the "hotter" aspects of Western medicine. Hot and cold states of the body were loosely linked to food groups and physical states of the body.

Based on these self constructions this chapter will specifically show how in Egypt the concept of fertility control through modern contraceptive devices, linked as they are to a medicalized physiology of the body, coexists with other diverse forms in which women experience their bodies. The following description should not be understood as a comprehensive discussion about local constructions of the body and self. I emphasize women's experiences primarily to deprioritize the individualized self and autonomy model of the family planning program.

*Daya*s AND WOMEN'S BODIES

To acquire a distance from the focus group methodology, I decided to spend more time within the village itself and also started visiting my urban site. This move entailed, as mentioned in the introductory chapter, putting myself in a different configuration of power where others had control over me.

After our initial introduction in the focus group sessions, I slowly got to know several *daya*s in the village. As a physician it was easy for me to ask them questions related to birthing and about their role in the general health of the mother and child. This also helped me, as a male, to understand birthing practices as well as local constructions of the female body.

Until the late nineteenth century more than 90 percent of deliveries in Egypt were performed by *daya*s.[4] The traditional midwife was increasingly blamed for infant deaths and unhygienic birthing practices and was under intense surveillance and attack (see chapter 7) by the colonial medical authorities (Morsy 1993a:23–25). By the early twentieth century these practitioners were rapidly being replaced by European-trained nurses and male medical doctors. The reorganization of women's healing and birthing practices hence meant the displacement of *daya*s by modern medicine.[5]

Egyptian research on health systems management recommends control of the birthing process by trained health personnel.[6] This intervention is said to be necessary to train women in child care, help in lowering infant mortality through immunization, and communicate the benefits of contraceptives to women (Burckhardt et al. 1980; El Kady et al. 1989). For example, a USAID family planning strategy focuses on home visits by health professionals on the fortieth day after delivery. This visit coincides with the traditional celebration at the end of postpartum convalescence and is considered a good time to introduce the mother to issues of immunization and contraception (Cobb et al. 1993). It is also a way to compete with local healers for influence over a woman's decision on future contraceptive needs. As a large section of Egyptian poor women still rely on *daya*s for their birthing needs, Ministry of Health and family planning doctors often feel excluded from what is considered a crucial time to help women decide on their future contraceptive needs.

The presence of *daya*s and other health providers in the village underscored the plurality of forms in which the body and related health issues were conceived by the people themselves. *Daya*s that I knew performed a range of tasks around childbirth and the general health of the mother and child. In addition to performing deliveries, *daya*s circumcised girls, prescribed treatment for problems of the female genital tract, helped women with fertility/infertility issues, and ritually washed the dead (women).[7] In my conversations with *daya*s in Qaramoos, they also acknowledged receiving training from the local family planning clinic on contraceptive methods. However, they felt it was not their position to give women advice on future childbirth or contraception. They thought these decisions should be left to the families themselves.

Delivering babies, however, remains one of the most important services that these women provide in the village. *Daya*s generally work alone or with one assistant while performing deliveries. Sameha, a *daya* with almost forty years' experience, asked, "How can these women relax with all these people around her?" She continued, "Our speech, unlike the doctors', makes the woman comfortable, and then everything is the hands of God." *Daya*s saw themselves as more knowledgeable than their peasant clients and constantly invoked divine intervention to distance themselves from the more secular medical practices. Sameha continued, "I am not afraid of any complications because God always helps us." These acts also socially legitimized their work in the eyes of the community.[8]

*Daya*s comprehend how the trauma of childbirth can affect the health of the mother. Prior to childbirth they prepare the mother by giving her massages with various oils, which helps ease the delivery and also avoids tears to the perineum. They sometimes use suppositories, which, they argue, hold the uterus in place after delivery because the trauma of delivery is thought to dislodge the uterus from its proper site. They then verbally admonish the uterus to stay in its proper position. As Ra'ifa, a veteran *daya* I knew, told me:

> We deliver the child, we massage the abdomen, and Allah willing the placenta comes out. After that we clean her up [the woman] and put the uterus [*beit al-walad*] in its right position and put a piece of cotton in and then say to the uterus three times, "Stay in your place until your time comes." And Allah makes her pregnant again very soon after that. It is only due to Allah that we succeed.

In her self-presentation Ra'ifa stressed the relaying of the message as an important act that demonstrated the relationship between the power of healing in her hand and in her speech. Her intervention in medical terms may be seen as precautions against uterine prolapse for which most gynecologists prefer to operate. In this case, Ra'ifa may have emphasized her role to show me that she not only knew about the condition but that she also actually prevents future prolapse from happening, saving her patients much expense and anxiety.

Doctors with whom I spoke in the village consider the *daya*s' delivery methods and use of suppositories to be unhygienic and prone to cause infection in the female genital tract. The *daya*s were aware of these criticisms. They respond by asserting that they do not exceed the limits of their competency. In difficult pregnancies they gladly refer women to the nearby medical doctor. Yet they maintain that in normal cases they have the expertise not only to deliver babies safely but, unlike the more distant social role of the doctor, they also provide an emotionally supportive environment in managing the birthing process.

One of the themes frequently repeated in our conversations was precisely this, how *daya*s were as capable as the male medical doctors (in Egypt obstetricians are mostly males) in handling delivery cases. In one of our meetings, Ra'ifa explained that once when she was called to deliver a child, she found that the baby had a breech presentation. *Daya*s normally do not intervene in such cases, so she asked the relatives to take the patient to a doctor. Ra'ifa said that she went with them and saw the doctor just push and pull at the legs of the patient (Ra'ifa made exaggerated gestures with her hands, imitating the doctor, indicating that he did not know what he was doing). She continued:

> I get very angry when I see something like this, so I said to him, "Doctor, I have delivered more than thirty cases like this, but the problem here is that this woman has become pregnant after a long wait. I would have delivered her if the risk of losing the baby was not so high, the rest is up to God." So he said, "Will you keep silent, or I will hit my head on the wall." So I replied, "The wall is next to you." But then the baby was delivered dead anyway and he still took the money. I just went to the woman and pressed on her belly and took out the placenta.

Ra'ifa might have related this to me to make a particular point. Aware of my medical training and also that I was friendly with the doctors in the nearby clinic, she was, in my opinion, relaying an indirect message to me as well as to them about her own competency in delivering babies. It may have concurrently reflected her understanding of and frustration with the fact that practitioners of modern medicine were slowly but surely making inroads into her livelihood. By listening to *daya*s like Ra'ifa and others, I started to understand the different ways in which poor women in rural and urban Egypt think of their selves, their bodies, and their health.

BEING FERTILE

Menstruation is primarily conceived by women as a time when bodily impurities are washed out. During pregnancy, it is believed by many that uterine blood may store these impurities from other parts of the body. The blood that comes out during childbirth is, therefore, considered impure and dirty. However, continuing on the theme of women's health, some *daya*s argued that stored blood during pregnancy also sustains the growth of the fetus. The notion of blood as a nutrient for the fetus was also commonly used by other women to talk about fertilization, as blood that nourishes the fetus (placental blood) is considered to have fertile qualities. *Daya*s told me how occasionally they would soak cotton wool with the blood that comes after delivery to make suppositories for women who had difficulty in conceiving. This blood, they would argue, when placed in the genital tract of a barren woman could get her pregnant.

Childbirth remains a cherished desire for most Egyptian families. It is the fulfillment of the idealized feminine role and establishes women as guarantors of the continuity of the lineage. Threats of infertility and delayed pregnancy by new brides are major sources of social anxiety in most Egyptian households. Women also talk about how children tie their husbands down. They reason that husbands of wives who give them the gift of children, especially of a male child, are less likely to seek divorce or another wife. The desire for children, women would say, forces men to marry again. Here, they also acknowledge the strong need for children in both men and women.

Fearing negative reactions, mothers urge their newlywed daughters to get pregnant soon after their wedding. Similarly mothers-in-law drop subtle and not-so-subtle hints to their daughters-in-law about getting pregnant. Women in both urban and rural areas would complain of being stigmatized as infertile if they did not conceive in the first few months of their marriage. Nafissa, an urban housewife who had four children ranging from 5 to 12 years, told us how she refused her mother's and mother-in-law's urging to go to the *shaykh* for treatment when she did not get pregnant within six months after her wedding.[9] She argued that she could resist because her husband disagreed with the suggestions and gave her hope that she would get pregnant when and if God wanted it.

Others, like Nagwa, another young mother in the same community, did make the rounds to *shaykh*s and midwives. At the time of our fieldwork she was seventeen months into her marriage and was still without a child. However, Nagwa, like many other women we spoke to, was ambivalent about the efficacy of treatments she was prescribed by the midwife[10] and was thinking of seeing a medical doctor instead.

These examples point toward the social importance of fertility in the lives of women and to the varied ways in which women respond to the pressure. They may simultaneously use traditional and modern methods of diagnosis and treatment. Once women had conceived children they would then, depending on their circumstances, use contraceptives to regulate their fertility. It became evident while speaking to women in rural and urban communities that most families do want to have children. The family planning program's insistence on birth control may, hence, be at odds with the preoccupation of women themselves, for whom childbirth is a blessing and infertility a social stigma (Inhorn 1994a).

The desire to remain fertile is emphasized in a variety of local ways that women conceive of their bodies. One of them is the complaint women have of *ratuba* (humidity) during their postpartum or postmenstrual period. I spoke to several traditional midwives who would use a uterine suppository (*sufa;* literally: wool) as a precaution against this malady. This suppository is inserted after childbirth because *daya*s suspect that, due to the openness of the body during delivery, some cold air could enter and potentially harm the uterus for the next pregnancy. This specific *sufa* is prepared by mixing lightly grilled onion (*basal*) with *shih* (wormwood) and sometimes with *helba* (fenugreek). The suppository is put into the genital tract and kept there for a while. The onion and *shih* mixture absorbs the humidity and makes the woman dry (also see Inhorn 1994a:82). A discharge is expected within a few days, which is a sign of the wetness leaving the body. This is sometimes also done when a woman is not conceiving. The reasoning is the same: During previous menstruation some humid air is thought to have entered the uterus, which needs to be dried before it can once again be fertile. These remedies should be seen as a local response to infertility problems. They also hint at how bodies are constructed as "open" and perhaps vulnerable at specific moments in a woman's life and how social forces can affect them at these junctures.

Kabsa AND THE CONSTRUCTION OF INFERTILITY

A male friend periodically invited me over to his house in a working-class district of Cairo. I became quite close to the family and would on occasion visit his parents. One day his mother, Umm Tayab, asked me why I did not have any children since my wife and I had been married for several years. My explanation of how both of us had decided to pursue professional careers and had postponed having children did not convince her. Umm Tayab quietly left the room and came back with a smooth stone. She said that she had received it from her mother. "If your wife is *makbusa* then I can help her, and this stone is the key to the cure," she told me. Being *makbusa* implied that my wife, in this case, had been ritually afflicted and suffered from *kabsa* (being bound, squeezed, pressed). There were several ways in which a woman could become *makbusa*. Umm Tayab continued:

> When a young bride sees a woman who is breastfeeding or one who has just given birth, then the bride may not be able to get pregnant. The answer is to do something so that the *makbusa* becomes better. I give these women this stone, they pass it through their dress seven times,

then they bathe with its water on the last days of the Arabic month. This is not *sehr* [magic] or the *ain* [eye], but it is the effect that the breast-feeding women have on the new bride.

Umm Tayab was a healer in her own right and would help in the diagnosis and treatment of women whom she thought were suffering from *kabsa* in the community. I was not sure how to proceed with her advice. With my own understanding of the situation I did not feel that our not having children was because my wife had *kabsa*. Yet Umm Tayab had introduced me to an important aspect of women centered ideas of inflicted infertility and its healing.[11]

Women in the village would tell me that fertility or the capacity to be fertile was the normal and healthy state of being for premenopausal married women. Infertility was considered a state of abnormality and liminality that needed attention and correction. An "open" body in some cases was thought to be more vulnerable to affliction and ill health. New mothers were considered open as they had just given birth and discarded impurities. So were newlywed women open due to the sexual act, as were women who were menstruating or girls who had been recently circumcised. Similarly, fresh burial sites were considered open and liminal. This notion of liminality signifies the "temporary" and the "open" in contrast to the "normal" and hence "closed." These open bodies and spaces in turn produced the effect of closing the generative potential of other bodies.[12]

Janice Boddy (1989), in her discussion of infibulation practices among the Hofriyati villagers in northern Sudan, gives a symbolically rich analysis of the female body and its relationship to its environs. Boddy suggests how the practice of infibulation or pharaonic circumcision prevents the loss of genital blood from within, as it protects the penetration of the womb from without. She argues that women are primarily responsible for reproduction of the family and lineage. Enclosing the womb is thus necessary for the nourishment of the husband's future "crop" and for continuing the family name (66–67). In this respect Boddy shows how the walled enclosure of the house yard, the *hosh,* symbolizes the womb. As the men's entrance into the yard opens into the enclosed area occupied by his children, his "crop," the door of the womb "also opens into an enclosed area where this 'crop' was sown and nurtured . . . just as the *hosh* protects a man's descendants. The enclosed, infibulated womb protects a woman's fertility; her potential and, ultimately, that of her husband" (Boddy 1989:73–74).

Following this symbolic construction of the reproductive female body, we can see why moments of celebrated openness, such as birthing or the first sexual act, also signify periods of vulnerability. The interior in these cases is laid bare to external manipulations. In Lower Egypt, where infibulation is not practiced, external threats are removed by physically separating the women who are in these stages of ritual openness. Hence, *kabsa,* as Marcia Inhorn points out, "entails the violation of these physical boundaries; it is literally and symbolically a problem over 'entrances'" (Inhorn 1994b:494).

Kabsa threatens women's ability to get pregnant or to breast-feed their children. This threat puts women's social role in the community at considerable risk. The cures are mostly women centered, and men seldom know about the ways women provide healing and support in these cases. As it primarily affects women and their social position of expected motherhood, this support is ever more important for women to retain their ability to reproduce. Women in the village told me that as *kabsa*-linked infertility was caused by a series of acts, the cure was in turn related to the original action. The ambiguity present in these acts needed to be reversed and reordered through inversion and restatement (Boddy 1989:106). These situations invariably involve the reconstitution and maintenance of boundaries (Douglas 1966). For example, if someone went to the cemetery to attend a burial or saw a funeral and then visited a new bride, the bride would become *makbusa* and hence infertile. The diagnosis can only take place when the woman does not conceive in the next year. The series of events are resurrected and a cure is found as an antidote for the initial event. There are several forms in which reversal in such a case may take place. *Daya*s informed me that they would keep palm fibers from the burial mat and also pieces of soap that were used in washing the dead to give to the *makbusa* woman so she could bathe with the soap: "We keep it *tetahhar aleyha* [so that she can clean herself]." Women may sometimes be asked to go to cemeteries and cross over graves seven times to reverse the initial act and become fertile again.

Here the conflict between birth and death may be another symbolic reasoning for *kabsa*. Death in popular Muslim belief[13] does create impurities. The corpse rots as it decays, becoming *najas* (impure), and the body is thought to become *turab* (dust). Yet death is also sacred as the *ruh* (soul) belongs to the *ālam il ghaib* (the invisible world) known to God, and the soul takes a journey from this world to the next. There is, however, the *ālam il barzakh* (the world of the tomb), where the soul rests until resurrected on the final day of judgment (*yom il qiama*). The length of this liminal stage is known only to God.

El-Sayed el-Aswad (1987), in a descriptive article on death rituals in rural Egypt, convincingly shows the symbolic linkages between birth and death. He argues that tombs in villages belong to families. They are also referred to as belonging to the same *rahm* (womb). Tombs are generally not opened more than once a year, like the womb for the birth of a child. Death here may be thought of as a passage to a second birth in which the dead enter back into a womb to be born yet again at resurrection. The deceased and the newborn are both wrapped in special clothes. There is a seventh-day celebration for the child. The mourning ceremony for the dead is performed on the day of the burial, the Thursday after that (*al-khamis as-saghīr;* lit. the little Thursday) and then the Thursday following the first (*al-khamis al kabīr;* the big Thursday, the seventh day) (el-Aswad 1987:222). Returning to the discussion on *kabsa,* the simultaneous opening up of two family houses, the tomb (for funeral services) and the womb (in childbirth), may create disorder and misfortune. *Kabsa* in these cases could be thought of more in terms of uncertain times and liminal moments in life's calendar.

Most women, however, argued for a central role of blood in the causation of *kabsa.* As Umm Tayab also suggested, if a woman who has recently had an abortion or has delivered a child enters into the room of a woman who has recently delivered as well, the woman who entered may cause the second woman's breast milk to dry up. Here body fluids like blood become significant. The power of fresh yet impure blood of women who have gone through abortion or of mothers who have recently delivered a child in essence can be harmful to other women. The solution takes many forms and may include a ritual in which both women who are related in this schema should step into a bowl of water together seven times and then bathe with it. Women are sometimes also asked to share menstrual blood in a bucket of water and bathe with it.[14]

In my discussions with women, *kabsa* was never understood as magic, a curse, a possession by spirits, or an act of the evil eye, the *ain*. The idea of an evil eye is linked to an expressed desire to harm another person, whereas *kabsa* is mostly an unknowing violation of boundaries. These boundaries cannot be reduced to the physical space that people occupy because not everyone is afflicted when the barriers are transgressed. However, for women in certain stages of their reproductive cycles, physical space does take on a far greater significance. In this case the poor living in close quarters in crowded housing conditions do not have the luxury of avoiding each other. Agreeing with Inhorn (1994a) I would argue that an inadvertent seeing of fresh meat by a new bride or the entry of a recently circumcised girl into a neighbor's house to see the newly born child is all that may be needed for the bride to become infertile or the new mother's milk to dry up.

This discussion of *kabsa* is important to understand in light of the model of the autonomous self propagated by the family planning program.[15] Some reproductive rights activists similarly stress that women should reclaim property in their bodies as a site of politics (Petchesky 1995).[16] This seemingly progressive political agenda remains embedded within the construction of an individualized sense of self whose rights are to be protected, and a bounded body whose integrity is to be maintained. In contrast *kabsa* informs us of how some female bodies in Egypt are related to the social aspects of life. Infertility, the drying up of breast milk, and the effect other people may have on one's bodily functions underlie the interconnectedness of ill health with social relations. The transgression of boundaries is done by humans who themselves may be in vulnerable states. This also entails a relationship between bodies of those who may unknowingly inflict and those who are afflicted. Similarly, it is about entries and exits. A person has to enter a room or a place occupied by another person. The first person comes from the outside to bound another, bringing with her the states of ambivalence that can cause reproduction and nourishment to cease. The cure also follows similar rules. The *makbusa* needs to go out to the cemetery or cross boundaries to become unbound. She may have to bathe with shared body fluids of another woman to bring her body back to its normal fertile state. Unlike the emphasis in the medical discourse, these situations help us to think of bodies and selves not only in their individuated forms but also in relation to bodies and spaces linked and essential for the normal health of one another.

In addition to *kabsa,* emotional states of people are also important in creating ill health and in some cases infertility. The affliction of disease on women who were sad was commonly reported to me.[17] In the following sections I shall discuss the linkage between fright, emotions, and the possession by spirits in order to further show how local ideas of self and personhood relate to reproduction and to the construction of the social persona.

EMOTIONS AND THE SELF

One day an elderly villager who knew me from when I worked in the clinic asked me to visit his home and see his ill daughter. I went with him and saw his daughter, who was suffering from a mild stroke that had affected the right side of her body. She was in her early thirties and in my assessment very young to have had a stroke. I asked them whether they had shown her to a doctor. The father informed me that she was under treatment by a professor of medicine at the Zagazig University (Zagazig is the provincial capital and the nearest large town). However, he felt that the treatment and medication were not helping his daughter, whose condition had not changed since she suffered the stroke the past week. I tried to assure them that the healing process was slow in such cases, and they should be hopeful that with prolonged rest and good care in her father's house she would be fine in a few weeks. As we were talking the woman's mother broke down and started telling me how her daughter was not happy with her marriage and was always sad (*zalaan;* lit. angry, yet also used for being emotionally upset or sad). Moreover, I was told that the daughter was prone to fits of anger, which she took out on her children. It was during one such emotional outburst that she suddenly fell to the ground and became listless. The parents transferred her to their own house to take care of her since they thought the husband's presence might further aggravate the daughter's health condition. The mother suspected that, due to her daughter's sadness, she might be possessed by a spirit. She wanted to consult a *shaykh* as well so that he could help in the physical recovery of her daughter. I visited the woman several times in her father's house, seeing her slowly get better. Perhaps as a physician I was never told whether they took her to the *shaykh.* Yet this episode gave me a glimpse into how some people constructed the relationship between extreme emotions and physical symptoms.

Extreme emotions were also believed to produce infertility. Some women would go to the village cemetery in the middle of the night on appointed days of the week and try to lie in the fresh grave of an infant or a child. The caretaker informed me that he would allow this practice so that women could cure their barrenness through *khadda* (fright). Women in Qaramoos told me that infertility can be caused by someone surprising them in the dark or by being frightened while crossing the railway track. Infertility due to *khadda* could only be cured by being frightened out of this infliction.

Khadda again challenges the forms in which the body is constructed in the family planning narrative. Fertility and infertility here are not linked to physiological or pathological processes but to everyday emotions of anger and fright. Like *kabsa,* the imagery of fertility and infertility in *khadda* was connected to being internally open or bound. Some women told me that fright could block the passages necessary for the female fluid that interacts with the male sperm to produce a child.[18] Others had a more vague notion of being constricted and ventured to argue that the female regenerative and reproductive functions ceased. Being frightened again, according to them, would undo this restriction and restore fertility. The relationship of emotions such as sudden fright or sadness to bodily functions is important to bear in mind. Socially produced emotions are not distinct from how the body is physically experienced by some women and is crucial to the construction of their self.

Another feature of *khadda* was that it could make women susceptible to the entry of spirits or *jinn*.[19] The belief in the presence of jinn as beings that are discussed in the Qur'an and that live a life like humans but on another plane of existence was quite widespread among people with whom I spoke. The point of contention between some of my more educated friends and others was whether jinn play a role in the life of humans.

*Jinn*s AND POSSESSION

In a direct critique of the notion of an individuated and bounded self, many of my informants believed that we all have counterparts just like us living in another dimension. They are called our *qarin* (masculine) and *qarina* (feminine). Sometimes they are also referred to as *akh taht al-ard* or *ukht taht al-ard* (the brother or sister under the earth).[20] This may mean that we always have a counterself that looks after us and helps us out. Normally men have female counterparts and women have male jinn as partners. At times we may anger these relatives and may suffer the consequences. In addition there are other jinn and *afarit* that in moments of our weakness and susceptibility can enter us and cause us harm. Women are mostly possessed by jinn because they have less control over their emotions and are thought to have *nafs* (lust, desire, emotions) and men more *'aql* (reason or rationality).[21] Women are also popularly considered more vain about their beauty. Hence, women who constantly look at themselves in the mirror are susceptible to possession. Similarly jinn frequent dirty places, like toilets and watering holes.[22] Cemeteries are also favorite abodes for these beings. Possessed women are diagnosed and treated at times by *shaykh*s, who are mostly men. A common female curative ceremony called *zar* is performed in urban and rural areas,[23] to cure the possessed. I always got evasive answers about the details of the ceremony and hence decided not to pursue the matter. However, I did talk to *shaykhs* who cured women suspected of being possessed by spirits.

One evening while having tea with a friend's family in an urban neighborhood, we were visited by a middle-aged couple that seemed worried. They were friends of the family and wanted to discuss the illness of their adult daughter who lived nearby and had three children. The daughter had been possessed almost one year earlier, and the family had taken her to a *shaykh*. The *shaykh* put his hand on her temple and prayed into her ear and forced the jinn to leave. They were all present and could see the spirit leaving through her left big toe, watching the toe expand and contract as the spirit left her. The problem now was that she was again possessed and complained that the face of a Christian man bearing a cross constantly stared at her.[24]

I was not able to follow the case further. Within a couple of weeks I met a *shaykh* while visiting another friend in the area. This *shaykh* was famous in the neighborhood for his curing abilities based on his knowledge of Islam and verses of the Qur'an that were antidotes to the jinn. I spoke to him at length about a range of issues and his curing abilities. He cured people by reading the proper verses of the Qur'an. He described a recent case to illustrate his point.

> Last week I was invited by this family in Mataryia [a neighborhood close to where we were] to cure their daughter, who was under the control of the jinn. When I arrived both her legs were stiff and the jinn was speaking through her. The jinn was a Christian. I spoke to him and offered to convert him to Islam. He agreed. I then asked him to perform *wudu'* [the ritual ablution before saying the prayers], then I asked him to recite the *shahāda* [the ritual verse that bears witness to the uniqueness of God and affirms Muhammad as his prophet]. I then asked him to go to the Ka'bah for Umrah [a ritual pilgrimage to Mecca although considered less important than the annual Hajj]. When he came back, I asked him to leave the girl, who had suffered a lot. The sign of his leaving was that one leg and an arm were held up and they went limp as he left. I did all this in front of the family and just by reciting the correct verses from the Qur'an.

It seems that different notions of relationships are at stake here but so are different notions of selves.[25] These examples may help us to think about how selves are constructed for those who get possessed in Egypt and those who live in the presence of their *qarin* and *qarina*. These selves cannot be thought of in terms of individuated entities with a coherent core and an autonomous agency that Western medicine and psychology direct us toward. If spirits cohabit with bodies that are already constructed in social and relational terms, as argued above in the discussion of *kabsa* and *khadda,* then their presence reemphasizes the construction of a non-unitary self.

It is also important to observe that medical literature seldom addresses possession in terms of people's own experience and understanding of the episodes. Western science, manifested in modern psychology, by and large regards these occurrences as mental abnormalities. In an illustrative case Stephania Pandolfo (2000) discusses the universalist categories used by Moroccan psychoanalysts to evaluate the traditional therapies of jinn possession in that country. She shows how modern psychoanalytic practitioners argue that the traditional healers, like the *shaykh*s mentioned above, essentially practice techniques of self as another by using suggestions to "make appear," "make speak," and "bring to trial" the jinn. Modern practitioners discard this suggestive mode that, according to them, only eliminates symptoms but does not cure. They accuse traditional healing of adding alienation to the alienation of illness. They argue that this practice mimics the illness that it presumes to heal and the "I," the subject, is never fully recovered. The patient never manages to recognize or take responsibility for his or her speech or desires and hence never reconstitutes into a responsible subject. The "I" always remains identified with the other within. Thus a grid is formed between the Imaginary, the space of jinn and traditional healers, and the Symbolic, the space of modern psychiatry and mental illness. A contrast is formed between traditional and modern, where the Imaginary is the realm of magico-religious and the Symbolic is associated with the psychoanalytically constituted self-identified responsible subject (Pandolfo 2000: 137–139).

I suggest that some selves in Egypt may coexist and cohabit in this world with spirits, animals, plants, stones, and God. These selves, always considered not to be true subjects, not possessing the true "I," are continuously monitored by development programs, as exemplified by the family planning program in Egypt, so that they may be managed or perhaps transformed into "modern and responsible subjects" (that is, to those who do possess the true "I") and be incorporated into the modern nation-state. Women's experiences in Egypt that embody different notions of self, time, and space, however, may enable them to postpone or defer this inclusion (Chakrabarty 1994a).

CONCLUSION

The Bangladeshi social activist and intellectual Farida Akhter (1992) questions the category of the individual self present in the arguments on reproductive rights and demonstrates its embeddedness in bourgeois liberal theory. Akhter argues that as citizens, individuals in a bourgeois democratic state are constitutionally free to earn wages, sell their labor, and enter into individual contracts with employers. Social reproduction takes place under circumstances of private production and the recognition of reciprocal rights between the employer and the employed. The product of our labor belongs to those who hire us to perform a required task. Labor thus becomes a form of commodity that we voluntarily sell. As capitalist relations of production extend into the realm of physical reproduction, procreation may take on commodity forms similar to labor power in a capitalist society. This would mean that as individual owners of our own production and procreative abilities we can conceivably manufacture products (babies) without recourse to the social. New reproductive technologies that make surrogate motherhood and in-vitro fertilization possible then become moments of celebration for this individualized self. Akhter cautions against this sense of individualization and emphasizes the risks of limiting the "demand to our individual body and not extending the demand to the body of the whole society" (Akhter 1992:37). She continues to say that liberal notions of individualism blind us from the social aspect of reproduction; "reproduction of human species is a social activity that is realized through individuals, but is never an individual affair" (Akhter 1992:38).

Elaborating on this idea of the social construction of the self, in an eloquent critique of the individual and the notion of individual rights, Mary Poovey (1992) argues that these categories are intertwined with the idea of a binary system of gendered norms. Poovey contends that women in bourgeois ideology have historically been constructed as maternal, making motherhood the normative identity. If women, Poovey argues, question their maternity, they not only question the "natural" basis of female identity but by oppositional logic that of masculine identity and the very basis of essentialist and individualized notions of gender and subjectivity. In proposing an alternative argument to the liberal narrative that only gives women identity "in relation to the identity and personhood of 'man'" (242), Poovey challenges the construction of the individualized subject and embeds the category of the individual in social relations. She persuasively suggests that no individual can conceptualize herself as an isolated unit, as a knower of all options, as this would evidently require the knowledge of social relations that structure options and outcomes. Therefore, personhood needs to be thought of not as an individualized unit but as inseparable from the social relations in which each person is inevitably bound. Poovey hence returns the construct "individual" into the fold of a heterogeneity placed within social relations (251–253).

Some feminist theorists similar to Poovey have long opposed traditional liberal accounts of individualistic self and argue for a relational sense of the self,[26] a self that is constructed and sustained in the social context. They have further shown the situatedness and identification of this social self with the body. Ethnographic work by anthropologist Emily Martin has clearly demonstrated how this embodied sense of self is experienced by many women during childbirth in the United States (Martin 1987).[27] A heightened sense of the body is also evident in the personal narratives of victims of torture and rape, and of holocaust victims. Susan Brison (1997), in a pivotal essay on trauma, shows how memory becomes embodied in many trauma victims and erases the philosophical distinction between body and self. In cases of repeated torture people may also find ways to disassociate their selves from their bodies. Similarly, some adult rape victims report a kind of splitting from their bodies and a separation from their former selves during and after the assault (Brison 1997: 18–19). One of the ways, Brison argues, that such victims seem to regain the coherence of their previous selves is by building a narrative that can be believed by an empathetic audience. In order to recover and be able to control her life and her environment, the trauma survivor may need an empathetic listener who bears witness and reinscribes a detached self. Autonomy is enhanced by dependency on another; autonomous self and relational self are "interdependent and even constitutive of one another" (Brison 1997:29).

These arguments are extremely pertinent for feminist debates on the construction of individuality and autonomous agency. The examples that I presented in this chapter, although similar in their emphasis to the socially constructed self in feminist literature, have different cultural situatedness in the understanding of the self. A self that already cohabits with *qarin* and *qarina,* I argue, is constituted as nonunitary prior to the nature of socialization needed in Western accounts of social constitution of self. There may not be an a priori unitary self that can be fractured or divided by trauma or interaction. This does not mean that these selves are not socially constituted. Rather, I want to stress a different kind of socialization that does not presuppose a unitary self before being multiplied or bifurcated through interactions with others.

As I suggested in the discussion on *kabsa, khadda,* and spirit possession, some women experience their bodies linked and situated in a larger social world. To be fertile or infertile may have to do with a folk or a scientific anatomical understanding of the body. Yet it may also have much to do with transgressions by other bodies, extreme emotions, and coexistence with other beings and the will of God. Among some members of poor households in Egypt the body and the self are, hence, experienced in a variety of forms. People exist simultaneously in different spheres. They participate as individuals within their own community and have relationships with their body, other bodies, and the spiritual universe. Simultaneously, however, they are part of a larger collective as individuals who are involved in wage work and participating in social processes with perhaps an increasing understanding of their rights within a legal framework of a modern nation-state.[28]

Chapter 5 | **Women's Choices**

"*Ihna rabish*" (we are rubbish) was how Rasha responded when I asked her whether she had any opinion on the family planning program in Egypt. She was a high-school-educated clerk employed by the family planning clinic near Qaramoos. Her disgust, expressed partly in English, was directed at the kinds of contraceptive pills available at the clinic. Women she knew had suffered multiple medical problems while on the pill and could not afford the luxury of a healthy diet that could counter their harmful effects.

While the Egyptian state implements its population management policy under the guidance of international donors and their development projects, the people's response to it is varied and, at times, defiant. Even for Rasha, who is employed by one such project, her relationship with fertility control methods was not entirely straightforward.

For many Egyptian women, accepting contraception is never an easy task. Rather, it is the outcome of a serious struggle. Either the woman fights against her husband's desires for more children, or she struggles with her own moral positions on the issue. Sometimes there is more than one obstacle. Fawzia, a thirty-year-old poor urban mother of four children whom we met in Behteem, was very ambivalent about her use of contraceptive pills:

A son of mine died of TB, and then I also had a miscarriage. At that time, I decided I would not take anything [meaning contraceptives] that makes God angry. I am still depressed with the loss of my two children. Now I am pregnant again and I am asking God to help me. When I took oral contraceptives [*huboob*] earlier, I would get weak. I wanted to use contraceptives as we are satisfied with the number of children that we have. Also, we live in just one room and my husband's income is not enough. Now I do not take anything. Sometimes I think of abortion. But when I think of the dead child and the one that came out dead, I decided that I will not disobey God anymore. I really wanted to have an abortion, I know it is a sin, but I also think about the hard life and conditions we live in.

Fawzia's situation encapsulates the dilemma of most women we spoke to. Her statement, added to my discussion on bodies and selves in chapter 4, shows how for many Egyptian women decisions on childbirth and outcomes of life's events cannot be understood without understanding their embeddedness in social relations and in people's beliefs.

In contrast, in league with international agencies, the family planning program in Egypt continues to emphasize the liberal notion of the individual through pedagogical discourses on self-denial, responsibility, and reason. Based on this individualized sense of self, development-oriented social science literature on Egypt highlights the possibility of women achieving high levels of personal autonomy through education, urban living, nuclearization of households, and employment outside the household. These attributes are positively related to lower family size and are statistically linked to an individual woman's increased ability to determine her family size (Nawar et al. 1995). This argument is embedded in the larger international discourse on how women in developing countries need to be empowered by being given the autonomy to step out of their traditional domestic roles. The literature on empowerment contends that women should be provided legal protection as equal citizens along with the knowledge, skills, and opportunities to make independent decisions (IPPF 1993). Some scholars linked to population policy advocacy emphasize economic activity as a road toward women's emancipation from dominating patriarchal structures (Mahmud and Johnston 1994). In this they seek to involve and challenge the state to consolidate women's status as citizens by providing a range of benefits and support structures that would empower women to seek employment outside their family domain (Mahmud and Johnston 1994:157; Correa and Petchesky 1994). As a confirmation of this argument the Egyptian Demographic and Health Surveys (EDHS) show how women in wage labor have lower fertility rates than those women who work outside the wage labor market (EDHS 1992).

Following these assertions development literature emphasizes how women, through wage work, create autonomous spaces that are concurrently organized in domains determined by the market and by the modernizing state.[1] Liberal economic theory considers wage work to be liberating because it assists in the production of a subjectivity that has a desire for industry, regularity, and individual accomplishment. Women as wage earners in modern economies are regulated through laws that grant them certain rights and privileges and incorporate them into the modern nation-state as citizens. The complex process of women moving from traditional control into perhaps the liberating arm of statal relations, a journey, as it were, from the household to the factory, is being documented by anthropologists in many cultures.

For example, Aihwa Ong (1988) shows how changing Malaysian socioeconomic conditions have increased women's access to wage labor. Women leave rural households to enter strict regimes of disciplined capitalist production and the world of modern consumption patterns where choice plays a major part in their individual self-fashioning. Similarly, Patricia Fernandez-Kelly (1983), in her ethnography of maquiladora workers in Mexico, details how exploited female workers anticipate the traditional roles of motherhood and prospects of marriage to opt out of the wage market. For the Middle East, Fatima Mernissi's (1982) work stands out for its analysis of the negative impact of capitalist development on Moroccan peasant women. Similarly, Soheir Morsy (1990) demonstrates in her ethnographic work how women's household and outside work responsibilities have increased with the advent of labor migration from Egyptian villages. The complexity of familial relationships and household structures, which I presented in chapter 3, also forces us to look more closely at the lives of women in the absence of their menfolk (Morsy 1990). In such cases, depending on particular circumstances, a recently married woman in a somewhat prosperous joint family household in rural Egypt may not be able to exert as much "autonomy" as an older woman in a less-well-to-do family.

For example, Fatima, a high school graduate from Cairo, was married to her mother's brother's son in a village near Qaramoos a year before I started my fieldwork. I knew her as a receptionist at the government clinic and also as the sister-in-law of one of the clinic managers. One day as we shared a taxi ride to Cairo, she informed me that this was her first trip back to the city since her wedding, and she had not seen her natal family in over a year. Fatima's in-laws had three feddans of land, most of her brothers-in-law had government jobs, and her father-in-law/uncle ran a general store in the village. They had one of the largest brick houses in the area and were considered a wealthy family. Her husband had left for Saudi Arabia three weeks after their wedding. It was only when her husband came back for his yearly vacation and then left again that we shared this taxi ride. This trip had materialized because her husband had given her permission to visit her relatives now. She was traveling alone and was, as an educated woman who had grown up in Cairo, trusted by her family to navigate the city by herself. Fatima was very matter-of-fact on this issue. Her structural position in the household did not allow her to make decisions independently although she had access to some of her husband's remittances and led a comfortable life. Hence, autonomy and women's work need to be, at least in the case of women like Fatima, thought about within the social, economic, and cultural parameters of their lives.

Further, social adjustment programs have caused rising inflation, a deteriorating job market, and increased economic precariousness for poor households in urban and rural areas. These economic and social changes, which include the privatization of health, education, and social services, have disproportionately negatively affected women's lives (Hatem 1994). As support structures for independent female-headed households are increasingly diminishing, the available option for some women may be to survive within the structure of their families. I would assert that women's work needs to be understood in the light of such practical matters as class differentials, access to off-farm work, employment possibilities, remittances, household formations, and competing moral ideologies that shape women's experiences, and not only in abstract formulations.

In many circumstances, work by both husbands and wives becomes crucial for the level of household income. Women who do opt to work may do so because the added income is a necessity for the economic survival of their families. Given an option many women, considering the lower wages they receive, might not want to engage in hard, day-long labor. For example, Ayesha, a peasant wife in Qaramoos who worked the full ten days of the cotton-picking season for LE 3 a day along with her two children and husband, was very clear on this issue when she said, "If my husband was a primary school teacher getting a monthly salary, maybe I could have stayed home and raised some poultry, but now I do need to work if my children are to go to school."[2]

Such accounts complicate the straightforward narrative of emancipation linked to wage labor. Clearly the issues are complex and varied, and much research, especially in the Middle East, needs to be done on women's work and its relation to class and the larger social, economic, and cultural context in which this work is available and performed. In the case of Egypt specifically, women's autonomy and its association to work needs to be rethought in relation to the multiple roles women play in contributing toward their families' welfare.

To push this argument and in light of the above discussion, I contend that autonomy is connected to the historic structures and possibilities that are available to a social actor.[3] Hence, before assuming changes in women's level of autonomy through the social processes of education, wage work, and modern living, it is necessary to investigate their lived experiences and see how social practices determine women's choices.

Based on ethnographic examples from my rural and urban sites, this chapter will guide us toward a greater understanding of the many ways women reach their contraceptive decisions. It will show how in the process their bodies become situated between multiple and opposing forces. There are the husbands demanding regular conjugal relationships. There are also the social and cultural pressures that often include the pressure to procreate. Finally, there is the state-sponsored family planning program that seeks to organize women's bodies by way of contraceptive devices. Yet, I will show how women, influenced by their own social circumstances, do demonstrate their independence and choices amid these conflicting forces.

As I present women's experiences in the following sections, it will become clear that their relationship to contraception is determined by a range of social variables. Some women in Egypt perceive their bodies and selves, as argued in the previous chapter, in relational terms and, therefore, may undermine the construction of the autonomous-subject model. Others use contraceptives informed by their own understanding of their bodily functions or invoke Islamic values that oppose use of contraceptives in all situations.

WOMEN AND CONTRACEPTION

Women with whom we spoke had specific practices that helped them regulate their fertility.[4] Primary among these methods were abortifacients. The range of abortion techniques included drinking a mixture of onion and garlic boiled in water, drinking frozen Coca Cola, and lifting heavy objects. Women in rural and urban areas told us how contraceptive pills taken in more than the required number over several days guaranteed a menstrual period. Somewhat literate women would sometimes purchase a stimulant of the uterine muscle from the local pharmacy and inject themselves to produce abortion.[5]

Abortions, although illegal in Egypt, are regularly performed in rural and urban Egypt. Women argued that abortion can be safe and successful only in the first two or three months of pregnancy. A woman who had aborted before said, "It is *haram* [forbidden] after the fourth month as the soul enters then." There is a broad theological debate in Islam on ensoulment of the fetus and the permissibility of abortion. Basim Mussalam (1982) argues that due to issues of inheritance and property rights, the juridico-legal aspect of sexual behavior became an important portion of the Islamic legal system as it evolved during the ninth through the twelfth centuries. Mussalam (1982) also cites examples of medieval Muslim medical texts containing descriptions of female contraceptive methods and abortifacients, suggesting a general tolerance for such practices. Historical evidence shows that popular acceptance of abortion was widespread even in nineteenth-century Egypt. In the 1830s Muhammad Ali Pasha decreed against abortion practices in peasant households in order to increase the supply of males for his army. Before that abortion was tolerated by the juridical system as customary practice that had legal value as subsidiary to revealed text (Cuno 1992; Panzac 1987). However, there is a difference of opinion among the schools of Islam specifically on when during pregnancy abortion is permissible. There are two major factors in this debate. One is ensoulment of the fetus, and the second is the health of the mother. Since the ninth century, Muslim jurists have not agreed on when the fetus becomes ensouled. The schools of Islamic jurisprudence range in their opinions from forbidding abortion at all and considering it as murder with stipulation of blood money, to tolerating abortion until 40, 90, or 120 days after conception. These stipulations are examples of when, according to the various schools of Islamic jurisprudence, the fetus is ensouled and hence meaningful life begins.[6] Abortion after these dates is akin to the murder of a human being.[7]

The idea of a fourth-month ensoulment invoked by women during our fieldwork may stem from these theological debates and from their popular interpretation in the communities we worked in. Abortion by an unmarried woman is of course a matter of shame, as is her pregnancy, and at times family members perpetuate violence against such a woman. But many women do have abortions as a means of reducing their family size. For an abortion women usually get help from *dayas* or from other women and speak of it as an unfortunate but necessary part of their lives.[8]

In addition to abortion, women have preferences for the kind of contraceptive they would like to use. Most of them hear about contraceptives through their friends, neighbors, or other women who are already using them. In this respect, media messages on the radio and television are also very important. Increased access to television in Egyptian households has helped policymakers to advance contraceptive use through media literacy. The state-sponsored media are used as a pedagogical tool and create opportunities for people to absorb and understand a range of social and political issues without the aid of formal schooling. Television drama serials, public service announcements, and other popular cultural media, like songs and theater, are regularly used to provide family planning information especially to poor and rural women. This information is then used by women to select what kind of method would be most useful for them.

Although statistically most Egyptian families are considered to be nuclear households (ROWIF 1991), for some of the men I spoke to the notion of family, especially in Qaramoos, was much broader and more inclusive. They used the term *aila* to describe the larger family/clan. An elderly informant explained to me the importance of the concept one day when he took me around the village pointing to the houses occupied by members of his *aila*. All of the male heads of these households were descendants of the same ancestor, his grandfather. He was proud that within a period of seventy years they, as a family, had become strong and resourceful. This resourcefulness, according to my informant, was strongly linked to the presence in the village landscape of households that had the name of the same *aila*. Having adult males not only signified strength in numbers to others but was also significant in bestowing favors and creating bonds of reciprocity outside the networks of state supervision and involvement.[9]

In contrast to this gendered position, among the media messages that particularly appeal to women is the name of the state-sponsored family planning program itself, Tanzīm el-Usra (Organization of the Family). Here the term *usra* is used for the family, signifying the smaller, immediate family in contrast to the larger concept of *aila* or extended family. In the last twenty years socioeconomic changes have led to a rapid urbanization of Egyptian rural areas, a spread of education, and a concomitant rise in modern consumption patterns. These influences have invariably had their impact on domestic relationships and have given rise to particularly modern notions of the private. As the *usra* becomes a lived reality for most Egyptian households, it also appeals to some women who want independence and privacy from larger joint households. Rural and urban women who were in such situations would, in casual conversation, sometimes tell me how they felt free in their own homes and did not worry about what they wore, for the sake of modesty, as the only people in the house were their husbands and children. They said that they could talk freely to their husbands and feel comfortable in doing what they pleased without their in-laws interfering in their lives.

Another message is the family planning program's emphasis on *tanzīm*, used in the sense of spacing, as opposed to *tahdīd* (root *hadd*: boundary, hence cutting off, complete cessation or control). This argument may be contrary to the more traditional fertility control model posited by the family planning program. Some women responded favorably to the spacing message as it gave them the option of postponing pregnancy while retaining their image of being fertile, intact.

Incorporating media images and pronouncements of spacing, women also at times used contraceptives to take a "rest" from periodic pregnancies. They may have used contraceptives to slow down their reproductive potential and allow their bodies to heal and recuperate from the trauma of delivery and the demands of breast-feeding.[10] Women's decision to take a rest was intrinsically connected to how they perceived their bodily functions.

MENSTRUATION, BODY FLUIDS, AND BLOOD FLOWS

As discussed in earlier chapters, local ideas of health and healing in Egypt incorporate the notion of an openness and fluidity within the body. In prevalent folk constructions objects and fluids may travel to other parts of the body that are thought to be in dynamic interconnectedness (Early 1988, 1993). Women's experience of their menstrual cycles is related to this construction. Some women told us that for them menstruation in regular cycles was linked with fertility and reproduction. At the same time the monthly menstrual cycle was also considered a time of much apprehension and anxiety. For example, Magda, a young urban housewife, explained it like this:

> This menstruation is a normal thing that has to happen. It is bad blood with a bad smell and I was brought up to shower and clean myself after it is gone. Everybody hates it. I feel it is better that women not have periods. If it were a creature we would have killed it and gotten rid of it. It hurts and makes me feel dizzy. I feel very uncomfortable when I have it. I feel unclean and do not know how to sit. My husband does not like it. Even young girls do not like it. When I was pregnant I felt good that I did not have it.[11]

Magda also told us that regular menstruation cleanses the body and removes the accumulated bad blood in the uterus. Women showed apprehension if the cycle was late as this could mean that impurities were being stored within their bodies. Further, menstruating women were considered unclean, and normally women would not pray or fast during their menstrual period. Most couples also do not have sex during this time due to religious and cultural sanctions.

Several other women explained their ideas of how modern contraceptive methods work by invoking body imageries that associated menstruation as a time when bodily impurities are washed out. Because one of the side effects of injectables like Depo-Provera is the cessation of menstruation, they are not very popular, especially among younger women. Women become anxious about the potential impurities retained within them. Also, a monthly cycle, however troublesome it may seem, keeps reminding women of their fertility. A missed period in Egypt, like anywhere else, is an indicator of a possible pregnancy. The amenorrhea related to Depo-Provera confuses many women about how to interpret a missed period. On the one hand, they were trying to avoid pregnancy. On the other they were experiencing little or no bleeding, a potential sign of pregnancy. This confusion needs to be further understood in light of these women's profound belief that although contraceptives may help in preventing pregnancy, God is the final decision maker.

Older women who were approaching menopause and had completed their family did accept injections. They asserted that as their bodies were older and not fertile anymore, menstrual blood was not produced as abundantly as in younger and fertile bodies, therefore, they worried less about retaining it. These women felt their bodies had changed and could absorb more harm.[12]

Given these connotations of menstrual blood, *daya*s and other women maintained that, if a woman shed little blood during childbirth, then she might have clean lactation (*bitrad'a nadīf*). The cleanliness in this respect referred to lactating without having menstrual cycles. Such women were considered protected from getting pregnant for an extended time without using contraceptives. The relationship of menstrual blood with body fluids, like milk, is important to understand in this body imagery. On the one hand, menstrual blood is considered impure and dirty, while on the other, in the case of clean lactation, the retained blood (during lactation amenorrhea) was considered to be converted into milk, a nutrient for the newborn child.[13] Women asserted that only those who have "clean lactation" were protected from becoming pregnant. Those women who started to menstruate while breast-feeding did at times accept contraception to postpone their next pregnancy.

Recent programs in Egypt on child survival, started under the auspices of UNICEF and USAID, monitor the infant mortality rates and the effect of various diseases on children. A major reason for this emphasis is to persuade women who have healthy and surviving children to have fewer birthing episodes. This program also encourages breast-feeding through the Ministry of Health clinics as a precaution against early-childhood diseases. Doctors advise women to visit clinics to periodically monitor the baby's growth and for immunizations. They give women special training on breast-feeding, proper weaning techniques, and general childcare. As much as breast-feeding is recommended by doctors for the child's well-being, prolonged breast-feeding is strongly discouraged as a method of contraception by the same clinicians. Rather, they encourage women to come for IUD insertion after the ritual forty days of confinement.[14]

Most women I spoke to, however, believed in the contraceptive effi-cacy of clean lactation. As Sara, a rural mother of three, proudly told me, "I lactated clean with all three and never needed to go back to the *laolab* (IUD) for two years after my children were born." Women like Sara who lactated without menstruating (clean lactation) would generally not use contraceptives during that period. In the pregnancy histories that we col-lected from women, many had intervals of two years between subsequent childbirth. Among our female informants two years of breast-feeding was considered a culturally appropriate duration. This period guaranteed the health and proper nourishment of the child. Closer pregnancies, women would argue, also meant competition for the mother's milk and would jeopardize the health of both the child and the mother.

Unlike some West African societies where there is postpartum sexual abstinence for two years (Bledsoe 1994), among my informants there was no cultural barrier to sex after a ritual wait of forty days.[15] Among those who did not have "clean lactation," therefore, some, as mentioned above, did take precautions against getting pregnant.

A case in point is that of Naeima, a poor urban housewife of forty-five whom we would meet in her small Behteem apartment. Naeima was married at the age of sixteen. She had had nine full-term pregnancies out of which five children, ranging in age from seven to twenty-four, were still alive. At the time of our meeting Naeima used an IUD and did not want to get pregnant again. She told us she periodically got pregnant at an interval of two years. She claimed that the two-year intervals were primarily due to her continuously breast-feeding her children. But she also affirmed that she would intermittently use the pill to prevent get-ting pregnant soon after childbirth. There were two occasions when she became pregnant within a year of giving birth. The first time was when one of her children died within seven days of birth. The second time, she got pregnant a few months after childbirth. She blamed this on not using oral contraceptives because she felt unwell after taking them. It was diffi-cult to get precise information from Naeima on her past contraceptive history and its relationship to her spaced pregnancies. She may have, judging our interest in family planning, felt forced to provide us with a compliant narrative about her past life. At this stage of her life these events may have been remote and not central to her concerns of day-to-day living. Yet the periodic nature of her childbirth, the emphasis on breast-feeding, and the intermittent use of oral contraceptives guides us to think how women like Naeima may pragmatically use contraceptives to postpone and space their pregnancies. Naeima's example also makes us aware of the ill effects of contraceptive use on women's bodies.

SIDE EFFECTS AND WOMEN'S BODIES

Women who did want to use oral contraceptives sometimes felt that the pills had a deleterious effect on their health. So they used oral contraceptives to prevent pregnancies, but they would stop using them to take a "rest" from the ill effects of contraceptives on their body. For example, Nafisa, another urban housewife and the mother of five, told us how, after having breast-fed her child for two years, she decided to start using contraceptive pills. She said, "I only take the pill [*huboob*] at times of need. I stopped them two months ago because I got headaches, dizziness, and complete loss of energy."

Similarly, women such as Fayza, an urban housewife and a mother of four, articulated clearly how different contraceptives affect women's bodies and health in relation to the circumstances of their lives. When we spoke to her, Fayza had been married for ten years. At the age of twenty-seven, she felt that her health was deteriorating due to periodic childbirth and her poor economic condition. Her husband, a janitor in the sewage department, wanted another son. She refused to get pregnant, since they already had a son, and started using contraception after her last delivery. Fayza used the pill irregularly for six months. She never liked the pill because, she explained, "Every time I used them I would spot blood, and if I took them the whole month I would spot every day of the month. I hated it and so did my husband. I felt unclean and always felt restricted with the spotting and also it interfered with my sexual relationship with my husband." Still she persisted with the pill as she feared that the IUD would perhaps harm her more. She argued, "I am using the pill now against my husband's will because I cannot raise a fifth child. I take it [the pill] even though it makes me *ta'baan*."

The word *ta'baan* here means to be tired. Yet in colloquial Arabic it is also used to convey a range of negative physical and emotional states. For women on contraceptive pills the word means to be unwell due to either weakness, headache, or general listlessness. Women on oral contraceptives, like Fayza and Nafisa, would sometimes talk about how they tolerated the ill effects of contraceptive pills on their health for a period of months and then took a few months of rest from them because their bodies would be *ta'baan* from prolonged contraceptive use.

Women invariably used the opportunity to talk to us as an occasion to inform us about their health. Ammal, an urban mother of two, had decided that she would not like to have more children because of her financial circumstances. "It was my decision," she said. "Men only bring in the money, it is the women who have to raise the children and worry about the expenses." She had tried the pill after her first pregnancy but had suffered weight loss and a drop in her blood pressure. She continued, "I also had dry milk [meaning that she could not breast-feed anymore], and my body was tender and painful." Linking the taking of oral contraceptives with good nutrition, she stated: "We need to drink milk and eat a lot of meat and chicken, and since we cannot afford it I decided to change the method."

Another woman in Qaramoos similarly argued: "We are farmers, we are not strong and we are not healthy, so we cannot take the pill every day and also work at home and in the fields." Other women in the village would state that they put on weight while using contraceptive pills. Oral contraceptives, women would argue, besides other symptoms, cause obesity and also produce breakthrough bleeding. Being heavy/full is a part of local notions of beauty and bodily aesthetics, as it reflects women's better health and nutrition. The weight increase, however, in oral contraceptive use, women told me, was due to the retention of fluids (bad blood) that then get stored under the skin, producing swelling with no concomitant gain in strength, making them lethargic and weak.

These women would say that only a proper diet (primarily meaning meat) can cure this feeling of tiredness and loss of energy. Poverty and lack of resources put a healthy diet out of reach for many. Further, breakthrough bleeding is also undesirable as, besides other problems relating to general weakness and complaints of dizzy spells, it also hinders carrying out of religious duties. These women thus associated oral contraceptive use directly with their socioeconomic circumstances.[16]

The emphasis on interchangeability of body fluids and the interconnectedness of different parts of the body also informed women's use of contraceptives. Women with whom we spoke experienced their bodies as linked to flows that expelled impurities and other flows that were converted into nutrients. This knowledge caused some women to reject

IUDs because they feared that besides producing breakthrough bleeding an IUD could travel up into the heart and cause serious problems. IUDs, women told me, could also travel upward and penetrate the head of the fetus if there was a pregnancy despite contraceptive use (everyone knows that contraceptives cannot compete with the will of Allah).

In some cases women did prefer to use IUDs, especially while they were breast-feeding. They also used them when oral contraceptives caused them physical discomfort. For example Naeima, the woman introduced earlier who had had nine pregnancies, had decided to get an IUD inserted after her last child was born seven years ago. Her husband, according to her, had always opposed her using contraception, arguing that as long as he was alive she would have to go on bearing children. "Now," she said, "he cannot argue with me anymore, he sees how my health is deteriorating and knows that I cannot bear any more children." She continued, "My daughter has a baby now and it would not be appropriate that I have more children at this stage."

When she had her IUD inserted the doctor told her that she might suffer from episodes of bleeding. She indeed did complain of heavy bleeding during her menstrual periods and also of intermittent bleeding during the month accompanied by dizziness, backache, and general malaise. "I am used to all this," she told me, "now that I have had them for six years." She acknowledged that she had been asked to go to the doctor for regular checkups, but she stated very matter-of-factly: "Look around you, what do you see, this is a harsh life, how can I afford to go to the doctor every now and then? I have young children to raise, there are other expenses."

Besides showing a complicated preference for contraceptive use, Naeima's example also contradicts the image of poor women as silent sufferers presented in development-oriented literature (e.g., Khattab 1992). Her reluctance to seek treatment for her ailments also sensitizes us to the economic pressures families suffer and how women continuously sacrifice their own needs for the family.[17]

SOCIAL FACTORS

As discussed in the introductory chapter, the structural adjustment program pushed by the Egyptian state under the advice of the IMF and the World Bank has eroded long-term subsidies on food. In addition, a 50 percent increase in energy costs in 1991, removal of subsidies in the agricultural sector (subsidies for items such as fertilizers and pesticides were removed in 1992–1993), devaluation of the Egyptian pound, higher transportation costs, and the raising of indirect taxes have all had an impact on the Egyptian poor (Korayem 1993).

These social processes directly influence the lives of the people with whom I spoke in rural and urban areas. Cairo's urban poor neighborhoods, as discussed in chapter 3, are particularly vulnerable to changes in the economy. In contrast to the villages, most low-income households in the city depend on fixed wages and on the market for their food requirements. Some of these neighborhoods, as in the case of Behteem, do not have the extended-kin support available to families in rural areas and in the older popular neighborhoods of Cairo itself.

For women who lived in Behteem, going to a family planning clinic meant taking two buses to reach their destination. This entailed a round-trip expense of at least one pound fifty piasters. Some government clinics now charge fifty piasters as an admission surcharge.[18] Add to this at the very minimum three to four pounds as the cost of antibiotics that were usually not available at the hospitals or clinics at subsidized rates. We arrive at a total of five or six pounds. It should be made clear, however, that if anything remains subsidized in Egypt it is the availability of contraceptives. In the clinic that I visited regularly (see chapter 2), IUD insertion cost two pounds, an injection of Depo-Provera that lasts three months only three and a half pounds, and a month's supply of pills could be purchased for just thirty-five piasters. Yet the combined expense of even a few pounds was enough to make a dent in the household budget, where the total monthly income might be less than one hundred Egyptian pounds for a family with at least six mouths to feed.

Women would tell us how they had been living with foul discharges due to IUD use but did not have the time or the resources to go back and get themselves examined by a doctor. Some women did not want to be examined by male doctors, finding the experience to be immodest. But by and large the expenses of transportation, the hospital fee, and in case of infections, the price of medicine/antibiotics, discouraged these women from visiting the clinic.

Yet women do use contraceptives and make choices, negotiating their way through a range of opinions and options. In rural and urban Egypt, as nuclear families rely more on themselves than on the extended family, the burden of raising children routinely falls on women's shoulders. As discussed earlier, with the burden of domestic work and the increasing pressure to find wage labor to sustain the household, women complain of how multiple and periodic pregnancies drain their health. Zeinab, a *fellah* woman in Qaramoos with three children, one day complained about her sister's husband: "She has been pregnant eight times and is *ta'baan*. Only four of her children survived, all are daughters. The husband now wants to remarry, my sister has told him not to disturb her. 'Go do what you want,' she told him. Men do not give up. It is our *jism* (body) that is *ta'baan*."

Zeinab helped her sister get an IUD inserted so that she would not accidentally get pregnant. "She is my sister, how can I see her ill?" Women like Zeinab and others that I spoke to do use the contraceptives available through the family planning program to space their pregnancies and also at times to prevent any pregnancies at all. In this they may be supported by their husbands. When I asked Zeinab whether women consult their husbands or take this decision on their own, she replied that it was forbidden to use contraceptives without the husband's knowledge and all decisions should be made together. Then, after a pause, she continued: "I take care of the animals, the children, all the things at home. You think I cannot make this decision?"

Like Zeinab, other women make independent decisions, too. Yet some also struggle with their husbands to use contraceptives. Amal, a thirty-three-year-old mother of five in Behteem, decided to start using contraceptives because of the hardships of life. She said: "If my life was better, I would have had more children. Our house is too small for us, there is no room for more." When Amal told her husband of her decision to use contraception, he became upset. He believed that contraceptives are forbidden in Islam, and that it was a sin to use contraception. She complained that he now slept away from her in another room, refusing to touch her as long as she continued to use contraceptives. A number of women we spoke to, like Amal herself, pragmatically situated their argument for accepting contraceptives in narratives of socioeconomic necessity. In contrast, attitudes that argued for Islam's opposition to contraception, like Amal's husband's, were also constantly invoked in our conversations with other women.

ISLAMIC IDEALS

Sausan, a twenty-four-year-old mother of two, lived in Behteem at the time of my research there. She was educated through the tenth grade, and her husband had a high school diploma and worked in a publishing house.

Sausan told us that she could not get pregnant for three years after her marriage. She was worried but thought that this was what God wished for her. She went to the doctor and also took some medicine, but it did not help. She related:

> I was very upset in those days, not because of my husband or that I was getting old. I believe in God and I know He has reasons for everything. I knew my husband also wanted to have children, but he is a patient man and also gave me money for the doctor. Sometimes I used to cry and feel sorry for myself. I was upset that people viewed me as infertile. I wanted them to come and congratulate me for having a child. I used to ask God for a baby every time I prayed. I did not want to remember the dates of my period, believing that if I remembered it would come, and I wanted to miss it. I did not want to feel its pain when it came and I always engaged in all kinds of work to forget about it. I remember once when I had my period and wanted to go to the Eid [the feast after the month of Ramadan] prayers. I did not want to acknowledge that I was menstruating, so I showered and went and said my prayers, asking for God's forgiveness for my unclean self. After a month I missed my period and got pregnant. I know God listened to me, He is all knowing.

In Behteem, we periodically met women like Sausan, women who had joined religious groups that met every week to hear sermons on the life of the Prophet and to discuss other moral and ethical questions. In their self-presentation to us, these somewhat younger and more educated women sought to distance themselves from the traditions of their mothers and grandmothers. They criticized women-centered veneration practices at tombs and *zar* ceremonies as un-Islamic and argued that these practices were backward, superstitious, and ignorant (also see Bernal 1994: 52). Many of them, hence, did not believe in the ability of jinn, *afarit,* or *qarin/qarina* to manifest themselves in people's bodies and cause them harm. These women would forcefully condemn these beliefs and talk of those who believed in spirits as living in *jahillaya* (ignorance, not enlightened). Religious and modern in their approach to health and the body, these women would argue against going to midwives or other female healers and would always prefer the medical doctors.

In folk belief that other women related to us, women were supposed to have less ʿaql (characteristics from the realm of reason) and more *nafs* (characteristics from the realm of disorder). Sausan and her friends on the contrary thought of themselves as well versed in the intricacies of religion. This knowledge of Islam made them consider themselves to possess ʿ*aql* like most men. As male-centered Islamic knowledge was viewed as true Islam linked to progress, the women saw themselves to be equals to the extent that they could attain the same level of learning and understanding of Islam as men. Their move from *nafs* to ʿ*aql* could be interpreted as symbolic masculinization. Indeed, older women in the community would sometimes taunt these women for speaking and acting like men. It should be emphasized that the women were aware of this criticism. They would reply that Islam is not gender blind, and it is imperative for women and men to learn and acquire knowledge to improve themselves and become better Muslims. Accordingly they would argue that, by becoming more knowledgeable, they could also raise better Muslim children who would be trained in the correct practices of the religion. It was not seen as competing with men or following some preordained male trajectory, but rather as following a path that God had chosen for all Muslims, men and women alike.[19]

These women not only resisted contraception but also considered the issue of autonomous choice as contradictory to their own sense of agency. It was their subservience to God that profoundly questioned the liberal agenda of individual agency promoted by the family planning program. For them the presence of God in their day-to-day decision making was crucial. They were unwilling to grant themselves an autonomy that would not take into account Islamic doctrine. Their opposition to contraceptives was also informed by what they considered to be God's wish, that they populate the world with large numbers of believers. Given this outlook most of them wanted to have a large family.

CONCLUSION

In her work on medical discourse and women's bodies, Emily Martin (1987) shows how lower-class African American women in Baltimore, Maryland, registered less acceptance of the dominant medical model than is the norm. This was not only due to racial and gender oppression but also because these women were left out of the medical system's pedagogical project.

Along these lines, we can see the practice of family planning in Egypt as one case of deployment of modern regimes of social control embedded in modern management and behavior modification techniques. For the women we spoke to, being fertile was extremely important, as it offered them social acceptance and respect. The option to use contraceptives was always delayed until they had proven their ability to become pregnant. Even when these women did use contraceptives, they placed their use within a framework of an already constituted self, as shown in chapter 4, that is linked and situated in broader social relations and environment. Ideas propagated by the family planning program may be pragmatically incorporated within patterns in which the self constructs itself, but these ideas may not have the exclusive and unique space desired by the program.[20]

Socioeconomic pressures have compelled many in Egypt to curtail their family size. Ideas of modern living linked to the desire to educate children, which is evident in most households, have forced families to think differently about resources and their own future. Yet, poor Egyptian women have still retained a certain level of independence in part because of the breaches in the pedagogical project, and in part because they have not seen themselves as isolated individuals targeted by the programs. Even the planners have started to understand this.

Program planners comprehend that independent decision making for women is related to a set of complex relationships within the household and beyond. The social actors in this process include men. In a move to address this issue they have, as I show in chapter 2, started research and information campaigns to increase male involvement in the family planning decision-making process. The next chapter further situates some of these multiple contexts that influence and determine the acceptance of family planning within Egyptian households.

Chapter 6

Men and Family Planning

Jean and Simone Lacouture, two French journalists writing in the late fifties, elaborate as follows on the relationship between Egypt's demography and geography:

> The population in Egypt increases by one more human being every minute. The Nile Valley, over populated like all oases, is so crowded that it can no longer feed its inhabitants. The political and diplomatic history of the country revolves around this problem: There are too many Egyptians in Egypt.
>
> LACOUTURE AND LACOUTURE 1958:357

The Lacoutures continue by emphasizing that "the population increase in Egypt, from a social point of view, is linked to ignorance, superstition, ill health, poverty and the Islamic customs themselves (polygamy and divorce)" (1958:358). Like many authors of the colonial and contemporary eras, the Lacoutures argue that these demographic and social problems could be corrected only through education and social development and by "restoring women to a sense of their human dignity and men to the sense of their responsibility" (360).[1]

Leila Ahmed (1992) reminds us that arguments that linked Islam and its traditions with the subjugation of women, epitomized in the practice of veiling and seclusion, were essential discourses for Western colonialism in the Muslim Middle East to undermine and eradicate the culture of the colonized people. In this process the colonial authors and administrators sought to undo the victimization of Muslim women by Muslim men and Islam. One of their prime targets was the Egyptian peasant, the *fellah*. Described in the colonial literature as coarse, uneducated, lazy, docile, submissive, and carefree, the peasant was also portrayed, however, as lord and master within his own household, where he degraded, secluded, and inhumanely treated his womenfolk.

An early ethnography on the Egyptian peasantry by Father Aryout, a Coptic priest who studied the *fellahīn* of Upper Egypt, describes the presumed psychological makeup of the Egyptian peasant:

> The truth is that the Fellah does not think outside the immediate present; he is fettered to the moment. No time and place except the present have much effect on his mind, because they have none on his senses. He is like a primitive or a child; his intellect is controlled by the things he is feeling and doing.
>
> ARYOUT 1963 (1938):140

This infantilization of the Egyptian man created a justification for intervening in the lives of these men in order to modernize, educate, and civilize them. Hence, not only women needed to be liberated but men also were to be educated to become rational, responsible beings leaving behind their perpetual status as adolescents.

Despite generations of such representations of Egyptian social life as "traditional and static," the socioeconomic situation in Egypt and other Arab countries for the better part of the twentieth century has seen extensive urbanization, increases in commerce and wage labor, and a spread of formal education. In this context, the expanded participation of women in the labor force and increased female education have changed the organization of the household and redefined female space and boundaries. Feminist anthropology related to the Middle East has astutely described these sociological changes (see, for example, Abu-Lughod 1986, 1998; Altorki 1986; Morsy 1978, 1993a; Nelson 1974, 1996; Rassam 1984). Demographic research, however, continues to maintain the household primarily as female space. The association of reproduction and fertility with femaleness effectively perpetuates the domestic/public dichotomy and splits social analysis into female/male spheres.

Unraveling the pervasive processes through which gender asymmetry is maintained calls for the inclusion of experiences of both sexes and their roles in reproducing or subverting the system. This chapter will seek to present ethnographic data on the construction of the male body and sexuality as they relate to the debate on fertility control in Egypt. The endeavor is to show the linkages between the political, social, and economic conditions prevalent in Egypt and the lived experience of the men with whom I spoke. I shall further hint at historical and contemporary efforts to use development models to modernize the Egyptian masses, especially the poor, and how these efforts are linked to emergent constructions of gender and domestic life in Egypt.

MEN'S REPRESENTATION

A series of advertisements aired in Egypt seek to address the issue of men's role in contraceptive decision making. The advertisements are produced by the State Information Services under technical guidance from the Johns Hopkins University Center for Communication Programs, which is funded by USAID for the purpose. Through these television advertisements, men are increasingly made aware of their familial responsibilities as providers. Some of the advertisements represent men as heads of families yet simultaneously criticize them as defenders of the status quo, as conservative, traditional, and antimodern, that is, anti–birth control. Others encourage men to be flexible and uncritical toward female decisions to use contraceptives. Yet others use pervasive historical stereotypes showing an unconcerned peasant patriarch who rides on a donkey while his wife, walking next to him, carries a big load on her head. Some summon men to behave better toward their womenfolk and show images of modern urban men helping their wives in domestic household chores. Another shows a *shaykh* admonishing a poor man for failing in his duty as a father and for having many children without thinking of the consequences. In another, a social worker scolds a father for his son's psychological distress due to the son's lack of education and hence reduced opportunities to earn a living. The father is blamed for the large family and the sense of deprivation and inadequacy it creates for all. In many advertisements, authority figures like the *shaykh* and the social worker stress the responsibility of men to live up to their role as provider. By invoking this image the family planning policy makers seek to shame men into being "real men," that is, being more responsible individuals and, therefore, producing fewer babies. Family planning is presented in terms of the health and future of the wives and children, evocations with strong appeal to the men.

The men who are shown in these advertisements as opposing contraceptives are depicted in traditional peasant clothes, while men who seem to be more open to family planning are shown wearing modern Western clothes. These simplistic markers again dichotomize the debate into a traditional-modern scheme. They invariably also play on stereotypes that the Egyptian elites hold about poor Egyptians in general and the rural poor in particular.

Further, the issue of responsibility of the head of the household toward the social good is being emphasized at a time of general economic instability for the Egyptian poor. The state's argument for men's responsibility toward their families is put forward even as the opportunities to fulfill that role are rapidly diminishing. By concentrating on issues of birth control the state may deflect resentment against itself onto the domestic sphere, as couples with large families are themselves held responsible for their economic plight.

One of the major concerns of the family planning program, as discussed in the analysis presented in chapter 2 (in contrast to lived experiences), is to create a progressive, positive, and modern family space devoid of pressures from other kin, friends, and relatives on reproductive decisions. There is an assumption that the household is a nuclearized decision-making unit, free and open to discussion regarding fertility choice and the sole locus of social respectability.

In liberal political theory the family is regarded as the natural basis of civil life. As a location of biological ties and affective emotions among its members, it may, however, stand opposed to the working of the liberal state. Family can be "thus simultaneously the foundation of the modern state and antagonistic to it" (Pateman 1989:21). Hence, the family needs to be reconstituted on modern grounds. Its allegiance has to reside with the state, linked as it is to the ideology of social good. To emphasize this point further, I would, following Michel Foucault's (1980) argument, suggest that the father is not necessarily the representative of the sovereign or the state, nor are the latter projections of the father. Yet the reconstitution of the father's role within the family is necessary to accomplish the transformative requirements of the modern state, whether for the control of the population or the medicalization of sex (100). Therefore, while the Egyptian state may still need fathers as head of the household, a new kind of patriarch is desired, one who is responsible about his civil duties and subservient to the state.

In the following sections I present the responses of rural and urban men with whom I lived and spoke. I show how men themselves give meaning to the language and practice of fertility control as it enters their households and affects the notions of their bodies, fertility, and sexuality. I emphasize the conflict that these men have with the prescribed notions of the individual and the domestic and how social and economic changes reinforce or destabilize their positions by impinging on gender relations within the household. It should also be emphasized that the responses of these men reflect their presentations of themselves to me, a man whom they considered to be a friend and a co-religionist, yet somewhat different due to my education and nationality.

MEN AND THE FAMILY

After I had been in Qaramoos for a few days, Ismael, the brother-in-law of my friend and host Atef, invited me to see his feddans,[2] planted in cotton. While walking toward his fields, Ismael casually asked, "*Ya daktor,* how many times should I have sex in a day?" I was caught unaware. I had never been asked such a direct question before. What could I say? "Any number of times"? "I do not know"? "Ask your wife"? I gave the best answer that I could think of: "Any number of times, as long as both of you agree to it." Then, in turn, I asked him what had prompted him to ask me such a question. He answered that he worried about the health of his wife and did not want to burden her with too frequent sex. As our conversation developed, he told me further that he had always opposed any kind of contraception for his wife on religious grounds. But now that he had six children, childbirth might start affecting her health, youth, strength, and fullness. Therefore, he had given her permission to use the IUD. He resolved the apparent contradiction in his statements by asserting that, if Allah really wanted him to have another child ("if Allah wishes"), then no contraceptive could prevent it. Moreover, there is a distinction, according to him, between *tanzīm* (planning, spacing) and *tahdīd* (root *hadd:* boundary, hence cutting off, control, complete cessation). He did not disagree as forcefully with *tanzīm,* which he used more often in the sense of spacing, viewing it as sometimes necessary for women to recuperate their health after delivery and also to breast-feed the child.[3]

Ismael was a minimally educated (primary-school-level) farmer who had inherited some land. By local standards he was somewhat prosperous. In Qaramoos, as discussed in chapter 3, some men had college degrees or high school diplomas and worked for government agencies, yet many men that I spoke to were farmers with an educational profile similar to Ismael's. The concern for one's wife's health was the prevalent idiom through which these men spoke to me about relationships with their spouses. Their use of the health idiom may be partially due to their knowledge that I was a physician. Yet, I think it also showed the deep sense of caring and affection they felt for their wives and children. The dominant representation of Middle Eastern gender relations in anthropological and social science literature is one of stark contrasts. The separation of the male and female sphere, with the dominating patriarch, is an exaggerated depiction of lived experience. Inequalities do exist between the genders, but analysis needs to move toward understanding the dynamics of how these differences are maintained and undermined within constantly shifting social contexts. Cooperation and sharing between genders may exist simultaneously with male practices and rhetoric that seek to generate power and authority.[4]

For the poor (and my informants were mainly poor), cooperation within the structure of the nuclear household and larger networks of clan/family is a very important part of their lives. In the rural areas, as changes in the economy translate into the nuclearization of the household and as men migrate to the cities or the Gulf countries, people depend increasingly on the recruitment of household labor to perform daily agricultural chores. In these situations, husband and wife become a team in the management of household affairs, and the distinctions between public and private, male and female spheres are frequently blurred. Men spoke to me about their wives as partners who shared the vagaries of this life with them. Men, from both urban and rural areas, were proud of the hardiness and strength of their women in contrast to the upper-class women who were portrayed as lazy and weak. These men also felt emotionally attached to their wives and found them physically desirable and aesthetically pleasing (the notion of fullness and beauty was repeated several times).

In this regard studies mentioned in earlier chapters on women left behind by male migration in Egypt rarely emphasize the increased responsibilities and labor that overwhelm these women in the absence of their male partners.[5] Even those women who have the social space to make independent decisions feel burdened by the increasing workload of single-handedly taking care of the farm, raising children, supervising house repair, and maintaining familial responsibilities. Women spoke to me about feeling quite exhausted by all these responsibilities, especially when other kinsmen were also away from the village. Another aspect that is often ignored in representations of women left behind by their migrating spouses is the emotional loss that women may feel when their husbands are away for long stretches of time.

Seldom does literature on gender in the Middle East address the issue of affection between husbands and wives and how bonds of mutual support and caring are constructed within households. Most studies take the unequal gender relations as a given, rarely questioning how they are maintained, perpetuated, or changed in linkage to the social changes in society. The socialization processes through which gender asymmetry is maintained, hence, calls for the inclusion of experiences of both sexes.

Lila Abu-Lughod's (1986) work on the Awlad Ali helps us to see how women in this community use poetry to convey very strong emotions. She analyzes these poems as subdiscourses of resistance by the socially weak. The poems also give us a window into the private lives of the women and inform us about their romantic desires and their relationships with their husbands. The affective linkages that the women invoke binds both sexes into a single symbolic bond and hence undermines the sharp representations of public and private spheres.

Similarly some women in the village spoke to me of the loss they felt when their husbands were away. Hala worked as a servant in a government facility in the village. Her husband had been away for over two years in Saudi Arabia. She had a teenage daughter, and she had one-third of a feddan of land that she rented out. As an uneducated rural woman married to a poor, almost landless peasant who had gone abroad to make a living, Hala suffered from taunts and jokes from her coworkers about how her husband had left her alone with her daughter and would never come back. Hala was always anxious about the well-being of her husband and felt alone and tired in dealing with life by herself. "*Daktor,*" she would say to me, "could you not get my Ibrahim here through your *mashru'a* [project; meaning my work]. Why does he have to work so hard there when he can get some guineas [Egyptian pounds] here?"

Hala's direct lament was an interesting episode in my understanding of how some peasant women talk about general life situations. Depictions of gender relations in rural Egyptian households always portray women as oppressed without ever mentioning relationships of kindness, sharing, and mutual love between husbands and wives. These representations may follow a long history of how the "Arab" family is historically placed in a classification of themes. Some of the repeated themes are the nonconsensual marriage, where men are dominant and the family is more important than the individual, the cross-cousin marriage patterns, the honor of women, the social powerlessness of women, and the threat of polygyny, dangling as a sword over women's heads (Tucker 1993 : 196–199). I do not seek to locate a Western-influenced concept of "love" within the *fellah* household in order to "humanize" the subjects of this ethnography, but at least I would like to question the terms in which relationships within these households are portrayed.

Caring for his wife is intrinsically linked, for a man, to her reproductive and childrearing capacities: she is the mother or potential mother of his offspring. Motherhood, especially with respect to sons, is a culturally valued position, and almost all recently married women I spoke to were eager to attain it. For men, the ability to fertilize affirmed their virility. It also guaranteed the continuity of their name, lineage, and the traditional values of their families.

My male informants conceived of their wives as bearers of tradition and repositories of cultural knowledge. In their worldview a woman's place was at home, taking care of the children and maintaining the household. The necessity of spacing births was therefore not only to safeguard the health of their wives but also to guarantee the well-being of their children. Frequent pregnancies might not give the mother enough time to recuperate, thus affecting her health, and might also affect her ability to take care of the babies, jeopardizing their health as well.

Procreation of sons is especially linked to social prestige and authority. It is, not surprisingly, also linked to notions of virility to which these men adhere. The famous Egyptian writer Yusuf Idris, in his story *You Are Everything to Me,* explains this in a not-so-subtle manner. He describes the life of Sayyed, a traffic police officer who becomes impotent after an illness. Sayyed seeks remedies from *shaykhs,* faith healers, and medical doctors, with no success. He becomes very depressed because of his inability to perform sexually. Eventually, at the end of the story, he decides to divorce his wife rather than face endless humiliation. His wife refuses to accept the divorce and vows to stay with him forever. At this stage Sayyed realizes that he is not impotent after all, for he has a son, a son who will be an extension of his virility and have the erection that he has lost.

Just as they extend their father's virile qualities, male offspring guarantee the continuation of the family name. The eldest son especially is said to *yiftah il-bab,* which literally means that he "opens the door."[6] This signifies that, in the case of the death of the father, the eldest son takes on responsibility for the mother and younger siblings. Under present inheritance laws in Egypt, which are guided by the *Shari'a* (Islamic religious law), male children become crucial in retaining inheritance within the family. A widow receives one-fourth of the estate if there are no children and one-eighth with children. If there are sons and daughters, then the daughters receive one-half the share of the son. A single son may inherit the entire property, while a single daughter can only inherit one half. Failure to have a son may mean that a portion of the inheritance reverts to the parents, brothers, or, in some cases, cousins of the deceased (Rugh 1984).

Also, during specific days in the month of Ramadan (the month of fasting) and on days of cultural or religious festivals, like the Eid, the Moulid il Nabi (the birthday of the Prophet), or the sixteenth day of the Muslim month of Shaban (a day when people go to cemeteries and pray for deceased relatives), fathers send meat or appropriate sweets to their daughters' homes. Sisters expect the same cultural tradition from their brothers after their fathers pass away.[7] Along with these ritual gifts comes the added responsibility of mediating familial disputes and protecting the women of the family.

Further, great importance is placed on the ceremony of receiving condolences when family members pass away. People feel anxious when there is no surviving male member, especially a son in the family, to accept the condolences. Men with whom I spoke took all these responsibilities very seriously and wondered how these traditional support networks would continue if they did not have sons. A house without a son is thought to be orphaned of its ritual obligations and importance.

This rhetoric of caring is an aspect of popular notions of masculinity that call on men to be responsible and provide for their families. Accordingly, as in my conversation with Ismael, men seldom expressed worry about their own health while discussing sexual activity and its potential for procreating children. Being men, sexual prowess and potency were intrinsic to their very nature. They did not themselves need medical advice. It was only the weak, or, more precisely, the women and children, who needed to be helped and protected.

Caring and affection for their household members did not, however, always translate into equal gender relations in household chores or even in the distribution of food within families. Men do attempt to exert authority within the household, and the rhetoric of protectiveness and responsibility may itself be related to systems of distribution of power within the family. Power connected to the larger kin ties of parents and parents-in-law is also very important, especially with regard to fertility decisions within the household. Moreover, as children give pleasure and provide happiness to the family, infertility can lead to the threat of divorce.

We can highlight two conclusions. First, there are many more actors involved than assumed in the ideal image of the nuclear household. Second, the reality of gender roles is much more complex than what is assumed in the simplistic depictions of Middle Eastern men in the ethno-graphic literature and in the popular imagination of the West. Men's no-tions of body, sexual pleasure, gender roles, and responsibility include both a rhetoric of concern for their wives and a desire to retain control and power over them. The following section illustrates some of the ways in which modern contraceptive methods are understood and used within the family against the background of gender differences.

MALE BODIES AND SEXUAL PLEASURE

Survey data in Egypt have shown that many men leave the choice of a specific contraceptive method to their wives after the initial decision to practice birth control has been made (Egypt Male Survey 1992). In my own fieldwork I came across men attempting to influence these decisions much more systematically than is assumed. Women still play a much larger role in choosing the contraceptives for themselves, and the knowl-edge that men possess is mostly through information that their wives give them. Men, however, make systematic use of that knowledge especially as it relates to the health problems caused by certain contraceptives.

Most men I spoke to were aware of negative effects of contraceptives on women's health and general well-being. Yet, as they spoke about the dangers of specific female contraceptives, they also encouraged and toler-ated their use if repeated pregnancies were affecting the health of their spouses. Like Ismael, they would recommend contraceptives to help their wives space their pregnancies.

In the communities where I worked, impotence along with sterility destabilized male positions. Impotence was periodically blamed on curses and magic (sehr) by rival men. I would constantly hear stories of how some men were tied (uqm) and rendered impotent by magic performed by some amil (faith healer) in the service of some enemy. The sexual act was also intrinsically connected for men with their procreative ability. Steril-ity was considered shameful enough for men not to go to doctors, and they considered getting a semen analysis done a humiliating experience.

An informant in Behteem, who was childless after fifteen years of mar-riage, went for the first time to get a sperm count. He showed me the re-sults, which indicated oligospermia (low sperm count). He asked me not to share this information since he was ashamed and had long blamed his wife for their being childless. After this he consulted with a gynecologist who told him that a test-tube child (IVF) would cost almost LE 3,000, an amount beyond his means. The man started getting treatment from an *attar* (herbalist), and I was told later by others who knew the story that he secretly married another woman.

Attar are very popular in rural areas and in popular urban neighborhoods. Men and women go to them for a variety of ailments. The *attar* also deal with a range of male sexual problems of sterility and impotency. An *attar* whom I visited many times would tell me about the different herbs and their healing effects on men's sexual drive and impotency. Men would also tell me of commonly used natural oils that decrease sperm count. Cottonseed oil (*zeit il kafoor*), for example, my male friends and the *attar* told me, was rumored to be used by the military in preparing food for the male recruits ostensibly to control their libido and perhaps their ability to reproduce. Such conspiratorial stories exposed these men's anxiety over losing their sexual potency, yet they may also hint at people's resentment of a state that seeks to curb their procreative abilities.

Men, like women, conceive of their bodies also as open and internally connected especially when warm, as after a sexual act.[8] If they used condoms, they feared that some sperm might travel back into their urethral orifice. I interviewed men who complained of pain in their inguinal regions when they had used condoms. They attributed this to the fact that sperm traveled back and lodged in the muscles, hence causing them pain. They argued that sperm might even travel to joints and cause arthritic pain. Similarly, men dreaded having intercourse with women who were menstruating. It was not only considered unclean and religiously impermissible, but according to some, menstrual blood could enter into them and lodge in their joints.[9]

One of the reasons that men did not use condoms was that they felt that they did not receive, and were incapable of giving, sexual pleasure. Both rural and urban men insisted that women receive heightened sexual pleasure when they feel the ejaculation passing through their vagina into their uterus. This pleasure was mixed with the gradual cooling down of female bodies from a hot state. Moreover, there was a general consensus among my informants that women take longer to reach orgasm. Men sometimes took medications to maintain sustained erections so that they could help their wives reach sexual climax. I spoke to several pharmacists in the urban and rural sites. The pharmacists would show me antidepression medications that were popular with men. These medicines had priapism as a side effect, giving men a painful yet prolonged erection. Men would also buy local anesthetic sprays for the same purpose.

Women may have different constructions of pleasure, but as a male, I could not explore their ideas to the same extent. These constructions may or may not overlap with those specified by men. Still, men's concerns with their spouse's orgasmic pleasure indicates a sense of sharing and giving sexual pleasure. This is not to deny that these concerns may also pertain to worries about male performance linked to prolonged erection.

Indeed, notions linked to local and popular interpretation of Islam encourage sexual relations not only as a procreative act but also as something to be enjoyed by both sexes. Yet, there is room here for subtle forms of social control. As women are constructed as wives, mothers, and daughters within systems of prestige with various ideological underpinnings, there is a competing construction of woman as an essentialized chaotic figure who represents disorder or *fitna*. This popular description emphasizes women's overpowering sexuality. Thus my male informants' emphasis on female orgasm may also reflect the fear that the unsatisfied woman may seek others to fulfill her needs.[10]

Anxiety over the spouse's infidelity makes some men restrict their wives' movements and also at times leads to extreme forms of domestic violence. On the one hand, this fear exposes the popular imagery of women as oversexed and unfaithful. On the other, it points toward a construction of competing masculinities where men fear other men with more erect penises as potential rivals for their women. Impotence therefore becomes the extreme insult. An erect penis and its power to satisfy are directly linked to the rhetoric and practice of power that men believe is needed to control women. So, as condoms may reduce pleasure for both men and women, their use may destabilize certain constructions of gender linked to practices of power and control.

The dissonance between medico–biological notions of the body and the folk imagery helps us understand further the receptiveness toward new contraceptive methods. It is an arena where multiple local understandings of health and healing and of sexuality and gender may conflict and "negotiate" with the standardized, rational, and unitary language of modern medicine. In the next section I connect these constructions to the contemporary social, political, and economic changes occurring in Egypt.

SOCIAL CHANGE AND GENDER

During the years 1992–1994 the ongoing privatization of state industries led to widespread layoffs with shrinking possibilities of employment. As opportunities to earn a livelihood in the Gulf countries and in Iraq also diminished, people returned home to reduced chances of employment. Inflationary tendencies had, furthermore, made certain food items, like meat, unaffordable for many. These living conditions created immense pressures on men who were at times the only source of livelihood for families. My informants would speak of their inability to have pleasure in life if they could not provide a "decent" living for their families. To be laid off under these circumstances was catastrophic. Even those who held steady jobs as factory workers or who were low-level public servants spoke of their inability to provide for their families. Some of my luckier informants held two or three jobs: working as a civil servant (*muwazzaf*) in the morning, driving a taxi in the afternoon, and selling home-cooked *tamiya* (falafel) at night. They, like others, complained of a shortage of money. One of the less fortunate among them, Bilal, told me:

> I earn one hundred pounds a month while working in a factory. I live in this room with my wife and four children. I share the toilet with three other families. My upstairs neighbors have nine people living in the same space as ours. Where should we go? Housing is so expensive. So is meat, I bought it today for fourteen pounds a kilo. This is the only time we are going to have meat this month. There is no money left after all the other expenditures.

School fees for children, rising transportation costs, expenditures for household clothing, monthly house rent, union dues, and monthly installments for a stove were other household budgetary items that were linked to the social worries of my informants in the urban areas.

In addition, people believed that certain food products enhanced the physical state of the body. For men, meat and meat products in particular were crucial energy-giving foods (popularly called *protienat*) and were essential to leading a healthy life and for sexual performance. As Bilal added, "Without meat and with all these worries I ejaculate in a few minutes, whereas the rich man can keep his erection for half an hour and satisfy his spouse."

The inability to sustain a sexual act goes back to the imagery of not being able to control one's woman through prolonged sex. The rich are thus constructed not only as wealthy and fortunate but also more masculine as they can keep their women happy and provide for their families. Wealth and access to better-paid jobs guaranteed a reduction in social worries and the income to consume more meat products. My informants felt that poverty undermined their virility as men. Rural and urban poor men generally consider themselves potentially more masculine than upper-class men; however, poverty may be undermining these positive self-constructions. As their sexual performance has suffered, simultaneously their own standing as men has suffered. Economic deprivation has made them socially and physically impotent. In essence poverty has de-masculinized them in their own eyes.

Julie Peteet (1994) describes how physical violence perpetuated during the first *intifada* by the Israeli security forces on the bodies of young Palestinian men became their rite of passages into adulthood. She argues that Israeli security services shifted their techniques of torture and violence once they realized that acts of bodily violence had taken on a meaning of empowerment and future political agency for the tortured men. Rape and other kinds of sexual violence started becoming more common to deprive men of their masculinity and manhood (Peteet 1994:45). Although the circumstances are very dissimilar, I would argue that the social and economic deprivation of the Egyptian poor and the concomitant drive on families to curtail family size is experienced as a form of violence that socially castrates and humiliates the men with whom I spoke, in the process depriving them of their masculinity and manhood.

In this global moment of New World Order, employment remains the only source of male dignity (Spivak 1996a). As poverty levels increase in urban and rural areas of Egypt, families struggle to manage under increasing adversity. Women are forced to seek employment outside their homes to help pay for the increasing costs of educating and rearing children. In urban areas, women from lower classes are seeking employment as domestics and as factory laborers. For men, their wives' excursions outside the house cut through the rhetoric of idealized domesticity. Men grudgingly agree to their wives working because of the need for the additional income. Yet they also complain that their spouses are neglecting domestic duties, including the proper training of the children. The fact that their partners need to work to support the household destabilizes the male role as provider and challenges the man's authority within the family. Men also fear competition from potential female applicants in an already shrinking job market. Mustafa, a primary school teacher in the village, complained about women teachers in these terms:

> Why should they work? By working they just lose their house and husband. Anyway, the inclusion of women teachers has meant less work for all of us and also less salary. Men can do all the work that these women do and we should be paid double what we get.

The anxieties of men over employment opportunities are also reflected in the nature of the marriage arrangements they face. Customary marriage practices call for men to provide a *sha'a* (apartment), *shabka* (gold bangles, at least a pair), *mahr,* (male dowry/bride-price), and *'aima* (*quaima,* a list of household items). These days, with increasing job insecurity and inflation, men find it difficult to fulfill these prerequisites for marriage. The economy and the changing nature of society were occasionally blamed by my unmarried friends for inability to marry even into their thirties. They complained that in their parents' time, men got married with minimum requirements, but now the girl's family demands, besides *mahr,* a list of goods like a color television and an automatic washing machine.

Men who spoke to me may have couched their reluctant acceptance of contraception in terms of caring for their wives' health. Yet, modern forms of residence, the emphasis on education, and socioeconomic factors are also pushing them toward using modern family planning methods. As a male informant explained, "I would like to have four or five children, maybe three boys and two girls, but to use an IUD is better than having a baby that might breed on the streets."

CONCLUSION

On the one hand, the Egyptian state seeks to produce socially responsible fathers who follow the state's advice on family planning and restrict their family size. On the other, the high unemployment rate, socioeconomic deprivation, and the undemocratic political environment push most people to the margins of the system, creating political conflict and deep resentment. These constructions, in the case of Egypt, hence, are on very slippery terrain. Moreover, the popular notions of the body, healing, fertility, and sexuality undercut the desired dominance of state-sponsored medical and social impositions.

Discussing the notion of hegemonic and subaltern masculinities in the Middle East, Deniz Kandiyoti (1994) places the production of masculine identities in generational and institutional terms and shows how masculinities are produced as men move through the life cycle. Through a reading of life histories and literary texts, she shows the ambiguities of stereotypical representation of males in the Middle East. She shows how, in early-twentieth-century Turkey, the unstable gendering of younger boys in relation to older men in the household, the homoerotic relationship within all male institutions, and the physical experience of boys in female *hammams* (communal baths) created complex realities for the construction of masculinities. Similarly, Lindisfarne (1994) argues that if hegemonic constructions of masculinity are linked to sexual performance, then the humiliation of impotency and the failure to deflower brides may also construct subordinate forms.

I have sought to complicate the representations of Egyptian men in particular (and Middle Eastern men in general) as they respond to the introduction of modern ideas and practices of contraception. Dominant notions of masculinity are unsteady concepts that are increasingly challenged as economic and social circumstances change. Further, as masculinities are created in gender-relational terms, they are also, as I argue, intrinsically linked to social and economic aspects of life.

Rapid socioeconomic changes are not only undermining traditional male power. Even for women the economic insecurity of their male partners undercuts the few benefits of the "patriarchal bargain" (Kandiyoti 1988) that they enjoyed.[11] Data show that the ill effects on nutrition and health linked to structural adjustment are worse for women and children (Nassar 1992). As old support structures are disappearing, new forms are yet to evolve. It continues to be a time of much apprehension and uncertainty for the underprivileged in Egyptian society.

Part Three

Constructing New Selves | *Chapter 7*

The population debate in Egypt has many actors. As much as it is a site of dialogue between the Egyptian state and international donors such as USAID, it is also an arena of discussion and confrontation between the state and other social forces in contemporary Egypt. Among them are the women's groups, who criticize the state's population policy from a secular women's/feminist perspective,[1] and the Islamists, who take a religious perspective.[2] These political and social groups compete with the Egyptian state on the terms on which modern domestic spaces should be incorporated into a future nation.

Through ethnographic examples and textual analysis this and the next chapter will socially situate these two broad political tendencies. In doing so I do not present a comprehensive survey of the various Islamist political parties or secular women's groups.[3] Rather, I critically discuss an internationally funded reproductive health study to represent the larger argument made by some secular women activists on reproductive rights. In the following chapter I analyze how certain Islamist groups, specifically the Muslim Brotherhood, respond to the state-sponsored population policy to demonstrate how some Islamists question the morality of the Egyptian state in propagating family planning. By presenting these arguments I seek to illustrate the expanded discursive and political context of the population debate in Egypt.

Prior to discussing the debate on reproductive rights, I draw a connection between contemporary efforts to reorganize people's notions of the private and their body and the debates generated in late-nineteenth-century Egypt on good motherhood and proper domesticity. I do this to emphasize how the modern women-sensitive developmental agenda is subsumed in a larger history of transformation of traditional behavior and custom in Egypt. I show below how, already in the late nineteenth century, modern medicine and the science of home economics regulated the domestic sphere. This historical context enables me to associate present-day family planning practices with a longer chronology of interventions into people's lives.

DOMESTIC REALM IN THE COLONIAL PERIOD

Ranajit Guha (1993), in an article on the relationship of the Indian national movement with the Indian masses, borrows the Gramscian concept of hegemony to show the processes through which consensus was built by the nationalist elite leadership. He argues that these leaders needed to harness the intuition and enthusiasm of the people so that order could evolve out of chaos. The subalterns' popular initiatives and autonomy of function, the immediacy in their politics, and the spontaneity of their actions needed to be disciplined by the bourgeois national elite for it to control and hegemonize the national movement. An undisciplined and autonomous subaltern collectivity needed to be made into a disciplined, controlled national movement that would respond to the desires of the leadership. It is within a similar framework, I suggest, that modern national governments seek to hegemonize and change the independent and autonomous practices of the lower classes.

In a comparable context, Partha Chatterjee (1989) convincingly argues how, in colonial India, Bengali nationalists sought to close domestic spaces to colonial penetration by constructing the categories of home/world and spiritual/material. He argues that the reason the issue of "female emancipation" disappeared from the public agenda of late-nineteenth-century Indian nationalist discourse was that the nationalists refused to negotiate with the colonial power on the "women question." The middle-class male nationalists could not permit the colonial regime to enter an area where the nationalists considered themselves sovereign.[4]

These discussions are relevant to the Egyptian case because similar debates among colonial authorities, the nationalist elite, Islamist reformers, and educated women in the late nineteenth century framed the question of reform within Egyptian domestic life (an analogous configuration may exist today in the form of international donors, the Egyptian state, Islamist parties, and secular women's groups). In the late nineteenth century many colonial administrators in Egypt attributed the low status of women in Egypt to Islam. The social system of Islam, according to these authorities, was a total failure because Islam kept women in a position of marked inferiority (Cromer 1908:134). Orientalists and European intellectuals would similarly argue that the degradation of women in Islam was like a canker that began its destructive work early in childhood (Ahmed 1992:152).

The modernizing Egyptian elite started replying to such writings by the end of the nineteenth century. For those who read Middle Eastern history, a familiar name from among this elite is that of Qasim Amin. Amin was a prosecutor in the Europeanized legal system and belonged to the Turko-Circassian landholding class. He wrote several books on women's emancipation in this period in which he agreed with colonial critics of Muslim social life regarding the backwardness of women. He argued that their backwardness was not due to Islam but rather to abandonment of the central traits of Islam. In one of his books, *Tahrir al-Mar'a* (The liberation of women), Amin concentrates on how customs of divorce, polygamy, female inheritance, lack of female education, and the veiling of women in Egyptian society were detrimental to the progress of the nation as a whole.[5] He particularly attacked seclusion among upper-class women as being responsible for their mixing with the lower classes and hence leading to their coarse and undignified behavior.[6] Women had to be tamed and refocused, he argued, toward becoming educated and unveiled. This process meant that upper-class women had to restrain their former expressiveness in language and practice and impose new forms of "silences" upon themselves (Abu-Lughod 1998:259; Najmabadi 1993).

For late-nineteenth-century modernist reformers like Amin, education of women was related to their responsibility in raising children. It was hoped that educated mothers would create a modern political order that would begin at their knees. The future organization of society in which women would be liberated was conditioned on the premise of following new ideas of science and progress learned from the European experience (Mitchell 1988:113; Cole 1981).[7]

There were competing visions to this essentially upper-class male discourse of creating citizen-subjects for the future nation. Upper-class Egyptian women in the late nineteenth century contested male-centered representations of the domestic and called for more education, autonomy, and independence for women (Badran 1995).[8] Educated women responded to modernist male attempts to reorganize domestic life by arguing for a more equitable relationship between husbands and wives and by asserting the idea of marriage for love rather than economic consideration (Baron 1994:165). There was a diversity of opinion among these women on issues of gender segregation, wage work, secularization, veiling, and Islamic revival (Baron 1994:121), yet there were also areas of shared agenda and agreement with liberal writers like Qasim Amin (Baron 1994; Cole 1981). One of these was the crucial interest in the process of motherhood.

Female writers concentrated on instructions for pregnancy and postpartum health care for the mother and the child and showed extreme interest in the organization of childbirth on more scientific lines (Baron

1994:159).[9] They advised mothers to take care of children and not to delegate child rearing to servants and relatives. These women writers also praised breastfeeding and actively discouraged the use of wet nurses.[10] Their recommendations were clearly meant to "redefine maternal responsibilities and invest them with greater importance" (Baron 1994:161).

The emphasis on motherhood and on domestic reform aimed at the creation of a modern citizenry at least among the privileged classes. The responsibility for raising children, the future of the nation, could not be left to uninformed or uneducated women. The reproduction of the nation itself depended on the scientific reorganization of how and under what circumstances children would be born and raised.[11] To produce new kinds of individuals in the emerging moral order, women needed to be trained and trusted to fulfill the task.[12] Not only procreation and child rearing were important at this juncture; rather, as Deniz Kandiyoti (1998) argues in discussing social life in early-twentieth-century Turkey, the emotional and moral tone of the family was to be reoriented. This mandated new disciplinary mechanisms for both women and men, not only to remake women but to refashion gender and gender relations as well (Kandiyoti 1998:281).

Concurrently the male-dominated medical system competed with the local midwives, seeking dominance in controlling the health and well-being of women. At the turn of the century more than 90 percent of deliveries in Egypt were performed by midwives. Some of these midwives were called *hakima*s and were graduates from official midwifery schools. *Dayas,* the more traditional midwives, were, however, the mainstay of most maternity cases in urban and rural areas. The effort to reorganize women's healing and birthing practices meant the displacement of the *daya*s and other women healers by modern medicine.[13] This meant an increasing interest by medical scholars in what was deemed to be the traditional customs and beliefs of Egyptian women. An example of this concern was evident in the publication of *Tibb-al-Rukka* (Old wives' medicine) in 1892 by an Egyptian physician, Abd al-Rahman Ismail.[14] In several volumes of this book, the author gave detailed accounts of the various health practices of the poor. The aim of the texts was to expose the negative and "foolish" aspects of these people's beliefs. His texts sought to display the falsity of the popular healing system and argue for the supremacy of scientific facts of medicine.

In an article published early in the twentieth century, Gorgy Sobhy, a graduate of the Kasr-el-Aini Medical College in Cairo, similarly admonished women for seeking treatment from a scientifically trained doctor only when their life was in danger (Sobhy 1904). The article goes on to present a study of the customs and superstitions of Egyptians on child-birth and pregnancy. Sobhy's detailed description of traditional birthing methods displayed the importance medical reformers in Egypt put on the context of indigenous beliefs. A knowledge of these beliefs would in turn help them to implement policies to transform traditional practices.

Arguments regarding women's education, household organization, and female birthing practices created opportunities to ensure that the fu-ture of the Egyptian nation would be different from the past. The debate on female practices in Egypt also spoke to the split between the modern-izing elite and the yet-to-be-modernized poor.[15] To be sure, the advice that the middle-class women gave in the Arabic press was restricted by and large to the small female readership from the urban middle and up-per classes. Late-nineteenth-century reformers primarily concentrated on the improvement of their own class even as they saw themselves repre-senting the entire future Egyptian nation.

As I have argued in earlier chapters, the debates continue even today on the health and hygiene of poor Egyptian women. Although the shift in emphasis toward the poor reflects historical changes in the political economy of Egyptian life, the arguments follow the reformist and mod-ernist preoccupations of Egyptian intellectuals in the colonial period. The last twenty years have evidenced positive increases in individual income and in other developmental indices, yet the gradual removal of welfare structures and state subsidies in the food, education, and housing sec-tors have adversely affected the economic well-being of the rural and ur-ban poor. Within this social and economic framework, Egyptian NGOs funded by international donors, as suggested earlier, play a vital role in propagating ideas about self-help, personal responsibility, and fertility reg-ulation. These NGOs are largely staffed by educated men and women from the urban middle and upper professional classes. Motivated by a de-velopment agenda of "social good," some of these groups conduct re-search seeking to transform the "unmodern" living habits of the peasantry and the urban poor.

THE REPRODUCTIVE-RIGHTS AGENDA

Many Egyptian NGOs with a women-and-development component are funded by larger international development programs. These NGOs include, among others, the Cairo Family Planning Association, Coptic

Evangelical Organization for Social Services (CEOS), the Association for the Development and Enhancement of Women (ADEW), and Appropriate Communications Techniques (ACT). They generate debates within Egypt on internationally defined positions on women's reproductive rights. Under the auspices of the Population Council, Ford Foundation, USAID, and the UN agencies, such groups, along with other activist women and secular women's groups, organize seminars and write position papers on issues of women's individual rights and autonomy related to reproductive health. International literature on reproductive health supports the role of such NGOs as crucial in making governments comply with international treaties on women's emancipation and sex discrimination (Cook 1993:83; Toubia and An-Na'im n.d.:18–24). Hence, some women's groups and NGOs operate as pressure groups (as shown in chapter 1), bridging the gap between international legal standards and the Egyptian state's position on these issues. In such instances these formations remain within the parameters of the debate set by the larger agenda of international development. By speaking the language of liberal democracy, and in their quest to make the Egyptian state conform to international rules and forms of conduct, these groups become interlocutors for the international donor agencies.

Following the 1994 International Conference on Population and Development (ICPD), there emerged a consensus among secular women's groups, NGOs, and aid agencies in Egypt on a more comprehensive notion of rights that includes provision for the health of the mother and the social well-being of women. A larger agenda of reproductive rights, according to this view, needed to be more inclusive and give equal opportunities to all classes of women. By propagating this argument these groups pushed the debate on reproductive rights beyond the mere provision of contraceptives toward becoming more sensitive to women's health in general.[16] This argument generated much interest among feminists in Egypt even prior to the ICPD. In the early 1990s international NGOs such as the International Planned Parenthood Federation, International Women's Health Coalition, and the International Reproductive Rights Research Action Group (IRRRAG) expanded their efforts to create a dialogue and debate within Egyptian society on women's rights issues such as abortion, sexual freedoms, and domestic violence and bring these under the rubric of reproductive rights (see Seif El-Dawla et al. 1998 for an Egyptian feminist's perspective on this debate). Below I present a comprehensive analysis of the evolving attempt to incorporate the reproductive-rights perspective into research on Egyptian women.[17]

I present this example of a research project in some detail to show how international groups concerned for the health of poor women seek to influence policy on fertility issues. The Population Council assembled a multidisciplinary team consisting of a physician specializing in obstetrics and gynecology, an anthropologist, and a social demographer among others, to conduct a study (1989–1990) on the sexual and reproductive health of women in the Giza governorate south of Cairo. The research focused on gynecological morbidities in the community under study. The ages of women included in the study ranged from under twenty-five to sixty. Most women were uneducated and of poor socioeconomic background.

In a series of published papers that analyzed the project data (Younis et al. 1993; Zurayk et al. 1994; Zurayk et al. 1995), the authors show a high rate of prevalence of reproductive-tract diseases in the given population. They argue that most of these diseases go unnoticed because women do not complain about their problems and endure the diseases in silence (Zurayk et al. 1994:4). All women in the study, a total of 500, were given a clinical gynecological examination performed by female physicians. It was found that over 50 percent of the women suffered from reproductive-tract infections. More than 50 percent were also diagnosed with prolapse of the genital tract. Other conditions such as cervical ectopy and premalignant cervical cell changes were present in almost a third of the women. There also was incidence of high blood pressure, anemia, and urinary-tract infections in the community. The severity of the situation was underscored by the researchers' finding that many women had multiple diseases (Zurayk et al. 1994:5).

Reproductive-tract infection was reportedly higher among women who were sexually active. The research associated current IUD use with high incidence of vaginal and cervical infections, anemia, prolapse, and a predisposition to pelvic inflammatory disease. Women who, according to the researchers, had unhygienic practices during menstruation, were also deemed susceptible to infections of the reproductive tract. In fact, the findings indicated that only one-fourth of menstruating women either boiled their protective garments or used disposable products (Younis et al. 1993:180–184).[18]

An important aspect of the research was the attention given to women's own perception of their bodies and health status. Respondents were asked about vaginal discharge in order to assess genital-tract infection. The researchers found that very few women ("only 13%") reported having a discharge other than ordinary. In contrast, the researchers' medical examination found that at least 64 percent of all women had medically suspicious discharge. They presented this information to highlight how "women may not perceive certain symptoms as dangerous or abnormal, considering them part of their reproductive reality" (Zurayk et al. 1994:11).

The study follows recent arguments by international women activists who work on reproductive rights.[19] In broadening the reproductive-rights mandate for the developing world, these activists assert that a comprehensive sense of these rights entails that state-sponsored family planning policy focus not merely on fertility control but also on expanded notions of social welfare, political freedom, and personal security. They maintain that state and social support given to women should empower and enable them to achieve equal status with men as full moral beings and, hence, equip them to determine their own bodily integrity, sexual freedom, and reproductive choice. Arguments are made for health policies that treat women's lives holistically throughout their life cycle, for reproductive services with well-trained staff, for a culture of health awareness that empowers women to make claims for their sexual and reproductive needs, and beyond this, for a reordering of economic policies to favor social welfare and primary health care (Correa and Petchesky 1994). Defenders of reproductive rights stress that women should be aided to reclaim ownership of their body as a site of politics as their arguments seek to connect this self-ownership to communal resources (Petchesky 1995:403).

These social concerns are reflected in the analysis of the Population Council's Giza study because it sensitizes us to the prevalent gynecological and health problems faced by poor women in rural Egypt. The shift in the rhetorical emphasis from merely providing contraceptives to the inclusion of broader health priorities for women is clearly a welcome change in family planning policies and programs. In their analysis of the data the researchers recommend a sensitivity to women's needs in designing health delivery systems and encourage training of health care providers on cultural issues related to women. Suggestion is also made for the presence of female doctors in the clinics who could provide hygienic and safe reproductive-tract examinations. These suggestions stem from hearing women's complaints about the available health delivery system.

However, not unlike the turn-of-the-century arguments on the unhygienic and superstitious practices of women, the researchers for the Giza study also blamed the birth attendants (*dayas*) for causing obstetric trauma (Younis et al. 1993). They labeled women's own personal habits as "unhygienic" and stressed that women did not understand their own health and needed to be educated about their abnormal discharges. The substitution of women's own understanding of their bodies by medicalized notions of female reproductive health does expose us to the somewhat elitist nature of these arguments. The liberal fear of female disorder resurfaces here under the guise of humane assistance and social welfare (Pateman 1989). As Gayatri Spivak (1996b) asserts, international funding of initiatives for women in developing countries produces upper-class feminist activism that tries to organize poorer women in their own image.[20] The desire to learn more about women's perceptions in this instance should also be seen as a conflict between the researchers' own perception of health and that of the women themselves.

This argument becomes clearer when we again consider how international advocates of reproductive rights respond to the diversity of views and practices found globally among women. Women belonging to different cultures and religious beliefs with distinct bodily experiences and sexual practices, as discussed earlier, may challenge the language of equality, personhood, or bodily integrity put forward by international feminist groups. Reproductive-rights literature contends that local beliefs and practices, even those enacted by women, can never take precedence over the social responsibility of governments and intergovernmental groups to ensure the propagation of human rights, promote women's development, and respect their self-determination (Correa and Petchesky 1994:118). Similarly, recommendations by the Giza study give precedence to a universalized notion of rights and the concomitant individualized construction of self and personhood over local beliefs and practices.

In the above-discussed accounts the emphasis on local practices is primarily to change the "harmful" aspects of people's culture and behavior. Culture may be deemed important, yet cultural particularities tend to negate universalism. There is a liberal desire to understand women's own perspective, but their practices are viewed as secondary to international standards of health and hygiene. This universalization narrative clearly privileges an assumed solidarity among women by abstracting out specific histories and local experiences.[21] International unity is achieved through the excision of the "cultural" and the subsumption of difference in the name of unifying and universalistic principles (Butler 1998). Therefore, arguments on reproductive rights tend to create a humanitarian social dilemma by constructing poor third-world women as victims who need assistance from international standards propagated by the United Nations and other global bodies. This move to unify may also reinscribe diverse cultures and practices into the continuing "Great Family of Man" narrative (Malkki 1998).[22]

Taking the above discussion into account and following Soheir Morsy's excellent critique of maternal mortality discourse in Egypt (Morsy 1991), I would also suggest that the recommendations of the Population Council's Giza study are basically meant to strengthen the family planning program itself. Although the research closely follows the politically progressive arguments on reproductive rights, the localized implementation of this agenda, at least in the case of Egypt, remains enmeshed within the political and social power of the lending agencies and the Egyptian state. In essence the desire to understand female bodies and health problems remains subservient to the goals of the family planning program. For, if women's health was this study's primary focus, then the emphasis should not have been only on improving the health delivery system but also on alleviating the poverty and socioeconomic problems of the community, which were deemed to be responsible for most disease conditions.

The policy solutions advocated by these studies call for further reflection. For example, in the face of evidence that IUDs cause reproductive-tract infection among most users, nonuse of IUDs was never a recommendation. On the contrary, suggestions were made to improve insertion techniques, to better train providers in the health facilities, and to encourage women to have regular check-ups (Younis et al. 1993; Zurayk et al. 1994). If IUDs were one of the major sources of infection, then why was there no suggestion to stop the use of IUDs for the poor and susceptible groups of women who have recurrent infections with their use? Training providers and placing counselors in the community to aid women in their health problems (Zurayk et al. 1994:20) are no doubt important public health interventions. Yet these interventions also consolidate the health delivery system and make it more efficient and consistent with the larger international family planning policy goals of improving the state programs.

It is important to note here that the neo-Malthusian emphasis on policy goals that seek to restrict birth rates through contraceptive acceptance at times conflicts with the broader agenda of women's health and welfare advocated by reproductive-rights activists. I would assert that in practice there may, however, be a narrowing of the ideological differences between these two social tendencies (Hodgson and Watkins 1997). The internationally supported reproductive-rights agenda may play a complementary role to the family planning program by helping it to be more "sensitive" to the needs of the clients (Population Council 1994) and, hence, address the weakness in the program through an agenda of cultural sensitivity, counseling, and persuasion.[23]

I discuss this study not to make a blanket assessment of all NGOs or secular women's groups but to show how a certain kind of internationally sponsored women-sensitive development agenda works itself into localized research.[24] During the 1992 to 1994 period, the link between the secular women's groups and the discourse of the donor agencies was one of pragmatic cooperation and critical distance. In the political agenda of the development agencies, however, there was a hint of a tactical alliance, as UN agencies and USAID sought to introduce the international human rights debate in Egypt prior to the ICPD as part of their emphasis on the "democratization" process and emancipatory politics based on the rhetoric of rights and legal reform of the women's groups themselves. One of the debates in which this language was periodically invoked had to do with family planning. As is obvious this language helped the potentially emancipatory argument on the right of a woman to choose a contraceptive or to plan her family.

WOMEN'S GROUPS

Many activist women who participate in secular women's groups have suffered personally and collectively in their struggle for rights of women in Egypt. The politics based on the invocation of "rights" may yet be important and valuable in the sphere of local struggles against undemocratic structures. Moreover, the insistence by some groups (e.g., Al-Mar'a al-Gedida and Markaz Darasat al-Mar'a: Ma'an)[25] on a more egalitarian and inclusive health delivery system challenges the state's political agenda of removing social subsidies for the poor.

Many Egyptian secular women's/feminist groups strive to change laws that control the private and the public life of Egyptian women. They operate mostly by organizing seminars, lectures, and other intellectual and cultural activities on women's issues. These consciousness-raising forums are meant for the interchange of ideas among the educated group of feminist women and men. In demanding the emancipation of women, some groups link their politics to the larger political struggles in the country on social and economic rights, reforms in labor laws, and the freedom of assembly and association. Some seek to struggle within the parameters of state-imposed legality to increase the legal and political space of permissible democratic politics. For those that are more radical and politically active, it is, however, extremely difficult to survive as a legal entity. Under Egyptian law all not-for-profit groups need to be registered with the Ministry of Social Affairs, which retains the right to close down any organization that it deems subversive. Law 32 of 1964 regulates the legal and administrative structures of all NGOs in Egypt. The Ministry of Social Affairs and its governorate-level directorates are responsible for the registration, control, supervision, oversight, and appointments of these voluntary organizations. A new law, Law 156, was imposed in 1999. In addition to earlier restrictions, this law requires NGOs to seek approval from the Ministry of Social Affairs before accepting foreign donations and grants, prohibits NGOs from participating in political and unionist activities, and closes the legal loophole used by some NGOs to register as not-for-profit "civil companies" to avoid the provisions of the earlier Law 32 (El-Gawhary 2000).

I interviewed members of various secular women's groups. I occasionally attended seminars and presentations organized by them and visited the groups at their offices. I also interviewed women working on gender issues in NGOs and international development agencies. The groups had varied ideological positions, ranging from overtly Marxist to liberal. (The self-expression of these groups as feminist is beyond the range of arguments presented here.)[26]

Most women's groups with secular modernist leanings exclude Islamic-oriented women's groups from their midst. The dialogue remains within the realm of those who agree on the liberal democratic ideals of modernity. Their exclusionary politics toward the more Islamic-minded women may alienate such groups from a sizable portion of women in society. For example, practices of poor women, under the guidance of Islamic-oriented groups in the *sha'bi* (popular) neighborhoods of Cairo, do not always figure in the possible political strategy of secular women's groups. Their encounter with the Islamist political phenomenon is, not unlike the Egyptian state, perhaps a threat to their own modern and secular ideals.[27] Very little attempt is made to reflect on the potential of a democratic alliance against an oppressive state or an alliance to address an issue such as domestic violence. This is not to deny that the Islamist groups have themselves been extremely critical and aggressive against the secular women's organizations and periodically resist any attempt to reform laws that discriminate against women.

A few secular women's groups and NGOs contribute to the developmental debate from a specific women-centered and nationalistic point of view. They argue that their efforts can help direct international funds to appropriate targets related to issues of women and development. This, according to them, guarantees a diminution of waste and corruption in the development process and sets priorities designated according to "real need."

Afaf (not her real name) is a member of the group Markaz Darasat al-Mar'a: Ma'an. This group has held seminars on women issues and has politically cooperated with other human rights and labor groups. While the group has socialist political leanings, its seminars were open forums for discussion among different political tendencies in Egypt. Talking to me on the issue of family planning, Afaf argued that "We are caught between the state, the international funding agencies, and the Islamist groups. We are not recognized by the state and need to register ourselves as commercial companies with tax-paying status. Where will we get the money, when we do not generate anything?" This specific group had a policy of not accepting international funds. Afaf continued: "International funding is readily available in Egypt these days, but it binds us activists into certain kinds of priorities, discourses, and engagements."

Like Afaf's group, other women's groups are also critical of the internationally funded Egyptian family planning program on methodological grounds. They oppose the use of poor urban and rural women as objects of experimentation for testing new contraceptive technology by international donor agencies. A member of the group National Council for Women, the women's wing of the left-leaning Tagammau party, showed her opposition to donor agencies by stating, "They use the bodies of poor Egyptian women to experiment with their contraceptives."

These critiques notwithstanding, such groups play a marginal role in the population debate in Egypt, which is dominated by the women-centered NGOs with international funding. The majority of the internationally funded NGOs implicitly assist the family planning program by advocating reproductive rights, yet they do not criticize the government on its lack of social welfare initiatives for women or on its policy to remove social subsidies with the subsequent effect on women's health.

In doing so they align themselves with the international feminist arguments on rights and individuality that write women's bodies into a juridico-legal discourse that helps to produce the modern individual liberal citizen (Spivak 1996a:248). It may also dovetail with practices of global capital that present the introduction of coercive population policies as vehicles for free choice and development for women (Spivak 1995:3). In doing so they may paradoxically also strengthen the state. The politics based on the agenda of "rights" and "consciousness raising" are historically linked with the effort of creating citizens and strengthen-

ing the state along with its capacity for coercion, "the continual forgetting of which fact constitutes the kernel of the citizen's 'everyday life'"
(Chakrabarty 1994a:331).

CONCLUSION

The history of the modern Egyptian nation-state is eminently linked
with transformations within its domestic sphere. As Dipesh Chakrabarty
reminds us in the context of colonial Bengal, "The public sphere could
not be erected without reconstructing the private" (Chakrabarty 1994a:
58). Similarly, the internal ordering of the domestic sphere was the key
to the progress envisioned by the turn-of-the-century educated Egyptian
elite. Here the issue of motherhood was crucial. Women were supposed
to shed their unhygienic habits, superstitious beliefs, and untidy lifestyles
and be educated into becoming proper mothers.[28]

As I have shown, upper-class women had competing visions to this essentially upper-class male discourse of creating citizen-subjects for the future nation. In these terms the new disciplining powers were not only re-
pressive but created opportunities to challenge older forms of authority.
As new orders create new possibilities, they also create new forms of governance. As secular powers, modernizing states like Egypt assume the task
of remodeling the moral and the material conditions of the lives of their
subjects. Where debates on proper motherhood in the late nineteenth
century were primarily organized around modern notions of the domestic (Baron 1994), now, new arguments incorporate the rhetoric of health
risks and population control to again reorder female bodies. In this regard
the process of acquiring knowledge through surveys, focus groups, and
anthropological research in Egypt today increasingly focuses on the lives
and bodies of the Egyptian poor. In the context of family planning this
research agenda is inherently linked to issues of emancipation of women
and the reorganization of the domestic space. As these new ideas create
opportunities for women to rethink categories and reassemble possibilities, they invariably also coexist with, as I demonstrate elsewhere in this
text, other ideas of the individual, the community, and the social sphere.

It is important to note that some Egyptian scholars opposed the late-nineteenth-century liberal agenda of scientific progress and domestic change. Many Egyptian male intellectuals of that time took a critical stance against the advocacy of unveiling and female education by female writers and liberals like Qasim Amin.[1] Their opposition to women's public education and participation in the workforce indicates a different response to colonial cultural pressures by some within the educated class. Omnia Shakry (1998), in an important essay on domesticity in late-nineteenth-century Egypt, argues that the changes in the domestic sphere arose out of a dialogue with colonial discourse, where certain aspects of modern reform were accepted while others were put under moral and religious scrutiny by the more Islamic-oriented scholars. Islamic thinkers of the period, such as Muhammad Abduh and Rashid Rida, engaged with the notion of Muslim backwardness in relation to European modernity by attempting to reform society through their interpretation of Islamic traditions and practices.[2] These and other reformers did not attribute the stagnation in Muslim societies only to technological or industrial retrogression but primarily to a digression from the teachings of Islam (Shakry 1998:152). Islamic scholars drew upon an indigenous body of knowledge and writings from within the tradition to argue for children's proper training and education. This emphasis on children's pedagogy depended on the reformation of the household. There was a call by Islamic reformers quite like that of the secular nationalists to organize the domestic sphere by training women in proper child-rearing and housekeeping techniques. However, there was a crucial difference from the secularist position. Children were not supposed to grow up with the sense of self-actualization and individuality embedded in modern liberal notions of the self. Rather, the emphasis on Islamic household training was to guarantee that the next generation would be raised as ethical beings with Islamic moral virtues. This training ensured the salvation of the children's souls and sought to place them within the collectivity of the Muslim *umma* (Shakry 1998).

Not unlike the liberal influence on contemporary Egyptian politics, nonsecular ideas continue to inform Egyptian social and political life. These arguments increasingly constitute the basis for opposing the state-sponsored family planning program. This chapter will map some of the positions that contextualize that opposition.

THE DEBATE

I became aware of the popular dimensions of this opposition while doing fieldwork among a group of urban working-class men in Cairo. Some of my male informants/friends invoked the notion of a large powerful family, the *aila* (also discussed in chapter 5), in linking themselves to larger group solidarities. This view became especially evident when these men spoke about the fertility control program in Egypt. As world events evolved over the period of my stay (1992–1994), the news from Bosnia was the most ominous for my rural and urban informants. The perception that Muslims were being persecuted because of their religion evoked anger and frustration among them. The situation in Palestine and the *intifada* against the state of Israel also immensely affected them, more so because many of them were veterans of earlier wars against Israel. They interpreted these and other world events as discrimination against Muslims and took them as personal humiliation. For many the internationally assisted family planning program was part of this series of events and of a larger Judeo-Christian plot to weaken the Muslims of the world. Ishaq, an urban informant, explained further:

> Allah is the creator, and the world belongs to Him, then accordingly, the national boundaries are meaningless and the whole universe was created to be populated by Muslims. People should be allowed to travel, work, and spread the message of Islam wherever they please. Therefore, it becomes a religious duty to enlarge your immediate family so that the larger family may become stronger.

These articulations point toward some important issues. Given a chance, most of my friends sought to travel as migrant laborers primarily to escape the lack of good employment opportunities in their lives. Keeping this background in mind, and the framing of their position in religious terms notwithstanding, they deemed family planning as a contrived social issue. They thought that, if only they were allowed to travel, the world would have enough resources to accommodate them. The imagery of a larger family and the critique of artificial geopolitical boundaries simultaneously challenge the modern discourse on the geographical boundedness of nation-states. Their view is also a criticism of the internationally sponsored family planning program, based as it is on the thesis of limited assets within given borders of a nation-state, seldom arguing for international or local redistribution of resources.

During the years 1992–1994, these thoughts were echoed in the media critical of the Egyptian government. *Al-Shaʿb,* a newspaper with strong links to the Islamist movement in Egypt, regularly published articles criticizing the family planning program. For example, in a piece published before the International Conference on Population and Development (ICPD) held in Cairo in September of 1994, the columnist argued that the United States and the West are threatened by their declining population growth in the face of the population growth potential of the Islamic world. Hence, the article stated, the United States in particular defines this population growth as a security and defense problem and allocates resources to fertility control measures rather than investing in real and meaningful development to help the Muslim countries (*Al-Shaʿb,* 24 June 1994). Editorials in the paper periodically attacked the Egyptian state's support of U.S. policies in the region and connected it to the rhetoric of "benevolence" embedded in the foreign-sponsored development projects.

Similarly, in a 1994 publication the Muslim Brotherhood, one of the more organized and popular political groups in Egypt, criticized the state-sponsored family planning program on at least three broad levels. First, it viewed the family planning program as a Western conspiracy to contain the number of Muslims in the world. Second, it argued against the corruption of the Egyptian state and asserted that the problem was not lack of resources but inequitable distribution. Third, it claimed that contraceptive use would destabilize the moral fabric of society as women could secretly use it to fulfill unrestrained female sexuality (Muslim Brotherhood 1994). Fertility restriction, the publication stated further, also cast doubts on God's guarantee to provide sustenance to the believers. Finally, the publication took a firm position on the boundaries of the nation-state. It argued for the concept of a single Muslim *umma* that needs to be unified but has unfortunately been kept forcefully divided by non-Muslim forces. The claim is made that integrating the Muslim countries into a single political and economic system will eventually expose the false claim of the population problem (not unlike the statement made by Ishaq), linked as that argument is to the lack of resources within a bounded nation-state (Muslim Brotherhood 1994).

In this perspective, debates on fertility control and the control of women's reproduction constitute codes for the sources of tension between the Egyptian state and Islamist political parties like the Muslim Brotherhood. It is a competition over the control of the domestic sphere, but the physical reproduction and the geographical mapping of the nation are also at stake here.

The state's desire to transform people to its own interpretation of Islam at times finds tests in the acceptance and use of contraceptives by primarily poor Egyptian families. The state may see contraceptive use as a symbolic parameter to gauge support and identify opposition toward itself. Sensitive to criticisms from the Islamists, the Egyptian state and international development agencies also use the family planning program as a conduit into the debate on the "authentic" interpretation of Islam being waged in Egypt today. This debate itself has a history that can be traced at least back to the Sadat era in the 1970s (Hatem 1994). In his desire to form an alliance with Islamist parties, Sadat moved to distinguish his government from Nasser's earlier more secularist rule and instituted laws that called for *Shari'a* to be one of the leading sources of legislation (666). Sadat's emphasis on both science and religion as important pillars for progress continues to inform Egyptian politics today. The present government argues for modernity in accordance with Egypt's own cultural roots, a desire for harmonious coexistence of authenticity and progress (Armbrust 1998:290). This process also helps the state fight the Islamist groups' social and political influence.

For example, remaining sensitive to local practices, the state-sponsored family planning policy emphasizes the right of the family as a unit to decide on the appropriate number of children it desires within the framework of religion and the cultural norms of society (Sayed 1989, as quoted in Naguib and Lloyd 1994). However, in practice services are primarily provided to women, and spousal consent is not required for the use of most family planning methods (Naguib and Lloyd 1994). International donor agencies favor this approach by championing the right of the individual, in this case "the Egyptian woman," to decide the method of contraception. As the choice of contraception by women is linked to their emancipation, the family planning program and the donor agencies present themselves as the defenders of the rights of women. International donors view the policy emphasis on couple rights as a direct infringement on the individual rights of women to decide in reproductive matters. They invoke the UN's Convention on the Elimination of All Forms of Discrimination against Women to struggle for the individual rights of women.[3]

These arguments, like those mentioned in earlier chapters, evidently create frictions between the state policies and the international agencies. Yet there are many areas of cooperation as well. To counter Islamist arguments the state and the donor agencies rely heavily on the state-sponsored religious leaders (e.g., the *shaykhs* of Al-Azhar University) to interpret Islam as favoring family planning. They also increasingly favor, as discussed earlier, a male component in family planning programs to educate men toward its own position. Among the range of arguments put forward by the state-sponsored publications and campaigns on Islam's relationship to contraception[4] is the key proposition of a strong nation. Based on one of the established rules of Islamic thought, that harm should be eliminated at any cost, the state-sponsored literature argues that, although procreation is important to preserve the entity of the nation, a large population dominated by ill health and weakness is useless (Ministry of Waqf and Ministry of Information 1994:18−25). This is reiterated in the writings of Mohammad Sayed Tantawi, who was the grand mufti of Egypt in the 1980s. He wrote:

> Once more we say: Welcome to a good, big, strong, productive population, but not to a weak, poor, and big population that goes astray from the right path and depends on others for its necessities. A small population is far better.
>
> TANTAWI 1988:5

The Muslim Brotherhood, in opposition to the state's position on family planning, has its own stake in the matter. For example, on the issue of the household relationship between men and women, the brotherhood bases its arguments on a specific hierarchy of ideas and practices embedded in its reading and interpretation of the Qur'an and the tradition of the Prophet. Islamic doctrine, according to the group, accepts the spiritual equality of both genders, but the role of headship and decision making within the household has been given to men. This is consistent with the prescribed private and public spheres that the gender roles are divided into. Women are the child bearers and have the onus of motherhood, while men have the responsibility to provide for the family. Men have been given the *Qowama* (the right of decision making) over women; however, this headship is bound in duties and obligations. For example, men cannot force their wives to pay for the upkeep of the house or for domestic expenditure. Husbands also cannot direct their wives' financial dispensations, which they are entitled by Islamic law to manage on their own. Moreover, there is an emphasis on amity and consultation in spousal relationships to guarantee a stable partnership. The injunction of the headship role is from God, who has specified a higher degree of rights within the family to men as leaders of a Muslim family. This notion of the family as primarily subservient to the will of God rather than to individual or social motivations fundamentally differs from the notion of choice and individual freedom embedded in modernist liberal tradition.[5] The decision on fertility regulation is, therefore, retained with the husband in this formulation. This is the crux of the issue. The extremely important aspect of growth of the *umma* cannot be left to women alone (Muslim Brotherhood 1994:25–38).

Islamist groups such as the Muslim Brotherhood create a desire for definition of morally correct and incorrect practices according to their own doctrine and interpretation of the Islamic tradition. Intrinsic to this discourse is the disciplining of bodily practices and the redefinition of ritual acts and spaces. These rhetorical claims are within the framework of modern notions of domestic life, represented in the public-private/inside-outside divide. However, it needs to be emphasized that the attempt to establish boundaries between people, to standardize beliefs and practices, and to secure loyalties is essentially a secular project of the modern nation-state. The Islamist groups' aspirations to constitute exclusions and inclusions may then be seen as influenced by modern disciplinary techniques of standardization, homogenization, organization, and administration (Asad 1986).

Seen in these terms Islamist politics are a part of the modern terms of politics.[6] In this regard they may have similarities with the women's movement as much as they are antagonistic to it. Historically as well, as Omnia Shakry (1998) cogently argues, in the early twentieth century both secular modernists and Islamists structured their interventions as a defense of true Islam and as a criticism of *taqlīd* (blind imitation of custom and tradition). Islamist thinkers of the time also had arguments on health, hygiene, and the discipline of the body parallel to those propagated by the secular modernists. Where the Islamists diverged was in their constitution of the individual and the future nation. They emphasized a moral and religious outlook within the framework of a larger Muslim community, the *umma* (Shakry 1998:128, 158–159). Similarly, today there is a common (yet differently manifested) desire by Islamists and by secular women's groups to reorganize women's bodies and sense of self according to criteria deemed correct by them. There is also a shared agreement between the state, the women's groups, and many Islamists on the modern notions of health and hygiene.[7] As much as Islamist groups are opposed to sexual independence, or construct different notions of the sovereign subject, some among them seldom challenge women's right to work and education, a decidedly modern feminist agenda (Abu-Lughod 1998).

It may be argued that in Egypt the struggle between liberalism and Islamist politics may be seen as a tension between two competing views on inhabiting the world. Victoria Bernal (1994), in an article on rural Sudan, shows how Islamist forces propagate understandings that link local identities to larger and more universal sets of beliefs and practices (41). Similarly, in speaking informally to men whom I considered to be sympathetic to various Islamist groups in my rural and urban field sites, I found that there was always a construction of the nation that was larger yet also contained within the boundaries of Egypt. My informants had a sense of solidarity and connection with other Muslim states, like Sudan, and the Islamist movements in different parts of the world. These political connections were further enhanced by the identical ways that some Muslims discipline their bodies without regard to national boundaries. Therefore, the regulation of correct practices of how one prays, washes oneself, wears clothing and veils, maintains a beard, cuts hair, and behaves in public and private spaces is an important link to larger groups of Muslims in other parts of the world.[8]

Political and social groups, like the ones discussed in this and the previous chapter, seek popular allegiance by purporting to represent people's aspirations for their own good. Yet the rules and sets of injunctions of the Muslim Brotherhood or of the secular women's groups do not necessarily lead to the desired practices by the people themselves. The aim of a situated analysis can be expanded further to look at how women and men on the ground incorporate varied positions on family life, notions of body, health, and hygiene into their personal lives. This process could appropriate an understanding of how people locally create meaning and participate in the production of moral desires influenced by, yet perhaps different from, those articulated by the state, the Islamist movement, NGOs, or secular women's groups.

A cultural space in Egypt where some of these categories of inside/ outside and public/private are destabilized in practices of the people themselves are the annual *moulids* of the saints all over Egypt. I shall briefly present this aspect of Egyptian life to identify social spaces that may potentially cause anxiety to both the state and the Islamist movement. I seek to argue for a sphere within the Islamic tradition that provides certain windows into the life of the poor.[9]

Moulids AND POPULAR PRACTICE

Moulids, the yearly festivals of saints like Sayeda Zainab, are important for the thousands of people who visit them every year. People come to pay their respects to the Sayeda and also to ask her for help in their personally troubled lives. I present excerpts from a journalist's interview of some pilgrims to the *moulid* of the Sayeda in early 1994:

> Shaban says, "I went three times to al-Sayeda to make the vows, and maybe I will come next year. . . . I need to protect my lands because we are threatened with loss of our lands through the agricultural land reform people. We came here to ask for help from the *sitt* [the lady; referring to the Sayeda] to pay the rent on the land . . . They want 100 pounds, but how will we pay it? And if we do not pay it, we will lose our lands."
>
> *Sabah el-Kheir,* 13 JANUARY 1994

Another participant continues:

> My son left a month ago and I am here to ask Al-Sayeda to protect him and to bring him back. All the men are leaving the land for they do not want to cultivate it, and there are no jobs.
>
> *Sabah el-Kheir,* 13 JANUARY 1994

These peasant voices in search of consolation and hope are different from the organized protest of political parties in Egypt. Many among the rural poor who lived under an oppressive rentier state were barely surviving. The increases in rent levels on agricultural land from seven to twenty-one times the taxes along with the removal of land ceilings also made things worse.

Under these circumstances the annual pilgrimages to the shrines of the saints reorient people to an authority that listens to them and sometimes also grants them favors. This spiritual dimension of the life of the Egyptian poor represents a characteristic of Islamic practice that is more open and anarchic. People in these *moulids* indulge in expression of their love for the saints through *zikr* (ritual chants) and dancing. The festival always has a carnivalesque side to it where the poor participate with religious fervor and much gaiety. This is not to suggest that these practices based in Sufi orders do not themselves have conventions of inclusion and exclusion or that models of instituted practices are not learned and held up as correct. It may, however, be said that the effort to regulate boundaries is less rigid than in other, perhaps more orthodox interpretations of the Islamic tradition.

There are approximately seven female saints from the family of the prophet Muhammad buried in Cairo. Three among them, Zainab, Aisha, and Nafisa,[10] are the objects of large gatherings and year-long pilgrimages. Women from mostly poor classes visit these sites regularly to ask the saints to intercede in their family problems and for blessings related to fertility. Similarly I followed several women to a shrine in the Muqattam Hills in Cairo called Sitta Binnat (Six Daughters)[11] where they would go to pray and leave notes to the deceased female saint(s), primarily asking them for assistance in fertility matters.

The presence of these deceased yet living female saints is a source of authority and power for the poor. Villagers line the streets of the city during the annual event, pitching their tents on the sides of busy streets, living in unsegregated close quarters and dancing and performing *zikr* that at times dissolve the gender boundaries. These events have, since the nineteenth century, been condemned by the urban educated class and the modernizing state as threatening to civic peace and order. Timothy Mitchell (1988) argues that for the late-nineteenth-century Egyptian elite, these crowds were part of the disobedient, chaotic, and disorderly rural and urban poor who, although a part of the nation, could not partake of the liberal notions of justice and rights until they could be made industrious and orderly through educational and pedagogical projects (116–118). Similarly, Sufi traditions throughout the nineteenth century, with their popular following, threatened the state as inspirations for rural revolts against the capitalist ordering of Egyptian villages. They were brought under state surveillance in the last quarter of the nineteenth century with the establishment of village-level *Shari'a* courts that regulated and codified the Sufi orders by the more orthodox tradition of Al-Azhar (Rieker 1996).

Nowadays the state still seeks to control these events by either incorporating them (like the *moulid* of Husein), denying them permission to go on for more than two or three days, or condemning the whole event as morally corrupting and disruptive to normal social life. This popular expression of Islam in Egypt is also problematic for the Islamist groups that follow the Wahabi reformist tradition of Islam. The issue of feminine sources of power and the general use of saints as intermediaries between humans and God are at times condemned as *shirk* (the linkage of God to any other being) by some Islamist groups. These popular forms of religious custom, while remaining within the Islamic tradition, also call into question the more rigid categories of classification and organization of domestic life, self, and body promulgated by the Islamic groups like the Muslim Brotherhood. Embedded in the rhetoric of the Muslim Brotherhood (among other groups) on proper Islamic practice and the constitution of a singular Muslim *umma,* then, is a pedagogical effort to reform those who do not follow their interpretation of Islamic practice.

The *moulid*s constitute an invasion by the socially unmodern, the superstitious, and the unsophisticated into the space of modern life. They also represent the heterogeneity present in the Islamic tradition to show how the establishment of modernity in non-European spaces cannot be traced simply as a progressive teleological history ending in scientific truth, supremacy of secular ideals, and godlessness. Rather, these traditional practices constitute a major site where people's strivings against oppression and marginalization are embedded in the imagination and practice of religion.

Conclusion

International development agencies view the nuclearization of families as positively influencing contraceptive use by Egyptian women. In the last several decades Western social science has also portrayed the nuclear family as linked to progress and democratic norms and essential for the spread and consolidation of capitalism (Stacey 1996). The process of nuclearization of households may, however, have less to do with the desires of the international agencies or with academic fashion than with changes in social and economic parameters of living. These changes are more pronounced in urban areas, where the poor around the globe increasingly face a dismantling of the welfare state along with an eroding availability of traditional structures of familial and kin support.[1]

The crisis of the welfare state can also produce potential social dangers in the shape of a restless populace. As a result, many Western democracies have evolved policies in which individuals need to shoulder responsibilities for the level of potential risk that they may pass on to society. I argue that before the globalizing discourses on permanent retraining, self-management, and decentralized planning (Martin 1994; Donzelot 1991a) become a reality in states such as Egypt, there is a need to construct a population that can be governed by self-regulatory mechanisms and through people's voluntary compliance with the law. This potentially hegemonic project of consensus building and persuasion has the tools of coercion, in the strict Gramscian sense of the term, always at its disposal. This said, in studying the internationally sponsored family planning program in Egypt, I have been primarily concerned with one particular process that helps in constructing this disciplinary individualism. I have shown how family planning projects, through their reliance on counting, on mapping, and on interventions to construct bodies as the object of knowledge, further governing capabilities of modernizing states (Horn 1994; Tsing 1993). In addition, the Egyptian case combines high-pressure persuasion for contraception by planners and the deeper impact of socioeconomic coercion. I submit that demographic transition may eventually happen in Egypt. If it does, it will more likely happen as a re-sult of diminishing opportunities for a majority of Egyptians to make a living than as a natural response to better standards of living.

As international agencies have compelled the Egyptian state to follow the dictates of their economic restructuring policies, the Egyptian state has also periodically sought to negotiate the terms of the structural adjust-ment program with the international lending/donor agencies. In recent years, the Egyptian state stood up to the IMF on further devaluation of its currency, slowed the rate of privatization of public industries, dragged its foot on passing patent laws, and was slow in reducing import tariffs. It was, hence, continually criticized in international financial circles for de-creasing the pace of deregulation and liberalization of the economy (EIU 1995; Lofgren 1993; U.S. Embassy Cairo 1993). The Egyptian rulers were quite aware that the financial reforms were unpopular; they also knew that Islamist and other oppositional groups could take advantage of the gen-eral dissatisfaction caused by the adjustment package. Standing up to in-ternational lenders was a risk worth taking, as it increased the state's le-gitimacy as a sovereign body in the eyes of the populace.

Similarly the Egyptian state continued to champion the legitimate cultural values of the people. On the one hand, to calm foreign donors, it favored the rationalized organization of fertility within households. On the other, it retained laws that allow for polygamy and discriminate against women in marriage and inheritance, to pacify the more religious ele-ments in the society.

The government's support of the international agenda of women's rights and emancipation was further put to the test when, for example, the issue of women's work was raised. The international donor agencies pe-riodically called for women's autonomy and encouraged their participa-tion in the labor force. The Egyptian state, on the one hand, rhetorically favored such efforts, while on the other, it was not capable of expanding job growth to accommodate both men and women. Employment rates in Egypt are generally estimated just for men. If all eligible women were included in these estimates, it is possible that the statistical demand for employment would increase threefold in just a few years (Fargues 1994). Keeping this in perspective, the Egyptian Parliament in 1994 sought to re-vive a 1979 law giving working women the option of a three-day week at half pay. The law came under severe criticism by women's groups and human rights organizations as discriminatory and unconstitutional. The government, however, promoted the law for the sake of the harmony of the family and the well-being of female workers. According to state officials the law, if implemented, would help women cope with their jobs and their family duties and give working women more time to take care of their husbands and help them in raising their children (*Al-Ahram Weekly*, 21–27 April 1994).

Seeking to disguise its own economic limitations the state periodically used language that favored the domestic/public division of labor. In doing this it contradicted the more emancipatory discourse of the family planning program yet calmed the anxieties of a section of men and political groups and moderately reestablished its position as a "responsible patriarch." In this sense, while the economic impact of globalization was felt throughout the Egyptian economy, the state did retain certain political powers of adaptability in its capacity to manage and mediate international and domestic demands (Weiss 1997).

These posturings by the Egyptian state aside, it is still, I would argue, firmly entrenched in a program of economic restructuring espoused by international lending agencies. Arjun Appadurai (1996b) has argued that the translocation of a large number of people and the inability of nation-states to safeguard their international borders have led to the cultural and structural subversion of the concept of the nation-state itself. He contends that the logic of motion creates other histories, cartographies, and cultural logic that undermine the authority of the modern state.

This may be so. I would only contribute to this by suggesting that an imagined or constructed sovereign nation-state like Egypt is also threatened by the universalized (read Western) international standards of development agencies. As modernization gets related to representative democracy, liberal laws, and a free market, it frames the legalistic arguments of rights and law as elements of political strategies that enable modernizing states to destroy old options and create new ones (Asad 1992a:334–336). The international pressure on states like Egypt to comply with the production and management of "free individuals" and to conform to international norms is sometimes exerted through the promotion of civil society.

As I suggest in earlier chapters, the relationship between the social and the individual and between the responsibility of the state and that of its citizens is mitigated through NGOs. International development agencies and Euro-American governments celebrate internationally funded NGOs as the foundation for strengthening civil society in Egypt and as a counterpoint to the undemocratic and oppressive state.[2] This is a familiar refrain in the democratic politics of lesser developed nation-states. In this work I have, however, argued that the role of civil-society organizations in Egypt may also be linked to the neoliberal international political agenda and may serve as an extension of the political history of the West. Civil society cannot be thought outside the logic of the liberal nation-state itself. The debate and contestation over reproductive rights and arguments for the privilege for labor unions to organize can only exist if there is a fundamental agreement on the language used by the democratic project of citizenship.

Further, the transnationalization of global capital requires a post-state class system. The process of strengthening international civil society assists global capital in organizing the civil and legal boundaries of independent states according to its own prescriptions. It should also be reemphasized that the argument on autonomy of women and choice in fertility control is made as welfare structures are being dismantled (also under international pressure) in Egypt, leaving families, especially women and children, economically and socially vulnerable. This process of structural adjustment gets intrinsically connected to the push for universal standards of law and rights and as a move toward creating a civil society that guarantees political and cultural equity. Yet, as we enter the twenty-first century, this movement is "concomitant to the spread of markets, and it becomes identified with acceptance of social and economic inequity in the name of democracy" (Tsing 1997:264). The tensions, polarizations, and entanglements that accompany these processes across and within state boundaries shape new forms of historical categories that Michel-Rolph Trouillot calls "fragmented globality" (Trouillot 2001:129).

As Partha Chatterjee (1993) contends, there are two dominant arguments in modern European social theory on the relationship between the state and the individual. One proclaims the sovereignty of the individual and freedom of choice, insisting on the noninterference of the state. The other consists of the nation-state assuming the regulatory role in society, usurping civil society and family and blurring the distinction between the public and the private (234). Both these narratives of modern social thought, Chatterjee asserts, are embedded in the greater narrative of capital. He argues, "It is a narrative of capital that can turn the violence of mercantilist trade, war, genocide, conquest and colonialism into the story of universal progress development, modernization and freedom" (235). For this narrative to unfold, the earlier forms of social organization need to be destroyed. Other ways of constituting community or relationships, such as the ones I discuss in my arguments on *kabsa* in chapter 4, are relegated to prehistoric forms of existence that need to be overcome in the name of progress. As David Scott (1999) reminds us in his reading of

Michel Foucault's work, political modernity's "fabricated unity depends upon the exile, incarceration, ostracization and marginalization of specific other identities" (207). Neither the modern postcolonial state nor the related construction of civil society allow other forms of imagination to flourish except those subordinated to the narrative of accumulation.

The integration, albeit uneven, of global markets and media forms has no doubt produced universalized forms of consumptive desires. Yet social and spatial polarization inhibit the majority of Egyptians from satisfying those needs, producing conflict and tension. Free-market capitalism in Egypt has not been able to deliver the abstract cultural pleasures of freedom, democracy, and the ideal of citizenship. The state has through public health campaigns, austerity measures, political violence, police aggression, and the housing crises coerced people to become more compliant with their fate.[3] The desire to construct a modern atomized citizenry with its allegiance to the state rather than to local communities and networks of power has, thus, remained illusory. Rather, another way of thinking about it is that the desired process of "homogenization is at best superficial" (Trouillot 2001:129).

For women this argument has a different resonance when we recall how, even within the framework of parliamentary states, men are delegated relatively more power through family law, tax law, and laws of inheritance and through encouraging differential power of men over women in the labor markets (Gal 1997:41). Further, as discussed above, in Middle Eastern societies the claims of female emancipation have been periodically sacrificed at the altar of cultural integrity (Kandiyoti n.d.). Women themselves constitute communities and arenas that the Egyptian state has not been able to successfully penetrate. Yet women's inclusion in the national community has also historically been determined differently from that of men, as women have remained hostages to particularistic discourses about cultural authenticity.

In order to conclude the above argument I would submit that this text has implicitly tried to ride two horses at once. In describing people's attitudes toward the family planning program, I have shown their demands for social justice, equity of distribution, and inclusionary citizenship. However, I have also, with the help of people's own views and ideas on the body, self, and community, interrogated the politics of emancipation and individual rights.[4] The success of this theoretically eclectic effort is for the reader to judge. Yet following Partha Chatterjee's work on nationalism, I maintain that, in order to oppose the narrative of capital, linked as it is to the history of progress, freedom, and the nation, it is crucial to investigate the narrative of the community. This is a narrative that is unyielding through its alternate constructions of the individual and the social to the disciplinary and hegemonizing pressures of the modern state placed within a universalizing economy (Chatterjee 1993). This investigation does not mean a rejection of modernity or an attempt to resurrect some residual past. The idea is to situate other narratives of being and existence that are as much a part of modernity as are the globalized history of progress and emancipation (Dhareshwar 1995). To emphasize people's own experiences of their body or the popular practice of their religion as I do in the preceding chapters is to insist on a different trajectory of political subjectivity and political community, a future politics that cannot be completely encompassed within the narrative of the liberal state (Scott 1999:215).

The interconnectedness of the world in the cultural, political, and economic spheres forces us to engage in sharing empirical insights and theoretical propositions to emphasize the intersection of particular and global histories in complex forms. The issue is not to simply duplicate the language of an inherently progressive history to illuminate the popular struggles in different parts of the world, but to understand as well the historical situatedness of these struggles against poverty, marginalization, religious prosecution, and state-sponsored violence, perhaps in their own terms, before building constructs of emancipation.

This text has sought to historically and ethnographically investigate the social processes that are deemed emancipatory before celebrating the pleasures of their outcomes.[5] In this respect it is imperative that we historicize the processes that we live in. As Emily Martin has recently argued we need to brutally essentialize the forces of capital that oppress the poor and restructure public and domestic work. She asserts that these global-scale economic and cultural forces need to be named, their core features identified, and their effects exposed (Martin 1996:75).

In this text I have hesitated to build counter discourses on resistive politics. Rather, I have described how the process of globalization, manifested in the development process, seeks to change people's notion of their bodies and selves. Building on the above arguments I would further argue that there remains a healthy tension in participating in yet distancing ourselves from the history we all share (Trouillot 1995). It is imperative that, in being a part of this modernity, we appreciate the possibilities that arise from values like equity, inclusion, tolerance, participation, and appreciation of differences, yet think of a politics in which these categories do not always carry the valences that are predetermined by their history in the West.

Notes

1. Quoted in Wahba (1993).

2. Development projects are primarily geared toward changing the traditional practices and habits of the people in the developing world to help them make the transition from their lifestyle to that of the unmarked globalizing model of the West. The "West" here is used as a historical term rather than a geographical construct. It is, as Akhil Gupta refers to it, a conjugation of place, power, and knowledge (Gupta 1997:321). In this construct, I refer to those hegemonic tendencies by which the "West" has historically imposed its rationalities as a global phenomenon onto other societies (Gupta 1997).

3. I refer here to national agencies such as the United States Agency for International Development (USAID); to multilateral agencies such as the World Bank and the International Monetary Fund (IMF); and the affiliated development agencies of the United Nations.

4. The Egyptian state has introduced and encouraged the use of modern methods of contraception for women through the government health centers. In the period between 1980 and 1992, the program was successful in increasing current contraceptive use among couples, primarily in the form of IUDs and birth control pills, from 24 percent to 47 percent (EDHS 1992:xxiii). In the same time span it reduced the Total Fertility Rate from above 5 to 3.9. This success, although substantial, is largely limited to urban areas. During the early 1990s international donors became concerned that if funding sources decreased, the Egyptian state might not be as committed to continue the programs and the gains might be reversed (Futures Group 1992).

5. See Paul Ehrlich and Anne Ehrlich (1990) and Garret Hardin (1993).

6. In contrast, Amartya Sen (1994) argues that, while there may have been yearly fluctuations and regional differences in the last few decades on a global scale, overall the increase in food output has consistently outpaced the expansion of the world population. He further states that the major rise in food production has happened in China and India, countries with the largest populations in the world.

7. Egypt had a strong economic-growth performance in the 1970s and early 1980s. This growth was dependent on the high foreign exchange income from

petroleum, Suez Canal fees, tourism, and remittances from migrant workers. Between 1974 and 1984 the GDP grew at an annual rate of 9 percent, which doubled the per capita income from $334 to $700 within the ten-year period. There was increased state investment in social infrastructure in this period, elevating per capita nutritional levels (daily calorie supply) by 21 percent. Life expectancy increased from 55 to 61 years, and infant mortality decreased from 116 to 85 per thousand. There was a concurrent rise in primary and secondary school enrollment, rural electrification (from 19% to 79%), and provision of potable water to rural communities (56%) (Handoussa 1991).

8. Economic liberalization in the early 1970s produced a new capitalist class and a skewed distribution of income. There were strong inflationary pressures that further widened the gap between fixed-income earners and the emergent entrepreneurial classes. However, due to a regional oil boom and an expanding economy, especially in the construction sector, full employment was available for most segments of the population (Handoussa 1991).

9. This was a pre-1985 military debt. Since 1985 U.S. military assistance to Egypt has been provided on a grant basis (U.S. Embassy Cairo 1992).

10. As the economic boom ended in the early 1980s, the Egyptian state, under an earlier agreement with the International Monetary Fund (IMF), shifted resources from the annual employment of high school and university graduates toward debt service. Also by the mid-1980s, shrinkage of job opportunities in the regional Arab countries led to return migration. The decrease in remittances and investment threatened jobs in the construction sector. These factors contributed to the 14.7 percent unemployment rate depicted in the population census of 1986. Although later estimates found the unemployment rate to be somewhat lower (the Labor Force Sample Survey 1988 shows about 12%), they were still considerably higher than the 7.7 percent unemployment rate of the 1976 census. The largest group of unemployed were new entrants into the labor force with high school and university degrees. The government slowed down the recruitment of graduates in the early 1980s into its guaranteed employment scheme; consequently, these graduates had to wait five to six years to get a state job (Handoussa 1991:7).

11. Law 203 was enacted in 1991 to restructure and privatize 314 public sector companies, almost 70 percent of Egypt's industrial sector (U.S. Embassy 1993). By 1997–1998, 109 companies had been privatized (EUI 1998).

12. Subsidies for consumer items such as edible oil, sugar, tea, soap, and bread were reduced and the general sales tax on tobacco and petroleum goods was increased. Energy rates were also increased to bring them closer to international rates. Subsidies on fertilizers and pesticides were removed in conjunction with the gradual removal of pricing and market controls on agricultural products.

13. The agricultural sector has benefited from the removal of pricing policies. With high wheat yields, Egypt reduced its wheat imports in 1992–1993. However, Egypt still remains one of the largest importers of food grains in the world.

Further, new laws have opened agricultural land to market forces, jeopardizing the land security of small farmers (see chapter 3).

14. The decrease in social spending became evident with the government's success in narrowing the budget deficit to less than 1 percent by 1996–1997. This also helped in servicing of an international debt that stood at $40 billion in 1995, despite reduction and relief (EIU 1995).

15. It is necessary to emphasize that people experience the state in multiple forms and at different sites. For example, the encounter with a village public health official or an agricultural ministry loan officer is different than experiencing the state legal system in the courts or witnessing the head of the state greeting foreign dignitaries on television. The state in these interactions is constituted as a local, regional, national, or transnational phenomenon. This conceptualization leads us away from thinking about the state structure as a monolithic and unitary entity and opens up the question of how different levels articulate with each other in seeking to implement developmental goals (Gupta 1995:392–394).

16. This passage has been partly influenced by James Ferguson's critique of anthropology and its relationship to development. Ferguson (1997) places development as anthropology's evil twin, which it can discard but never get rid of.

17. The root of the issue was that by studying these deviances the state could intervene to improve social conditions. Social and personal laws were tested according to the statistical concept of probability.

18. Foucault (1991), in his explication of the history of modernity in Europe, argues that statistics, by measuring social phenomena that may not be reducible to the family or individual, creates social facts by quantifying the phenomena of mortality rates, prevalence of disease, epidemics, accumulation of wealth, and spirals of labor. The unseeable is changed into tangible social knowledge, helping in the organization and disciplining of life. Family and the authority of the father within it as a model of governance disappear to give way to governmentality. Foucault states, for example, that

> In contrast to sovereignty, government has as its purpose not the act of government itself, but the welfare of its population, the improvement of its condition, the increase of its wealth, longevity, health etc.; . . . The population now represents more the end of the government than the power of the sovereign; the population is the subject of needs, of aspirations, but it is also the object in the hands of the government, aware, vis a vis the government, of what it wants, but ignorant to what is being done to it.
>
> FOUCAULT 1991:100

19. Uday Mehta asserts that Locke's liberalism is primarily conservative. The pedagogical construction of the individual raises barriers against self-expression and eccentric and unpredictable behavior in order to impose a normality that is compatible with rather traditional norms and purposes (Mehta 1992:1–36). The

free will of Lockean liberalism is a will that has been husbanded, regulated, and educated into one of social restraint and submission to law and larger authority. The individuality is thus constructed as normative in contrast to social and individual pathology (126–174).

20. Similarly in South Africa, colonialism used the idiom of human physicality to generate and maintain inequality. Historically, in the early twentieth century, the task to redefine, regender, and discipline the Black body through the process of education and training in Protestant ethics was taken up by mission schools. The desire was to create communities of self-possessed Christians who could be drawn into the European moral economy by participation in the market (Comaroff and Comaroff 1992).

21. See Michel-Rolph Trouillot's text (1995) on how other histories are silenced in the production of historical narratives in the West. Also see Dipesh Chakrabarty's (1992) important essay on postcolonial histories and their relationship to Europe.

22. Roger Owen (1965) in an early essay convincingly shows how, after Egypt became a British protectorate in 1882, the imposition of colonial policy in Egypt was influenced by the experiences of the administrators in India. The consul general of Egypt, Lord Cromer, was convinced, Owen argues, that Egyptian and Indian conditions were basically the same. Therefore, the fiscal inefficiency, tyranny, and corruption of the native rulers needed similar reforms and the introduction of European goals of civilization (111). Based on mid-nineteenth-century notions of liberal economics, Cromer believed that fiscal responsibility by the state—linked with low taxation and the minimum interference to free trade—was the road to material and moral progress. The notion of low taxes, according to Owen, was partly to follow the injunctions of John Mill in keeping with the assumption that money in the pocket of the people will enhance their capabilities of thrift, self-reliance, and material prosperity. Low taxes in India and then in Egypt were, however, also administrative experiments to stave off local discontent and peasant revolts and to incorporate a section of the people who would be more sympathetic to colonial rule.

23. The newly urbanized intelligentsia, feeling alienated by Western ideals and the state autocracy, sought their nationalistic roots in the cultural lives of the peasants. There is a combination of denigration and glorification of the peasantry in late-nineteenth-century Egyptian nationalist discourse and literature. In both instances, whether treating them as backward, exploited masses or elevating them to a position of uncontaminated purity, the peasantry is always addressed as objects, not subjects, of the national struggle (Tamari 1992:82).

24. I borrow this argument from Dipesh Chakrabarty (1995:757).

25. Modern states are characterized by growth in urbanization, changes in subjectivities with increased individualizing tendencies, bureaucratic rationalisms, traditional/modern temporal grids linked to progress, mass media, mass production, and an emphasis on scientific thought (Ivy 1990:4–5).

26. Following Antonio Gramsci's major dictum, however, if pedagogy and developmental initiatives fail or the rhetoric of equality and justice does not succeed, brute force and extreme forms of violence are still used to tame and discipline.

27. When we evaluate processes of planned developmental interventions, we might find unintended results. David Horn (1994) describes how the pronatalist policies of the Italian fascist state between the two world wars did not have the desired consequence of increasing fertility rates. The practices "designed to reduce mortality, promote marriage and increase fertility worked to redefine reproduction, with specific and predictable social effects" (Horn 1994:125). The increased emphasis on child welfare, health care, and education of mothers did not lead to a high rate of pregnancies, yet it did enhance the value of the individual child and in the process limited the number of childbirths (Saraceno 1991:198; see Horn 1994:126).

28. The "failure" of a disciplinary regime does not mean the failure of the system of social control. Michel Foucault argues that, although prisons were created as correctional institutions where inmates were to be rehabilitated into good citizens who would reenter society as law-abiding "normal" individuals, the outcome of this social experiment did not produce "normality"; rather, it led to the proliferation of delinquency. The production of delinquency may be thought of as a failure, yet social control is enhanced as the political and legal category of "criminal" translates into the medico-pathological category of the "delinquent" (Ferguson 1994:19; Foucault 1979). As a consequence of these interventions, the prison may not eliminate crime, yet it succeeds in producing the controllable pathologized subject (Foucault 1979:276−277).

29. I borrow this argument from Talal Asad (1993).

30. See Marcus (1995) for a more detailed discussion. Emily Martin's *Flexible Bodies* (1994) is an important example of a multisited, multileveled ethnography.

31. In making this argument I am influenced by, among others, Kamala Visweswaran (1994).

1. HISTORY OF FAMILY PLANNING

1. All translations are from Roger Allen (1974).

2. Recently revised estimates show that the population of Egypt was higher in 1800 than indicated by the estimates of Napoleon's savants. Daniel Panzac (1987) argues, after carefully reviewing evidence of evasion and underestimation, that the population was closer to 4.5 million than the 2.5 million accepted by most European sources of the time. This figure is approximately half the population of 9.5 million at the end of the nineteenth century as estimated by the reliable census of 1897.

3. Muhammad Ali needed able-bodied men who could be forcibly recruited to provide corvée labor for his economic projects and military campaigns.

Muhammad Ali was aware of the effects of epidemic diseases on his population. To reduce mortality rates Muhammad Ali introduced smallpox vaccine into his army in the 1820s; by the 1830s almost half of Cairo's newborn children were vaccinated. In the late 1830s the pasha also initiated a vigorous campaign against the plague with quarantines imposed at the ports of Alexandria and Rosetta (Panzac 1987), resulting in the eradication of the disease by midcentury. Survival of the population was further linked to land drainage schemes that added more cultivable land and increased the food supply.

4. Egypt regained formal independence from British protection after the revolution of 1919. Self-governance was instituted in 1921; however, British troops reoccupied Egypt during the Second World War.

5. This census employed a number of European experts. It was generated to illustrate various indices of Egyptian development at the time (Owen 1986:457).

6. Roger Owen (1965) in an earlier important essay convincingly shows that the imposition of colonial policy in Egypt, after it became a British protectorate in 1882, was influenced by the experiences of the administrators in India.

7. In my experience the fear of surveys and censuses continues in the rural areas of Egypt. The *fellah* population has traditionally felt harassed by the tax-gathering state. It is still very reluctant to tell the "truth" to survey enumerators.

8. One feddan equals 1.038 acres.

9. Nine years later, before the 1926 census, Craig persisted with the same theme: "Inevitably then there would come a time when the whole cultivable land would be under cultivation" (Craig 1926:449). Censuses, Craig added, gave the state crucial information to curtail rapid population growth. He never advocated any specific population control policy himself; rather, he concentrated on the issue to advocate the benefit of periodic censuses.

10. It also included an anti-imperialist explanation for high fertility rates in most colonized and nonindustrialized societies. The theory argued that in colonized countries improvement of public health and prevention of epidemics decreased mortality rates while fertility rates remained high. This was due to the persistence of an agricultural economy that provided raw materials to the colonial system. The theory asserted that colonial powers had forcefully kept their colonies unindustrialized to use them as markets for industrially produced goods from the mother country (Hodgson 1983:9).

11. Ever since the 1950s, demographers have led the way in instituting family planning policy and documenting how fertility decline is correlated to rising living standards. The new survey methods and research tools were used to convince policymakers and to counter criticism (Hodgson 1983:23−24). KAP (knowledge, attitude, and practice) surveys, first implemented in the 1950s, provided a rationale for the implementation of family planning programs. These surveys were interpreted to show how a majority of the respondents had a desire to learn about contraception. By the 1960s almost 400 of such surveys had been conducted around the world.

12. They also blame high population density in these countries for deforestation and increased levels of atmospheric carbon dioxide. In the case of carbon dioxide emissions, most fossil fuels responsible for the increased amount of carbon dioxide in the atmosphere are burned in the developed industrialized countries (Myers 1994). Some serious analysts still suggest that population control measures are more cost effective in the long run to reduce atmospheric carbon dioxide than a direct tax on emissions from industries. Economic estimates, according to these authors, show that international family planning and the regulation of female reproductivity cost $4 per ton of reduced carbon dioxide levels, or less than half of the tax required to reduce emissions in industries (see Birdsall 1994 and Preston 1994). This language of preserving natural resources and protecting the ecology is one of the current strategies used by the West to regulate and reorder the cultural and economic life of the rest of the world. With such a management-oriented approach, who can deny the effectiveness of population control as a saving grace for the future of all of humanity?

13. The SIS (State Information Service) in Egypt, responsible for media announcements on family planning, is primarily funded by USAID. Johns Hopkins University's Center for Communication Programs, as subcontractor for USAID, provides the major technical assistance for most advertising and for the development of innovative advertising techniques such as television serials.

14. The crude birth rate is the number of births in a given population during a given period of time, divided by the total population, and multiplied by a thousand.

15. Since the late 1980s, Egypt has been the second highest recipient of U.S. foreign aid (the highest being Israel). Critics have long cautioned against this relationship of dependency that neutralizes Egypt's role in the Middle East conflict and also integrates the Egyptian economy into the U.S.-dominated world market (in particular, see Morsy 1986).

16. Since the mid-1970s USAID has been the largest single donor to Egypt's family planning program, providing about 75 percent of all donor assistance (USAID 1992). In addition the Egyptian population program has been supported by UNFPA, the World Bank, and European aid agencies. In 1969 UNFPA assisted the Egyptian government by providing contraceptives and technical-education support. This program, lasting four years, cost $5.8 million. Another five-year UNFPA program with further emphasis on research and documentation was launched in 1976 with direct support of $8–$10 million (World Bank 1984).

17. Another $2 million a year was given to private nongovernmental organizations for training, technology transfer, and community outreach programs. Indeed, unable to convince the state to follow its recommendations, USAID increasingly turned to NGOs. In keeping with the free-market approach of American aid, the nongovernmental organization receiving the major allocation of these funds, Family of the Future, developed social marketing schemes for selling contraceptives through private pharmacies.

18. The National Population Council (NPC) would develop national population *policy*, plan programs, and coordinate among different agencies. Public sector (MOH, Cairo Health Organization, Health and Insurance Organization, Ministry of Social Affairs) and private sector (NGOs) would provide *services*. State Information Services (SIS) and other IEC programs would be responsible for *information*. The Central Agency for Public Mobilization and Statistics (CAPMAS), NPC, Egyptian Fertility Care Society, Cairo Demographic Center, and the American University at Cairo would conduct *research* on contraceptive prevalence and compliance (USAID 1987).

19. Before the ICPD in 1994, a presidential decree upgraded the National Population Council in 1993 into the Ministry of Population and Family Welfare. This ministry was dissolved in 1996 and merged into the new Ministry of Health and Population. This event reflected turf wars among the higher echelons of the Egyptian bureaucracy; it also shows how international pressures on the Egyptian government forced it to give the population issue a higher profile (Fargues 1997).

20. This indicates the proportion of married women who were using some form of contraception at the time of the survey.

21. TFR is interpreted as the number of children a woman would have by the end of her childbearing years if she went through those years bearing children at currently observed rates. It is calculated by adding the age-specific fertility rates.

22. Biennial Contraceptive Prevalence Surveys and the Demographic and Health Surveys were both conducted by Macro International, based in Maryland.

23. Although both high- and low-dose oral contraceptives (OCs) were available generally in Ministry of Health clinics, more high-dose OCs were prescribed in family planning clinics that I visited. Clinic staff with whom I spoke in several family planning clinics argued that, although the low-dose pill has fewer side effects, it needs to be taken every day, and forgetting even one could lead to a failure of contraception. High-dose pills were thought to work even if women did not take the pill for a couple of days. Similarly, the progestin-only pill was never systematically introduced (although it is available in special clinics and the private sector) in the internationally sponsored family planning program in Egypt. The progestin-only pill has fewer side effects because of its low levels of hormones, but it require precise monitoring and compliance by the user.

24. The CuT380 was developed by the Population Council and is the longest-acting IUD on the market. The scientific literature claims that this long-term IUD can be used for eight years (Population Council 1992). The shorter-acting CuT200, which has a life of under three years, was never introduced in Egypt.

25. Women who use IUDs complain of becoming ill, of IUDs interfering with their sexual life, and also of a high incidence of infections (Zurayk et al. 1994). Patterns of IUD use in Egypt show that women generally remove the IUD within two to three years of its insertion (Hassan and Fathalla 1995). This time period is far less than what is desired by the program.

26. Depo-Provera and Norplant both have progesterone as the active ingredient. Depo-Provera is an injectable that theoretically protects for three months, after which time the injection is repeated. Norplant consists of slow-releasing needles that are placed under the skin for a period of five years. The removal of Norplant is a minor surgical procedure. However, the weight gain caused by Norplant causes fatty tissue to develop around the needles, and surgical removal is often difficult (see Morsy 1993b for a detailed article on Norplant trials in Egypt).

27. Introduction of vasectomy as a contraceptive method is resisted even by professional men who work for family planning NGOs. While visiting an NGO, the Egyptian Junior Medical Doctors Association, I asked a male medical doctor if he as a medical professional would agree with the introduction of vasectomy as a form of contraceptive. Moving his hands toward his lap, he shouted back at me, "Nobody can touch my vas (vas deferens), nobody!"

28. The Egyptian Fertility Care Society, a major recipient of research grants and consultant funds by USAID, was originally formed in 1975 to promote sterilization through physician training and education. During the 1980s it had centers in fourteen major hospitals in the country.

29. In an article, Mehr Mahran (1993), the secretary of NPC and ex-Minister of Population Affairs, states that educated couples have a better sense of responsibility toward their children. Such parents desire their children to be educated and tend to delay marriage of their children until the children's education is complete. They are also aware of the financial costs of having more children and do not need external motivation to use contraceptives.

30. In this specific argument, Ibrahim's notion of civil society incorporates only those organizations that have population policy positions identical to the international donors. He excludes those whose views differ from the donor agencies. For example, Islamic political groups do not represent the "correct" form of civil society organizations even though they also oppose the undemocratic nature of the Egyptian state.

31. These consulting firms receive their fees from the same monies that are initially allocated to NGOs. There is a similar relationship between USAID and the United States-based contraceptive industry. IUDs and condoms used in the program are donated by USAID to the Ministry of Health. These donations are bought by USAID from distributors in the United States with funds budgeted for the Egyptian government. There is an indirect subsidy to U.S. manufacturers whose products are bought from tax dollars meant for development in Egypt. This is done in a political atmosphere where USAID, the World Bank, and the IMF lean on the Egyptian government to lower tariffs, privatize, remove subsidies, and withdraw protection of its own industries. At the same time USAID policy and U.S. taxpayer money subsidize U.S.-based health consultants and the contraceptive manufacturing industry.

32. It was formed in 1977.

33. Although these subsidies are being rapidly dismantled, the middle-class university-educated NGO employees still berate the poor for relying too much on government handouts.

2. CHANGING BEHAVIOR

1. The emphasis on women echoed larger trends in family planning policy around the globe. See Watkins (1993) for an extensive review.

2. The preceding analysis is based on interviews with family planning officials in the government, international donor agencies, and nongovernmental organizations and on family planning reports and surveys.

3. For example, with regard to husbands' attitudes toward their wives' freedom of movement, it was shown that 31 percent of men in Upper Egypt did not allow their wives to shop alone, compared to 9 percent in Cairo, although the difference in these percentages narrowed for visits to relatives and friends (16% in Cairo versus 19% in Upper Egypt). There were differences within areas in Upper Egypt as the percentage of men who did not allow their wives to shop or visit alone was 16 percent and 14 percent respectively in urban areas, compared with 40 percent and 22 percent in rural areas, "thus confirming the conservative behavior prevailing in rural areas which might be related to activities outside normal family circles" (EMS 1992:53).

4. I use the word "sought" here advisedly. In late-nineteenth-century India, the changes occurring within the domestic sphere, especially among the middle class, were indeed an ongoing historical process. Chakrabarty (1994a), however, argues (similar to, for example, Qasim Amin on the emancipation of women in Egypt, see chapter 7) that these shifts were also driven by a modernizing reform movement that emphasized the desirability of conjugal marriage and portrayed it as modern and morally superior.

5. Ian Hacking (1990) shows how, historically, statistical categories have shaped and defined people's behavior. As the technology of statistical knowledge developed and was refined in the nineteenth century, its potentialities for social control were understood. It manifested itself among other things in better sampling techniques. Therefore, representative sampling, the kind used in the Egypt Male Survey, gives more accurate information on the population than a simple census would.

6. The above argument should not be understood as claiming that every move by the state goes uncontested. Rural or urban, women and men create their own preferences for contraceptive methods through formal and informal networks of knowledge and valuation. Indeed, we could interpret some of the EMS survey results as suggesting that in Upper Egypt women and their "traditional household patriarchs" are equal partners in rejecting modern contraceptives connected to the authority of the state and the development agencies.

7. Minya city is the capital of Minya governorate.

8. This has led to a policy initiative to create clinics in the private sector or under the supervision of an NGO (CSI, the Clinical Services Improvement project). It was argued that the clinical staff in such clinics could be carefully recruited and kept at a high motivational level through better pay and working conditions.

9. The training session was conducted in English mixed with Arabic during discussions and role plays. English was used whenever technical and medical information was discussed, and the written material was also in English.

10. These links are important to note, as they sensitize us to how research techniques and service delivery methodology, developed in public health schools in the United States, are transferred and universalized throughout the developing world by individuals who are educated (at times on very generous scholarships from USAID) in the United States and who then return to their home countries.

11. For an excellent discussion of such retraining techniques in the United States, see Emily Martin's (1994) *Flexible Bodies*. Especially in chapters 10 and 11, Martin shows how new forms of flexible work regimes require retraining and education of the workforce.

12. Consent, in the Lockean framework of liberal theory, is given to the government to exercise legitimate authority, hence, we consent to follow rules that may limit our own freedom through the act of our own free will (Hirschmann 1992). The act of consent binds citizens in a contract with the state; to consent enmeshes the actor in obligations.

13. This process is similar to the description provided by Rayna Rapp in her work on genetic counseling. Rapp (1988) suggests that the discourse of genetic counseling is caught in a contradiction. Although the field developed to provide pregnant women and families with more choices, it ends up reproducing and extending existing social hierarchies (144). Genetic counselors tailor the highly technical nature of genetic information to the needs of the individual pregnant women. As women do not have other models and experiences for understanding this abstract scientific knowledge, the counselors play a gatekeeper role between science and social experience (154).

14. The social nature of childbirth and familial relations are constantly undermined in this process by focusing on the individual health of the mother. Moreover, notwithstanding the rhetoric of female choice and autonomy, women are in fact charged with complete personal responsibility for their own health. Attention is thus diverted from the state's failure to provide for its people (Morsy 1995:172).

15. The staff, however, left at one or half past one.

16. It is obvious that in these settings the kind of privacy advocated in the training sessions was not possible. Counseling was done in front of all present and at times more than one doctor participated.

17. This schema is not different from the initial marketing of contraceptives in the West, linked as it was to a similar notion of female autonomy and the politics of giving women control over their own bodies. We have seen, in the case of Egypt, however, that this autonomy cannot be akin to anarchy and needs to be attained through persuasion (Mehta 1993).

3. SPATIAL CONTEXT

1. Nasser was president of Egypt from 1952 until his death in 1970.

2. The land reform law of 1952 required the forceful takeover and redistribution of all landholdings over 200 feddans (held by an individual) or 300 feddans (held by a family). This was reduced to individual holdings of 50 feddans and family holdings of 100 feddans by 1969. The reform law succeeded in economically crippling the regime's primary political rivals, the large landholding class. It also generated enormous political support among the peasantry.

3. *Al-infitah* (the opening), as this policy was generally called, was heralded as a new economic order after the mismanagement and socialist experiment of the Nasserite period. New laws were legislated to relax import and export requirements, privatization was encouraged in commercial enterprises, and foreign banks were allowed to operate for the first time since the 1950s (Ajami 1982:487).

4. One feddan is equal to 1.038 acres.

5. Those who owned between 5 and 50 feddans as individuals or up to 100 feddans as a family with dependent children.

6. Nicholas Hopkins (1983) shows that farmers owning less than one feddan are forced to look for off-farm work to supplement their household income. It is estimated that more than one-third of a feddan is needed to support one resident dependent on agriculture. Members of families with very small holdings have less than a tenth of a feddan each, while those with small holdings have 0.28 feddan each. According to figures analyzed by Robert Springborg (1990b:38), there are 1.9 million Egyptian families in these categories. He argues that almost 70 percent of Egypt's rural population in the 1980s may have been living below the level of subsistence, forcing a large percentage to seek labor outside the agricultural sector (Springborg 1990b).

7. It is estimated that by the mid-1980s almost 3.5 million Egyptians, 7 percent of the population at that time, lived in other Arab states (Lesch 1985).

8. In 1987 a new agricultural decontrol policy was instituted with the goals of removing government controls on farm prices, crop area, and crop procurement; removing restraints on private-sector procurement, processing, and marketing of farm products; and removing subsidies on inputs and limitations on land ownership by the state.

9. In essence the law reverses the contract between tenants and the state, which was the centerpiece of the 1952 agrarian reforms. The new law was unan-

imously passed with the support of all the major political parties in Egypt and a minimum of national debate. The law primarily lifts the ceiling on land ownership, allowing for accumulation of land by those who possess capital. Land rent was increased from a fixed value of seven times the land tax to twenty-two times the land tax. Sharecropping contracts were determined at 50 percent each, with provision for the sharecroppers to maintain the irrigation and drainage of the land. All prior contracts were to be terminated in the year 1997–1998, five years after the law was passed. The landowner would then have the right to sell the land or rent it to someone else. If the landowner wanted to sell the land before the five years, the tenant had the right of first refusal. If the tenant did not buy the land, then he was entitled to a compensation of forty times the tax for each remaining year of the contract (Hinnebusch 1993).

10. Commenting on this scenario, Timothy Mitchell (1995) argues that the major problem in the rural sector is neither lack of productivity nor a large population that cannot feed itself. Rather, the problem lies in the changeover from grain production for humans to fodder production for animals on the same acreage (135). In this shift to animal farming geared to meet the demands of the urban middle class for red meat, the regime has to import wheat in increasing quantities from the United States and other European countries. Mitchell (1995) further contends that the definition of a middle or large landholder has not changed since the late nineteenth century, whereas the crop yields have increased fourfold in the last century due to the use of fertilizers, insecticides, and better water drainage. Therefore, the yield of a 50-feddan farm may be as much as a farm of 225 feddans a hundred years ago (Mitchell 1995:138). Based on these findings, a redistribution of land as 3-feddan holdings to farmers, Mitchell argues, will not result in loss of agricultural productivity (Mitchell 1995).

11. During the colonial rule in Egypt in the late nineteenth century, the peasants were encouraged to grow cotton at the expense of food crops. Issues of food self-sufficiency were not affected in this period due to the size of the population and largely due to consumption patterns. This policy was put in place so that Egypt's national debt to European lenders could be paid off through export earnings (Mitchell 1995).

12. The area was a major producer of cotton, and landholdings were primarily large estates owned by the ruling élite. Gabriel Baer (1962) suggests that about a quarter of the cultivatable land in the Sharqiya governorate (36,000 feddans) belonged to the royal family. The figures for landholdings in Sharqiya for the years 1936–1937 show that 69 percent of small landholders possessed 13.6 percent of the land, and 0.5 percent of large landholders (more than 50 feddans) owned 34 percent of the land. Among the small landholders only 13.5 percent had more than 2 feddans of land, and most landholdings were below 0.5 feddan (called "pygmy holdings") (Ammar 1942).

13. *Izba* is a late-nineteenth-century and twentieth-century form of landholding in Egypt in which the landowners provided their peasants with dwellings

and small plots of land to grow their own food. The landowners controlled the title to the land, credit, and links to the market.

14. Actual holdings may be larger or smaller than the land ownership records show. Nicholas Hopkins (1987) asserts that landholdings in Egypt should be understood as land ownership plus the land rented subtracted by the land rented out. These patterns of renting land were present in the village, but details about them are hard to come by. The small landowners feared discussing money matters and agricultural profit. This should be seen in the context of how people respond to the long history of regressive taxation by the Egyptian state.

15. Twenty-four quirat equal one feddan.

16. Egyptian law at the time prohibited renting or selling of agricultural reform land; however, systematic renting and selling of this land goes on unofficially. The new owner takes on the government installment and debt and abides by the crop rotation schedule. In the year that I was doing fieldwork, the market rate for renting one quirat of land (1 feddan = 1.038 acres; 1 feddan = 24 quirat; 1 quirat = 175 square meters) was about LE 50 per year. The recent changes in the rent laws had raised the land rent from seven times the basic tax to twenty-two times. In 1992–1993 the basic tax was LE 33 per feddan per year for the area. The going market rate for renting a feddan was somewhat higher (24 × 50 as opposed to 22 × 33 with the new rent ceiling) than the new changes would allow. In changing the rent ceilings the state had brought the rental rates for the reform land nearer to the going market rate. Similarly, the sale price for one quirat of agricultural land was approximately LE 1,200. For house-building purposes it ranged from LE 4,000 to LE 7,000 per quirat, depending upon the land's proximity to the main road that passes through the village. As most of these transactions were technically illegal, the nature of sales and rental arrangements was very difficult to ascertain. Peasants feared being taxed over and above their normal dues. Only in lay conversation with some slips here and there could one start to understand the breadth of these practices.

17. Men usually complained that those persons who had agricultural land and were also employed were better off because their food bills were partially subsidized. Therefore, individuals with two or more feddans of land were looked at enviously in the village, as they possessed some level of food security.

18. Gender has traditionally been used in the agricultural sector to divide the labor market and reduce labor costs while increasing profits for employers (Toth 1991:231). The rates of daily wages in Qaramoos were LE 3.5 for women, compared to LE 5 for men in the farming sector. This discrepancy in wages has long been used to depress wages for male daily workers as well; especially in times of surplus labor, men have been forced to do traditionally female jobs to make a living.

19. Robert Springborg (1990a), who has extensively studied Egyptian rural relations, argues that male migration may have also resulted in a high birth rate in rural Egypt, as children were increasingly employed to perform intensive agri-

cultural activities along with their mothers. It is clear that population growth continues to play a crucial role for most present-day analysts of Egyptian agriculture. Even for those (like Springborg, for example) who are sympathetic to the peasantry, population increase is invariably blamed for peasant poverty and fragmentation of landholdings.

20. This process, although not central to the arguments being presented in this text, does help us in partially understanding the veiling patterns among women. Peasant women wore the traditional *hijab,* which did not cover the face. I suggest that the ability to refuse work in the village is at times linked to the socioeconomic status of the individual family. Wearing the *niquab,* the more restrictive veil that covered the face, may also have been connected with the enhanced wealth of some women and their families. This is a very complex topic and beyond the scope of this text; for a more detailed and nuanced discussion on the subject of veiling in urban Egypt, see Arlene Macleod (1991) and Fadwa El-Guindi (1981, 1999) among others.

21. With Egypt's population reaching 60 million today, Cairo accounts for almost one-fourth of the total population, whereas in 1897 it was not even one-tenth of the country's population. This also reverses the status of Egypt as being primarily a rural country. In 1907, 81 percent of the population was living in villages, whereas currently approximately 50 percent of the inhabitants live in the rural areas (Ministry of Development and New Communities 1979; CAPMAS 1986).

22. Migration is no longer a major source of growth for Cairo. In the period 1966−1976 natural increase accounted for two-thirds of the growth and inmigration the remaining one-third. Similarly, it is estimated that only 19 percent of Cairo's population was born outside of Cairo, whereas in a regional comparison approximately 60 percent of Istanbul's inhabitants were born somewhere else (Tekce et al. 1994; Greater Cairo Region Master Scheme 1991).

23. While many sectors of the population are crowded into tiny residential units, Cairo has one of the highest vacant housing rates among world metropolises. Almost 15 percent of the housing stock is left vacant due either to building deterioration or by owners leaving buildings empty for future use. Huge amounts of public and private investments are hence tied up in the process. It is estimated that with all the housing crises Cairo may still have a surplus of almost one million housing units (Meyer 1986).

24. Cairo grew at a rate of slightly less than 3 percent in the 1980s whereas the southern area of Giza, now incorporated into the city, grew at a rate of 5 percent. Similar areas in the north of the city, like Shubra al-Kheima, grew by about 8 percent (United Nations 1990).

25. Most houses were being built on legally bought land; their informality, for city planners, arose from their construction on agricultural land. Studies sponsored by the state and conducted by USAID use informality and illegality as interchangeable concepts. Accordingly, informal housing occurs when property

owners fail to comply with the land subdivision requirements, which results in their inability to register land or to obtain building permits (USAID 1982b). The principal issue is the conversion of agricultural land, which is prohibited under Law 52 of 1940 and 1975. Planning officials argue that this law has been ineffective since its implementation. As most requests for land development are rejected by the Cairo housing authorities, many developers do not even apply. The law is also very difficult to enforce. Once plots are sold and houses are built, removal is virtually impossible.

26. I accompanied at least two families to weddings in the Delta town of Bilbes in Sharqiya governorate and to a village in Qualubiya governorate.

27. Key money is an amount given to the owner of the residence in a lump sum. The tenant then pays a rent lower than the market rate. If the renter gives the apartment or house to a new person, he can receive the key money from the new tenant and thus recuperate his initial investment. The new tenant then continues to pay the rent to the original owner.

28. Similarly, while I was once sitting with friends in a café in another popular neighborhood, a police contingent came in and dragged away, beating and kicking, one of the waiters. The complaint was that he was a suspect in a burglary case. People later explained that this was a common occurrence and the purpose of the mistreatment was to intimidate people so they would refrain not only from criminal activity but also from political involvement with the Islamist "terrorists."

4. WOMEN'S BODIES

1. For the reasons cited in the introductory chapter, I conducted most of my community research in a village in the Delta and in poor Cairo neighborhoods. The Delta and Cairo are generally considered success stories for the implementation of the family planning program. The peasantry and the poor in these areas, according to family planning officials and literature, were thought to be more "modern" compared to the Upper Egyptian population. However, health campaigns and family planning officials still emphasize the noncontinuation and nonreliability of use of modern contraceptive methods in these populations. The strategy is to continue the program's emphasis on behavior change leading to a sustained use of modern family planning methods.

2. The participants were more familiar with the doctor, and I had no prior experience with this research methodology, a problem compounded by the fact that I was still struggling with the local dialect.

3. Agency as a modern concept is not transcendental or universal. Rather, it is linked and regulated by specific historical structures of possibilities available to the actor/agent (Asad 1996; Trouillot 1995).

4. *Daya*s, the traditional midwives, are in contrast to *hakima*s, who were official midwives and graduates from the midwifery schools. *Hakima*s also lost their prestige and dominance during the protectorate period. They received training in the basics of public health, surgical skills, and gynecology and obstetrics and had served the female population of Egypt since the time of Mohammad Ali Pasha (1805–1848).

5. The history of systematic replacement of midwives by allopathic medicine is not confined to Egypt or other non-Western cultures. Gertrude Fraser (1988, 1995) shows how, in the southern United States, the destruction of the midwifery tradition was carried out by modernization projects under the auspices of federal health programs. She demonstrates how African American women, the primary practitioners of this trade, were replaced by practitioners of modern allopathic medicine during the first half of the twentieth century, in the name of social and medical progress. This reform-based agenda incorporated the rhetoric of better health for women and children to justify the authority of scientific medicine and to push the traditional midwives to the edge of obstetrical practice (Fraser 1995:45).

6. Since the beginning of the twentieth century, the Egyptian state has included *daya*s in its health delivery system with varying levels of success. Until the 1960s, only those who completed official training were licensed to practice. This process was terminated in the 1960s in favor of licensed nurse midwives. In the early 1980s, with international recognition of the role traditional birth attendants played in childbirth and in the general health of the community (Pigg 1997), the state allowed the legal practice of only those *daya*s who had licenses from the earlier period. In recent years, there has been a widespread attempt to incorporate *daya*s into midwifery and family planning training sessions in order to use their moral weight in counseling women on contraception.

7. A function for which *daya*s traditionally were quite in demand was helping in the act of *dukhla,* the ritual defloration of the bride by the groom on the wedding night.

8. In the village, *daya*s would return on the third day after childbirth to check the navel of the child and put kohl around the child's eyes. They would come again on the seventh day to bathe the child and also to celebrate *subuu'* (the ritual celebration after the seventh day). They put the child on a *gharbal* (a sieve-like structure) with some grains that are thrown on people signifying longevity of the child and the fertility of the mother. Special candles are burnt and the naming ceremony also occurs on this day. It is on the seventh day that the *daya*s are given presents and also paid. The emphasis on hospital births under the supervision of doctors is eroding the important part *daya*s play in the social life of the community.

9. She also resisted the pressure to bathe with the menstrual blood of a fertile woman.

10. This consisted of a back rub to bring out the humidity (*ratuba*) from her womb and also a pessary with various ingredients.

11. Marcia Inhorn (1994a), in her excellent analysis of *kabsa* among lower-class urban women in Egypt, argues:

> In Egypt today, *kabsa* represents the unwitting and unexpected entrance of a symbolically polluted individual into the room occupied by a sacredly vulnerable female ritual initiate, whose bodily "boundaries" (and more specifically her reproductively significant genitalia) have been recently violated through circumcision, defloration or childbirth.
>
> INHORN 1994:115

12. Marcia Inhorn (1994a) analyzes *kabsa* as ritual pollution, whereas Janice Boddy (1989) links it to spirit possession. My understanding of the process is closer to and is influenced by Inhorn's rich analysis; however, at no time did my informants think of *kabsa* as a polluting occurrence. I would restrict my analysis by calling it an affliction.

13. Almost all of my informants were Muslims.

14. Vegetables that ooze fluid may cause *kabsa,* as does the sight of a black eggplant. Reversal occurs when the afflicted woman takes a bath with waters treated with these vegetables. Likewise, meat with fresh blood on it may cause *kabsa.* Further, as *kabsa* is linked to states of the female body, it is also connected to the liminal stage of the moon when it is ambiguously absent from the sky. These are the most vulnerable times of the month for *kabsa. Daya*s recommend that women who deliver in the last few days of the lunar month should not leave the room before the new moon rises again. Another name for *kabsa* is *mushahara,* derived from the Arabic word *shahr,* meaning "new moon" or "month."

15. The concept of the autonomous, individualized body that is considered the site of inalienable bounded property rights is ascribed historically to the works of Newton, Descartes, and Locke in Western political thought (Harvey 2000:100). It also incorporates the Cartesian construct of the mind-body dichotomy so common in the modern practice of medical science.

16. Rosalind Petchesky's (1995) argument partially accepts the construction of the individual as historically developed in Western thought. However, it does seek to co-opt the collectivist politics of sharing and communal living in opposition to a narrower definition of the individual linked as it is to the notion of property and market forces.

17. Like Soheir Morsy (1993a), who also worked in the Delta, I found that emotional states affect people's health. Morsy argues that women become ill in situations where they feel oppressed and take on the sick role that momentarily helps them recuperate and lessens the burdens of their life. There is a sense of voluntarism in the notion of taking on a "sick role" that I did not find in the communities I studied. Domestic violence and an excessive workload did make

women sad and unhappy with their life situations, but their illnesses could not be entirely willed into being. Emotional states, though, could be seen after the fact to have played a part in the illness.

18. Some women told me that women produce *mani* (colloquial for semen) or *maya* (lit.: water) that combines with the *didan* (lit.: worms, used also colloquially for sperm). According to them this mixture is important for conception. "Cold" (*bard*) women who do not have *maya* do not conceive (Boddy 1989 and Inhorn 1994a have similar findings in their respective works). Others, as mentioned above, insisted that it was their stored blood that continuously replenished the hungry fetus inside them, making their contribution far more than that of men.

19. Morsy (1993a), in her analysis of health and illness in a small village in Lower Egypt, describes spirit possession as a common explanation of illness by women and also some men. She argues that all illnesses had ultimate social relational causes, but spirit illness or *uzr* was most commonly attributed to negative emotional experiences, such as sadness, subordination, fright (yet fright can also cure women's infertility), and anger in individuals.

20. This construction is widely reported in Middle Eastern ethnographic literature as elsewhere.

21. Men also become possessed. I met two men who claimed to have been possessed. These men were extremely poor, with social responsibilities that they could not adequately fulfill. Due to these factors, in social terms they were considered weak and feminine.

22. People with whom I spoke would make associations similar to Aihwa Ong's (1988) description of used sanitary napkins and dirty toilets in Malaysia.

23. See Janice Boddy (1989) for a discussion of *zar* in the Egypt/Sudan region.

24. In the case of possession discussed above, there was an added complication. The Christian spirit now wanted to marry the woman, who was already married. This suggestion of sexual liaison became an acute crisis for the family's honor. They felt that while possessed the woman herself might not be able to resist the advances of the spirit. The host family advised her to find another more powerful *shaykh,* and one who had a clinic near the Cairo railway station was recommended.

25. Janice Boddy (1988) raises somewhat similar questions on women's self and personhood in relation to spirit possession in her analysis based on fieldwork in rural Sudan. She argues that in the village she worked in, feminine and masculine categories were not only ideally constructed but also relationally situated. Female and male selves were symbolically representative of the larger kin networks. When women became possessed they were further involved in a relationship with the possessing spirit. Boddy maintains the spirit within the woman was always considered distinct from her self. Unlike psychological readings of spirit possessions where such episodes are explained as "dissociated facets of the pos-

sessed woman's self" (Boddy 1988:18), the acknowledgment of possession in *zar* or healing ceremonies by the possessed and by others begins a process of healing and the realization that the woman is intrinsically related to another being inside her that is, however, separate from her person and self. This other self, the spirit, is in constant attendance and may influence the decisions and perceptions of the women, to the extent that Boddy found women referring to themselves as "we" in a gesture of incorporation of the other. In addition, the same spirit could possess other women, thus establishing relationships between different women which were beyond the links of selfhood created through kinship ties (Boddy 1988:17–19).

26. In this trajectory see the more recent edited volume by Diana Tietjens Meyers (1997), among others.

27. In another context, the notion of embodiment is eloquently presented in Marilyn Strathern's work (1988) on individual selves in Melanesia, where bodies and selves exist intrinsically enmeshed in social relations (302).

28. I take this argument from Michael Carrithers (1985).

5. WOMEN'S CHOICES

1. These arguments are emphasized in Egypt at the highest level. For example, President Hosni Mubarak, addressing a conference in 1993, stressed that increasing women's participation in the labor force and elevating their level of education would reduce the population growth rate (Fargues 1997).

2. Questions about how power and resources are negotiated within Egyptian households need attention beyond the models of conflict between genders. Rather, I would suggest that these issues should be addressed with an understanding of the caring and mutual support that may exist between spouses (see chapter 6).

3. Autonomy as a concept in liberal thought is embedded in the discourse of a self-understanding and a self-regulating individual that acts rationally and is partial to its self-interest. Similarly the liberal notion of agency as a concept is modeled on the idea of an autonomous subject "who possesses a will distinct from the will of others" (Asad 1995:15). Yet this construction of the individual overlooks the relations within which these subjects are "formed, situated and sustained" (Asad 1995:15).

4. The research and interviews presented in the following sections were partly done with the help of my female field assistant, Dahlia A. In this chapter, whenever appropriate, I consciously use the first person plural "we" to incorporate her contribution to the fieldwork.

5. As much as children provide meaning and happiness in women's lives, some, such as Fawzia, whom we met in the introductory section of this chapter, find it economically burdensome to raise many children. Also, older women who already have grown children sometimes abort if they get pregnant (Rageb 1995).

6. The Hanafi Sunni and the Zaydi schools allow abortion before 120 days. The Hanbali Sunni school allows it before 40 days, and among the Shafi'i Sunni schools some allow it before 80 days and some allow it until 120 days (Bowen 1997).

7. The qualification for the health of the mother is also very important in this regard. Abortion to save the life of the mother is never a sin or a prosecutable offense under Islamic jurisprudence (Bowen 1997: 166–168). In Egypt the penal law of 1937 explicitly prohibits acts of abortion although the law has clauses that permit women to obtain abortion services from medical personnel in life-threatening conditions (Hutington 1997). Like Egyptian law the recent anti-abortion position of the Islamic *ulema* and the Islamist parties is also a modern phenomenon. This contrasts with the equally modern advocacy of safe and on-demand abortion by international feminist organizations.

8. *Daya*s help perform abortions and in case of illegitimate births also keep the secret. As a *daya* told me, "The one who washes the dead should also hide the secret." In this sense as well, in addition to the services they provide (documented in chapter 4), *daya*s are an integral part of women's health practices.

9. This person was eighty years old and had been a peasant all his adult life. He had seen the changes in land tenure system from the days when almost all the agricultural land in the village belonged to the royal ruling family and the people primarily worked for them, to the present day when the land reforms instituted under Gamal Abdel Nasser were being threatened by new laws favoring accumulation of land in large private holdings. In this changing and uncertain period, the strength and the integrity of *aila* was a source of immense pride and sustenance to him and to many others. According to him, the larger the family, the more resourceful one could be in facing these turbulent times.

10. Bledsoe et al. (1998) show that in rural Gambia, women present similar arguments to avoid pregnancy. However, in Gambia the idea of resting helps women readjust to modern patterns of birthing practices since postpartum abstinence was widely practiced in this area.

11. Women generally complained of backache and weakness during the menstrual period and felt they did not have the energy to perform normal household chores.

12. See Bledsoe et al. (1994) for similar processes in Gambia.

13. This is in addition to the argument on how retained blood during pregnancy nourishes the fetus and the afterbirth has fertile qualities.

14. Popular publications also carry stories about women who claimed they would not get pregnant because of their "clean lactation" yet got pregnant after a few months (Al-Mussawer 26 November 1993).

15. Some women would laugh at this and say that men can never wait this long. Others would praise their husbands and tell us how their husbands wait for them to recuperate their health before demanding sex.

16. Rural and urban women would explain how upper-class women could tolerate the pill better because they had the appropriate diet to counter its side effects.

17. Similar to Naeima's predicament, another poor urban housewife in Behteem personally complained to me about how her health was constantly failing due to the use of different contraceptives. She had started by using the pill when she only had three children. Now she lives with her six children in two very small rooms. She had periodically used IUDs and an injectable contraceptive, which had adversely affected her health. Like others she continues to suffer the consequences of contraceptive use rather than have more children that she and her husband cannot adequately provide for.

18. The World Bank and USAID have pushed for a payer-supported health delivery system in Egypt. The Demographic Health Survey in Egypt periodically asks questions on how much women are willing to pay for contraceptive services. Moreover, government hospitals, in 1992–1994, were becoming involved in pilot projects on cost recovery schemes, where a variety of services were only available for a fee.

19. Aihwa Ong (1994), in her essay on women's role in the Islamic movement in Malaysia, similarly shows how by taking on the role of reasonableness some Islamic women's groups challenge male authority. Among other things, they criticize men for their lustful attitudes, exemplified by polygamy, and seek to inverse the reason-as-to-male versus passion-as-to-female ideology. However, Ong argues this critique can only develop if women create an aura of chasteness and are mindful of their unruly passions, thus reaffirming the original model in the process (Ong 1995:186).

20. I am indebted to Hanan Sabea for this insight.

6. MEN AND FAMILY PLANNING

1. Timothy Mitchell (1995) argues that in development texts the Nile Valley is imagined as a space where life has remained unchanged for centuries. This representation enables development agencies, such as USAID, to intervene and inject new ideas of technological change to overcome the imbalance between resources and population growth in this "static site."

2. Unit of land used in Egypt. 1 feddan equals approximately 1.038 acres.

3. The distinction between *tanzīm* and *tahdīd* should not be understood as a manifestation of an unmitigated voice of the people. The Egyptian state in its media announcements and publications of the population-planning program continually stresses the issue of spacing. Seeking to be sensitive to the culture of the people, the state announcements justify spacing as permissible in Islam in contrast to complete cessation, which may not be religiously allowed. Hence, local ideas about contraception may be influenced in complex forms by ideas propagated by the state information agencies.

4. However, see Abu-Lughod (1986) and Gilsenan (1996) for more sophisticated depictions of Middle Eastern gender relations.

5. See discussion on women's work in chapters 3 and 5.

6. The reference here is to opening the door to the burial chamber/tomb.

7. Due to lack of resources some of my informants were, as surviving elder brothers, not able to afford these gifts for their sisters. Sometimes better situated younger brothers would take on the responsibility and erode familial authority and respect of the elder.

8. I was constantly warned not to drink cold water after a sexual act, as it could go to my knees and cause arthritic pains.

9. Men have an immense fear of the power of menstrual blood. Rural and urban men would tell me that those women who seek revenge from men may spike their tea with a few drops of menstrual blood The man who drinks this may slowly lose weight and his normal defenses against infections fail. This may sometimes result in death. The hold of this notion in the popular understanding of health and illness is so strong that a case was registered by the police against a woman for murdering her husband by this method (Egyptian Gazette, 1 July 1994).

10. See Lila Abu-Lughod (1986) for a more nuanced reading of *fitna* as it relates to gender relations. In my interviews, this construct provided an overarching argument for the need to physically restrain women and also to circumcise them, as circumcision was thought to sexually cool women down. However, in private talks with my male informants, none of them believed that their wives would leave them as they were very much in love with each other, although most admitted that their sexual lives were affected by their poverty.

11. Kandiyoti (1988) argues that by letting men enjoy some privileges women traditionally guaranteed for themselves a secure social and economic environment.

7. CONSTRUCTING NEW SELVES

1. For the particularity of the argument I present in this chapter, I am only considering those women's groups that have a secular and nonreligious philosophical outlook.

2. All Islamist groups, parties, and formations completely or partially oppose the state-sponsored family planning program according to their own interpretations of Islamic doctrine. The Islamist movement in Egypt needs to be understood in all its diversity and complexity (e.g., the Muslim Brotherhood and groups such as Islamic Jihad and the Gamaʿat el Islamiya). In this text, however, I do not present a comprehensive and detailed analysis of the responses of various Islamist groups to the fertility control program in Egypt. I will instead concentrate on arguments put forward by the publications primarily of the Muslim Brotherhood and the politically sympathetic press, such as the newspaper *Al-Shaʿb,* as they offer a critique of the state-sponsored project.

3. See Nadje Al-Ali (2000) for a more in-depth analysis of these groups, their specific histories, and their political leanings.

4. Kamala Viswesvaran (1996), however, provides a critical analysis of this argument by showing how women political prisoners in colonial India had an independent social and political position from that of the male nationalists.

5. For liberals like Amin, however, Egyptian men and women were never seen as equals in intellectual capacity. On the contrary, his books viciously attack the character of upper-class Egyptian women. Seeking to reform women from his own social background, he chastises them for not taking care of their personal hygiene and appearance and thus remaining unattractive to their husbands. He further argues that their lack of intellectual capabilities made these women jealous and critical of their hardworking partners and portrays women as illiterate, shifty, and manipulative in their dealings with men. He demanded that women stop wasting their time in trivial pursuits and engage themselves in the vital aspects of organizing the household, of dealing with the domestic budget, of supervising the servants, and busying themselves in the proper upbringing of children. Educated and domestically organized women could only become social equals of their men and guarantee a harmonious relationship based on true love and affection. In short, the new domestic space needed to be tamed and educated to match the needs of the rising modernist male sensibilities [Amin 1992 (1899)].

6. Juan Ricardo Cole (1981) argues that issues such as veiling and seclusion in late-nineteenth-century Egypt were not relevant to the multitude of poor and rural women who worked as domestic servants or as peasants.

7. Amin is considered a major figure in the modernist narrative of Egyptian national history. His place as the foremost Arab intellectual of his generation who spoke for the liberation of women and raised his voice against the practice of veiling has remained secure in modern Arab historiography. However, see Ahmed (1992) and Abu-Lughod (1998) for critiques of his works.

8. In the late nineteenth century the majority of the Egyptian population lived in rural areas. Although there had been rapid urbanization in the last quarter of the nineteenth century with a concomitant rise in manufacturing, the major financial earnings of the country still depended on the cultivation and export of cotton. Since the early 1860s educational reform had produced thousands of male and female graduates in higher education, medicine, engineering, mathematics, law, and other secular subjects. This native population gradually started occupying professional positions as middle-level government servants, junior and noncommissioned officers, tax and revenue collectors, school teachers, doctors, and nurses (Cole 1993). The Egyptian middle class, along with the Circassian gentry that aligned itself with Egyptian nativism, was part of the emerging nationalist forces. Qasim Amin and the female intellectuals belonged to this elite that, influenced by ideas of modern science and liberalism, had started to socially assert itself.

9. Activists like Malak Hifni Nasaf belonged to the upper middle class of Egyptian society As a teacher and writer, she argued for unveiling, for broad and professional education of women, and against the practice of polygamy (Cole 1981:401). In addition to formal schooling she also advocated home education on child rearing (*tarbiya*). Her lectures and writings stressed that a school education for girls was useless in the presence of "ignorant mothers" and a poor home environment. Another activist writer of the period, Labiba Hashim, a Syrian editor who lived in Egypt, echoed this theme of constructing a proper home atmosphere. She argued that the central problem of Egypt was that mothers were ignorant about child-rearing principles, health, and hygiene. This, according to Hashim, reflected that these women lived in a backward nation (Shakry 1998:144–145).

10. Beth Baron (1994) suggests that the argument against the wet nurse may have been made as an economizing and modernizing measure by middle-class women intellectuals.

11. These processes were not dissimilar to the turn-of-the-century arguments on good motherhood and healthy children popular in Britain. There as well the focus was on middle-class women who were supposed to produce and train the future virile and healthy (male) citizens of the Empire (Davin 1989).

12. Qasim Amin argued that women's ignorance, non-hygienic nature, and superstitious beliefs were detrimental to the prospects of a future modern Egyptian nation. The solution lay in training young girls in the sound scientific basis of child rearing, so that they could better raise the next generation.

13. The *hakima*s were recruited from the times of Mohammad Ali Pasha (1805–1848) and trained in the basics of public health, surgical skills, and gynecology and obstetrics to serve the female population of Egypt. By the turn of the century these practitioners were allowed only to practice midwifery and were rapidly being replaced by European nurses and male medical doctors. Moreover, the traditional midwives, the *daya*s, were increasingly blamed for infant deaths and unhygienic birthing practices by the colonial medical authorities and were, by the early part of the twentieth century, under intense surveillance and attack (Morsy 1993a:23–25; Kuhnke 1990).

14. Relevant parts translated by John Walker (1934).

15. Cynthia Nelson's (1996) biography of Doria Shafik, a major yet tragic figure in Egyptian feminist history of the twentieth century, clearly shows the negative reactions of upper-class educated women to the uneducated and traditional women of even their own class. Especially see the first chapter regarding Shafik's childhood.

16. The most radical position on this issue was taken by the Markaz Dirasat al-Mar'a al-Gedida (the New Woman's Research Center).

17. Of course the poorest women of Egypt do not have the critical voice in these debates that are led by Western feminists or educated upper-class native "diasporics" (Spivak 1996a:248–249).

18. This information on women's personal hygiene can be essential from a marketing point of view as well. As more consumer commodities enter the Egyptian market, manufacturers of sanitary products may need this information to create new markets.

19. I refer here generally to groups like the International Women's Health Coalition, the International Planned Parenthood Federation, and a coalition of feminist activists that work in collaboration with the Population Council, US-AID, and public health schools in the United States and in Europe.

20. It is important to point out that the Arabic equivalent for reproductive rights (*al-huqūq al-ingabiah*) literally refers to the right of giving birth and does not have any clear meaning for most Egyptians (Seif El-Dawla et al. 1998).

21. This argument is partly influenced by Judith Butler's (1998) critique of Left/progressive intellectual positions that downplay identity politics as "merely" cultural (33) and accuse it of being unsympathetic to materialist issues. She argues that certain Marxist arguments construe cultural politics as factionalizing and particularistic and blame it for having lost a politics that unifies around a common goal, a common language, and a universal mode of rationality (34).

22. In a different register Nadje Al-Ali (2000) also raises the issue of universalistic ideals and cultural relativity. Al-Ali shows how some Egyptian secular women activists respond to the international human rights discourse by taking a culturally relativistic position. My concern here is different. I argue that the reproductive-rights agenda, in the specific example of the Giza Study, privileges universalizing scientific arguments over the bodily experiences of women themselves. My understanding of this phenomenon is indebted to my reading of Emily Martin's (1987) important work on medical discourse and women's experiences of their own bodies.

23. This further entails incorporating anthropological methodology to study women's own perceptions of body health, sexuality, and self. The researchers argued that such understanding would help providers in communicating with women and form a base for the health education campaigns. These campaigns would be designed to raise women's awareness of their own reproductive health and guide them toward seeking health care for disease conditions (Zurayk et al. 1994:18).

24. For a situated and culturally contextualized example see Seif El-Dawla et al. (1998).

25. These are two groups that have their roots in the socialist student politics of the 1970s.

26. In the following analysis I also do not include the Islamist women's groups and their political argument regarding development or family planning.

27. Saba Mahmood (1995), in an unpublished theoretical essay, discusses the problems Western feminist thought encounters in accommodating the views of religious Islamic women.

28. Qasim Amin's forceful admonishment to mothers is worth quoting:

> Is it not a mother's ignorance that allows her to neglect her child's cleanliness
> so that he is dirty and left to wander in the streets and alleys, wallowing in the
> alleys in the dirt as baby animals do? Is it not her ignorance that allows him to
> be lazy, running away from work and wasting his precious time, which is his
> capital, lying around, sleeping and dallying, even though childhood years are
> the years of energy, work and action? . . . Is it not a mother's ignorance that
> compels her to bring up her child through fear of *jinn* and evil spirits?
>
> AMIN 1992 (1899):26−27

The motherhood that guaranteed children would be well trained, would eat
a proper diet, would be regulated into work habits, and would have the correct
moral values was crucial to the aims of Egyptian nationalist leaders. This not only
meant a change in the lives of the women but also a redefinition of what childhood would mean from then onward.

8. ISLAMIST FUTURES

1. For example, Talat Harb, who was a major early-twentieth-century
Egyptian financier and the founder of the indigenous Bank Misr, earlier in his
career attacked Amin's adulation of European civilization. He argued that wom-
en's education must have an Islamic content and be restricted to knowledge
essential to manage the household and to raise children. He feared that giving up
the veil would be a step toward the disintegration of the indigenous values of
Egyptian Islam against the moral degradation of European mores (Cole 1981:
403−404).

2. The basis of the argument relied on the concept of *tajdīd,* which connotes
revival, especially the renewal of an authentic Islamic spirit embodying an ethi-
cal-moral dimension, and *islah,* referring to reform including the correct moral
and ethical behavior to increase righteousness of the community. At the core of
these concepts were the fundamentals of religion (*usul al-din*) underpinned by the
Qur'an and the *hadith* (Shakry 1998:151).

3. Egypt has signed the convention (CEDAW) with reservations.

4. Among other investments the international donors have funded an International Islamic Center for Population Studies and Research affiliated with the
Al-Azhar University, the oldest center of Islamic learning, in Cairo. Funding has
also been directed toward publishing books on the permissibility of family planning in Islamic jurisprudence, for example, *Family Planning in the Legacy of Islam*
(1992) by Abdel Rahim Omran, published with financial support from the United
Nations Population Fund.

5. Feminist critiques of liberal political thought have, however, systematically shown how men in contemporary Western democracies have as well retained their position as head of the household and, hence, legal and social power over women and children (Pateman 1989:183-184).

6. The insistence on God's sovereignty over that made by human laws may rhetorically subvert the liberal democratic project. It can also be viewed as a characteristic of modernity that shares some but not all the features of the liberal tradition of the West.

7. Soheir Morsy's (1988) ethnography of a hospital run by an Islamic philanthropic organization in Cairo shows how the entire system is based on modern medicine. This is not surprising since the National Syndicate of Medical Doctors (the physicians union) was governed by elected physician representatives who either were members of the Muslim Brotherhood or were sympathetic to its politics. Similarly, historical analysis of Egyptian public health in the 1930s and 1940s shows how during epidemics some Islamic groups like the Muslim Brotherhood advocated the establishment of modern medical and public health facilities (Gallagher 1990:110).

8. It needs to be clarified, however, that this hegemonic ambition geared toward Muslim bodies is different in emphasis and regulatory power from the universalistic arguments based in the liberal traditions advocated by the state and by some secular women's groups. The power of liberal thought linked to the globalization of capital leaves very few social spaces where other institutional arrangements of public life can be thought of as workable (although there may be some private spaces that are still somewhat independent from these processes of globalization). The project of rethinking liberalism is still an imaginative process among some intellectuals and political actors. Arjun Appadurai (1996b:33) has called for the critical construction of liberalism rather than its passive enjoyment as a universally valid assumption. Similarly Dipesh Chakrabarty (1998:479) argues that a gesture should be made toward the limits of liberal comprehension, hence challenging its all-knowing apparatus.

9. I am indebted to Martina Rieker for her insight and help in conceptualizing this section of the text. The depiction and celebration of Sufi Islam by the colonial authorities and Western travelers as inherently more tolerant and heterodox compared to the orthodox tradition, and the analysis by anthropologists of the high Islam of the urban elite and the low Islam of the urban and rural poor, put my argument at risk of a similar reading. Following Talal Asad (1986) I maintain, however, that these traditions have to be seen not as essentially incompatible but in their relationship to power and the social, economic, and political conditions that make certain traditions more dominant than others.

10. Huda Lutfi's (1993) unpublished work on the female saints informs some of the argument discussed here.

11. Nobody is really sure who is buried here, but the place refers to the six daughters from the prophet Muhammad's family who are buried in Cairo.

CONCLUSION

1. The economic and social violence perpetuated by the state in alliance with international capital is a globalized phenomenon. In this regard the diatribe against irresponsible African American men and minority single mothers in the United States is too widespread to be repeated here.

2. This is a role bravely played by some of the NGOs. The Egyptian Organization of Human Rights, among other groups, has been repeatedly harassed and intimidated by the Egyptian state security services.

3. Like the human rights NGOs, those that speak about democratic reform are also periodically harassed by the state security apparatus. For example, after the ICPD, the state apparatus put greater legal restrictions on the functioning of secular women's groups and NGOs. In recent years the Egyptian state has increased its monitoring of and restrictions on foreign funding of NGOs. In the process it has sought to stifle the voices of those groups that criticize the state.

4. I borrow the metaphor of the rider from Florencia Mallon (1994), who raises this issue while seeking to combine Gramscian and Foucaultian perspectives in social science research. The arguments are presented partly in analyzing the exchange between O'Hanlon and Washbrook (1992) and Prakash (1992).

5. I take my cue from Sidney Mintz (1971), who in an article published more than a quarter of a century ago, shows how modernization and the penetration of commercial competition for women traders in West Africa and the Caribbean meant they became stuck in low-paying jobs and lost their independence.

Bibliography

Abaza, Mona

1987   *The Changing Image of Women in Rural Egypt.* Cairo Papers in Social Science, vol. 10, monograph 3. Cairo: American University in Cairo Press.

Abdel-Aziz Sayed, Hussein, Fatma Hasan el-Zanaty, and Anne R. Cross

1992   Egypt Male Survey 1991. Cairo: Cairo Demographic Center, and Columbia, Md.: Macro International, Inc.

Abdel-Khalek, Gouda

1993   "Egypt's ERSAP: The Orthodox Recipe and the Alternative." Unpublished manuscript.

Abu-Lughod, Janet

1971   *Cairo.* Princeton, N.J.: Princeton University Press.

Abu-Lughod, Lila

1986   *Veiled Sentiments.* Berkeley: University of California Press.

1989   Zones of Theory in the Anthropology of the Arab World. *Annual Review of Anthropology* 18:267–306.

1998   The Marriage of Feminism and Islamism in Egypt: Selective Repudiation as a Dynamic of Post Colonial Cultural Politics. In *Remaking Women,* ed. Lila Abu-Lughod, 243–269. Princeton, N.J.: Princeton University Press.

————, ed.

1998   *Remaking Women.* Princeton, N.J.: Princeton University Press.

Ahmed, Leila

1992   *Woman and Gender in Islam.* New Haven, Conn.: Yale University Press.

Ajami, Fouad

1983   The Open-Door Economy: Its Roots and Welfare. In *The Political Economy of Income Distribution in Egypt,* eds. Gouda Abdel-Khalek and Robert Tignor. New York: Holmes and Meier Publishers.

Akhter, Farida

1992   *Depopulating Bangladesh.* Dhaka: Naringrantha.

Al-Ali, Nadje

2000   *Secularism, Gender, and the State in the Middle East.* Cambridge: Cambridge University Press.

Allen, Roger

1974   *A Study of Hadith Isa Ibn Hashim: Muhammad al Muwaylihi's View of Egyp-*

tian Society during the British Occupation. New York: State University of New York Press.

Altorki, S.

1986 *Women in Saudi Arabia: Ideology and Behavior among the Elite.* New York: Columbia University Press.

Amin, Qasim

1992 (1899) *The Liberation of Women.* Translated by Samiha Sidhom Peterson. Cairo: American University in Cairo Press.

Ammar, Abbas

1942 *A Demographic Study of an Egyptian Province.* London: Percy Lund Humphries and Co.

Appadurai, Arjun

1996a *Modernity at Large.* Minneapolis: University of Minnesota Press.

1996b Sovereignty without Territoriality: Notes for a Postnational Geography. In *The Geography of Identity,* ed. Patricia Yaeger, 40–58. Ann Arbor: University of Michigan Press.

Armbrust, Walter

1998 Terrorism and Kabab: A Capraesque View of Modern Egypt. In *Images of Enchantment,* ed. Sherifa Zahur, 283–300. Cairo: American University in Cairo Press.

Armstrong, David

1984 The Patient's View. *Social Science in Medicine* 18(9):737–744.

Aryout, Henry Habib

1963 *The Egyptian Peasant.* Boston: Beacon.

Asad, Talal

1986 *The Idea of an Anthropology of Islam.* Occasional Papers Series. Washington, D.C.: Center for Contemporary Arab Studies, Georgetown University.

1992a Conscripts of Western Civilization. In *Civilization in Crisis,* ed. Christine Ward Gailey, 333–352. Gainesville: University Press of Florida.

1992b Religion and Politics: An Introduction. *Social Research* 59(1):3–16.

1993 *Genealogies of Religion.* Baltimore, Md.: Johns Hopkins University Press.

1994a Ethnographic Representation, Statistics, and Modern Power. *Social Research* 61(1):55–88.

1994b Europe against Islam: Islam in Europe. *Nexus,* vol. 10. (In Dutch.)

1995 Interview, by Saba Mahmood. In *Stanford Humanities Review,* Special Issue on Contested Politics, 5(1):1–16.

1996 Comments on Conversion. In *Conversions to Modernities: The Globalization of Christianity,* ed. Peter van der Veer. London: Routledge.

el-Aswad, el-Sayed

1987 Death Rituals in Rural Egyptian Society: A Symbolic Study. *Urban Anthropology* 16(2):205–241.

Azmi, Hamed El Sayed

1937 The Growth of Population as Related to Some Aspects of Egypt's National Development. *L'Egypte Contemporaine* 168–169.

Badran, Margot
1995   *Feminists, Islam, and Nation.* Princeton, N.J.: Princeton University Press.
Baer, Gabriel
1962   *A History of Landownership in Modern Egypt, 1800–1950.* Oxford: Oxford University Press.
1969   *Studies in the Social History of Modern Egypt.* Chicago: University of Chicago Press.
1982   *Fellah and Townsman in the Middle East.* London: Frank Cass and Co.
Baron, Beth
1991   The Making and Breaking of Marital Bonds in Modern Egypt. In *Women in Middle Eastern History,* eds. Nikki Keddie and Beth Baron, 275–291. New Haven, Conn.: Yale University Press.
1994   *The Women's Awakening in Egypt.* New Haven, Conn.: Yale University Press.
Bernal, Victoria
1994   Gender, Culture, and Capitalism: Women and the Remaking of Islamic "Tradition" in a Sudanese Village. *Comparative Study in Society and History* 36(1):36–67.
Birdsall, Nancy
1994   Another Look at Population and Global Warming. In *Population, Environment, and Development.* Proceedings of the United Nations Expert Group Meeting on Population, Environment, and Development, January 1992. New York: United Nations.
Blackman, Winifred
1927   *The Fellahin of Upper Egypt.* London: George G. Harrap and Co.
Bledsoe, Caroline, Allan G. Hill, Umberto D'Alessandro, and Patricia Langerock
1994   Constructing Natural Fertility: The Use of Western Contraceptives in Rural Gambia. *Population and Development Review* 20(1):81–113.
Bledsoe, Caroline, Fatoumata Banja, and Alan G. Hill
1998   Reproductive Mishaps and Western Contraception: An African Challenge to Fertility Theory. *Population and Development Review* 24(1):15–58.
Boddy, Janice
1988   Spirits and Self in Northern Sudan: The Cultural Therapeutics of Possession and Trance. *American Ethnologist* 15(1):4–27.
1989   *Wombs and Alien Spirits.* Madison: University of Wisconsin Press.
Bowen, Donna L.
1996   Abortion, Islam, and the 1994 Cairo Conference. *International Journal of Middle East Studies* 29(2):161–184.
Brison, Susan
1997   Outliving Oneself: Trauma, Memory, and Personal Identity. In *Feminists Rethink the Self,* ed. Diana T. Meyers, 12–39. Boulder, Colo.: Westview.
Burchell, Graham, Colin Gordon, and Peter Miller, eds.
1991   *The Foucault Effect.* Chicago: University of Chicago Press.
Burckhardt, Robert, John Osgood Field, and George Ropes

1980   Family Planning in Rural Egypt: A View from the Health System. *L'Egypte Contemporaine* 37:41–69.

Butler, Judith

1990   *Gender Trouble: Feminism and the Subversion of Identity.* New York: Routledge Chapman and Hall.

1998   Merely Cultural. *New Left Review* 227:33–44.

Caldwell, John, Pat Caldwell, and Bruce Caldwell

1987   Anthropology and Demography: The Mutual Reinforcement of Speculation and Research. *Current Anthropology* 28(1):25–43.

Carrithers, Michael

1985   An Alternative Social History of the Self. In *The Category of the Person,* eds. Michael Carrithers et al., 234–256. Cambridge: Cambridge University Press.

Celik, Zeynip

1992   *Displaying the Orient.* Berkeley: University of California Press.

Chakrabarty, Dipesh

1992   Postcoloniality and the Artifice of History: Who Speaks for "Indian" Pasts? *Representations* 37:1–26.

1994a   The Difference-Deferral of a Colonial Modernity: Public Debates on Domesticity in British India. In *Subaltern Studies 8,* eds. David Arnold and David Hariman, 50–88. Delhi: Oxford University Press.

1994b   Marx after Marxism: History, Subalternity, and Difference. *Positions* 2(2): 446–463.

1994c   Labor History and the Politics of Theory: An Indian Angle on the Middle East. In *Workers and Working Classes in the Middle East,* ed. Z. Lockman, 321–333. Albany: State University of New York Press.

1995   Radical Histories and Question of Enlightenment Rationalism: Some Recent Critiques of Subaltern Studies. *Economic and Political Weekly,* 8 April, 751–759.

1998   Reconstructing Liberalism? Notes toward a Conversation between Area Studies and Diasporic Studies. *Public Culture* 10(3):457–481.

2000   *Provincializing Europe.* Princeton, N.J.: Princeton University Press.

Chatterjee, Partha

1989   Colonialism, Nationalism, and Colonized Women: The Contest in India. In *American Ethnologist* 16(4):622–633.

1993   *The Nation and Its Fragments.* Princeton, N.J.: Princeton University Press.

1998   Community in the East. *Economic and Political Weekly,* 7 February, 277–282.

Cleland, Wendell

1936   *The Population Problem in Egypt.* Lancaster, Pa.: Science Press Printing Company.

1937   Egypt's Population Problem. *L'Egypte Contemporaine* 137.

1939   A Population Plan for Egypt. L'Egypte Contemporaine 185 (May 1939).

Cobb, Laurel, Rogers Beasley, Donald Harbick, Keys MacManus, and Mary Wright

1993   *Final Evaluation of the Family Planning Systems Development Subproject of the Ministry of Health.* Cairo: USAID.

Cochrane, Susan, and Ernest Massiah

1995   *Egypt: Recent Changes in Population Growth.* Human Resource Development and Operation Policy Working Papers. Washington, D.C.: World Bank.

Cohn, Bernard

1987   The Census, Social Structure, and Objectification in South Asia. In *An Anthropologist among Historians and Other Essays.* Delhi: Oxford University Press.

Cole, Juan Ricardo

1981   Feminism, Class, and Islam in Turn-of-the-Century Egypt, *International Journal of Middle East Studies* 13:387–407.

1993   *Colonialism and Revolution in the Middle East.* Princeton, N.J.: Princeton University Press.

Colla, Elliot

1994   "Between Nation and National Subject: Tawfiq al-Hakim's *Yawmiyyat na'ib fi-l-aryaf* as National Allegory." Unpublished manuscript.

Comaroff, John, and Jean Comaroff

1992   *Ethnography and the History of Imagination.* Boulder, Colo.: Westview.

Cook, Rebecca

1993   International Human Rights and Women's Reproductive Health. In *Studies in Family Planning* 24(2):73–86.

Cooper, Frederick, and Randall Packard

1997   Introduction to *International Development and the Social Sciences,* eds. Frederick Cooper and Randall Packard, 1–44. Berkeley: University of California Press.

Correa, Sonia, and Rosalind Petchesky

1994   Reproductive and Sexual Rights: A Feminist Perspective. In *Population Policies Reconsidered,* eds. Gita Sen et al., 107–123. Harvard Series on Population and International Health. Cambridge: Harvard School of Public Health.

Craig, J. I.

1917   The Census of Egypt. *L'Egypte Contemporaine* 32 (April).

1926   The Census of Egypt. *L'Egypte Contemporaine* 96 (December).

Cromer, E., Lord

1908   *Modern Egypt.* London: Macmillan.

Crouchley, A. E.

1939   A Century of Economic Development, 1837–1937. *L'Egypte Contemporaine.*

Cuno, Kenneth

1992   *The Pasha's Peasants.* Cambridge: Cambridge University Press.

Darney, Philip, M. F. Fathalla, and H. Hammam

1978 "Modern and Traditional Midwives in Egypt: Cultural Roles and Medical Competence." Manuscript prepared for the 106th annual American Public Health Association meeting.

Davin, Anna
1989 Imperialism and Motherhood. In *Patriotism: The Making and Unmaking of British National Identity,* ed. Raphael Samuel, 203–235. London: Routledge.

Delaney, Carol
1992 *The Seed and the Soil: Gender and Cosmology in Turkish Village Society.* Berkeley: University of California Press.

Dethier, Jean-Jacques
1989 *Trade, Exchange Rate, and Agricultural Pricing Policies in Egypt.* Vols. 1 and 2. Washington, D.C.: World Bank.

Dhareshwar, Vivek
1995 "Our Time": History, Sovereignty, and Politics. *Economic and Political Weekly* 30(6):317–324.

Dixon-Mueller, Ruth, and Adrienne Germain
1993 *Four Essays on Birth Control Needs and Risks.* New York: International Women's Health Coalition.

Donzelot, Jacques
1991a The Mobilization of Society. In *The Foucault Effect,* eds. Graham Burchell et al., 169–180. Chicago: University of Chicago Press.
1991b The Pleasure of Work. In *The Foucault Effect,* eds. Graham Burchell et al., 251–280. Chicago: University of Chicago Press.

Douglas, Mary
1966 *Purity and Danger: An Analysis of Concepts of Pollution and Taboo.* London: Routledge and Kegan Paul.

Early, E.
1988 The Baladi Curative System of Cairo. *Culture, Medicine, and Psychiatry* 12:65–83.
1993 *Baladi Women in Cairo: Playing with an Egg and a Stone.* Boulder, Colo.: Lynne Rienner.

Economist Intelligence Unit (EIU)
1995 Country Report, Egypt. 2nd quarter 1995.
1998 Country Report, Egypt. 4th quarter 1998.

Ehrlich, Paul, and Anne Ehrlich
1990 *The Population Explosion.* New York: Simon and Schuster.

Escobar, Arturo
1992 Imagining a Post Development Era? Critical Thought, Development and Social Movements. *Social Text* 31/32:20–56.
1995 *Encountering Development.* Princeton, N.J.: Princeton University Press.

Fahmy, Khaled
1993 "All the Pasha's Men: The Performance of the Egyptian Army during the Reign of Mehmed Ali Pasha." D.Phil. thesis, Oxford University.

Fargues, Phillipe

1994   From Demographic Explosion to Social Rupture. *Middle East Report* 24(5):6–10.

1997   State Policies and the Birth Rate in Egypt. *Population and Development Review* 23(1):115–138.

Ferghany, Nader

1991   A Characterisation of the Employment Problem in Egypt. In *Employment and Structural Adjustment,* eds. Heba Handoussa and Gillian Potter, 25–56. Cairo: American University in Cairo Press.

Ferguson, James

1994   *The Anti Politics Machine.* Cambridge: Cambridge University Press.

1997   Anthropology and Its Evil Twin: "Development" in the Constitution of a Discipline. In *International Development and the Social Sciences,* eds. Frederick Cooper and Randall Packard, 150–175. Berkeley: University of California Press.

1999   *Expectations of Modernity.* Berkeley: University of California Press.

Fernandez-Kelly, Maria Patricia

1983   *For We Are Sold, I and My People.* Albany: State University of New York Press.

Foucault, Michel

1979   *Discipline and Punish.* New York: Vintage Books.

1980   *The History of Sexuality,* vol. 1. New York: Vintage Books.

1991   Governmentality. In *The Foucault Effect,* eds. Graham Burchell, Colin Gordon, and Peter Miller, 87–104. Chicago: University of Chicago Press.

Fraser, Gertrude

1988   "Afro-American Midwives, Biomedicine, and the State: An Ethnohistorical Account of Birth and Its Transformation." Ph.D. diss., Johns Hopkins University.

1995   Modern Bodies, Modern Minds: Midwifery and Reproductive Change in an African American Community. In *Conceiving the New World Order,* eds. Faye Ginsburg and Rayna Rapp, 42–58. Berkeley: University of California Press.

Freedman, Lynn P.

n.d.   "Women, Health, and the Third World Debt: A Critique of the Public Health Response to Economic Crises." Unpublished manuscript.

Futures Group

1992   Strengthening Egypt's Population Program. USAID: Cairo.

Gal, Susan

1997   Feminism and Civil Society. In *Transitions, Environments, Translations,* eds. Joan W. Scott, Cora Kaplan, and Debra Keates, 30–45. New York: Routledge.

Gallagher, Nancy

1990   *Egypt's Other Wars: Epidemics and the Politics of Public Health.* Syracuse, N.Y.: Syracuse University Press.

El-Gawhary, Krista Masonis
2000   Egyptian Advocacy NGOs: Catalysts for Social and Political Change? *Middle East Report* 214:38–41.
Gillespie, Duff, Constance Carrino, Charles Johnson, and Barbara Seligman
1989   "Egyptian Population Assessment: A Report for USAID Cairo." Edited and produced by Population Technical Assistance Project, Dual and Associates, Inc., and International Science and Technology Institute, Arlington, Va.
Gilsenan, Michael
1996   *Lords of the Lebanese Marches.* Berkeley: University of California Press.
Government of Egypt Ministry of Agriculture, and USAID Cairo
1989   "Conference   Proceedings   and   Recommendations."   Unpublished manuscript.
1989   Conference on Policy Reform in Egypt: Current Status and Future Strategy. *Benchmark* 3(2).
Greater Cairo Region Master Scheme
1991   "Implementation Assessment, Updating Proposals." Institut d'amenagement et d'urbanisme de la région d'île de France and General Organization for Physical Planning. Cairo.
Greenhalgh, Susan
1990   Toward a Political Economy of Fertility: Anthropological Contributions. *Population and Development Review* 16(1):85–106.
1995   Anthropology Theorizes Reproduction: Integrating Practice, Political, Economic, and Feminist Perspectives. In *Situating Fertility,* ed. Susan Greenhalgh, 3–28. Cambridge: Cambridge University Press.
————, ed.
1995   *Situating Fertility.* Cambridge: Cambridge University Press.
1996   The Social Construction of Population Science: An Intellectual, Institutional, and Political History of Twentieth Century Demography. *Comparative Studies in Society and History.*
Guha, Ranajit
1993   Discipline and Mobilize. In *Subaltern Studies 7,* eds. Partha Chatterjee and Gyanendra Pandey, 40–68. Delhi: Oxford University Press.
El-Guindi, Fadwa
1981   Veiling Infitah with Muslim Ethic: Egypt's Contemporary Islamic Movement. *Human Organization* 28(4):465–487.
1999   *Veil: Modesty, Privacy, and Resistance.* Oxford and Paris: Berg.
Gupta, Akhil
1995   Blurred Boundaries: The Discourse of Corruption, the Culture of Politics, and the Imagined State. *American Ethnologist* 22(2):375–402.
1997   Agrarian Populism in the Development of a Modern Nation (India). In *International Development and the Social Sciences,* eds. Frederick Cooper and Randall Packard, 320–344. Berkeley: University of California Press.
1998   *Postcolonial Developments.* Durham, N.C.: Duke University Press.

Hacking, Ian

1990 *The Taming of Chance*. Cambridge: Cambridge University Press.

Handoussa, Heba

1991 Crisis and Challenge: Prospects For the 1990s. In *Employment and Structural Adjustment,* eds. Heba Handousa and Gillian Potter, 3–24. Cairo: American University in Cairo Press.

Handwerker, W. Penn

1986 Culture and Reproduction: Exploring Micro/Macro Linkages. In *Culture and Reproduction: An Anthropological Critique of Demographic Transition,* ed. W. Handwerker, 1–28. Boulder, Colo.: Westview.

Hanna, Milad M.

1985 Real Estate Rights in Urban Egypt: The Changing Sociopolitical Winds. In *Property, Social Structure, and Law in the Modern Middle East,* ed. Ann Elizabeth Mayer, 189–211. Albany: State University of New York Press.

Hardin, Garrett

1993 *Living within Limits*. Oxford: Oxford University Press.

Hartman, Betsy

1995 *Reproductive Rights and Wrongs: The Global Politics of Population Control*. Boston: South End Press.

Harvey, David

1996 *Justice, Nature, and the Geography of Difference*. Cambridge, Mass.: Blackwell.

2000 *Spaces of Hope*. Berkeley: University of California Press.

Hassan, Ezzeldin, and Mahmoud Fathalla

1995 Broadening Contraceptive Choice: Lessons from Egypt. In *Family, Gender, and Population in the Middle East,* ed. Carla Makhlouf Obermeyer, 217–231. Cairo: American University in Cairo Press.

Hatem, Mervat

1994 Egyptian Discourses on Gender and Political Liberalization: Do Secularist and Islamist Views Really Differ. *Middle East Journal* 48(4):661–676.

Hinnebusch, Raymond

1993 Class, State, and the Reversal of Egypt's Agrarian Reform. *Middle East Reports* 184.

Hirschmann, Nancy

1992 *Rethinking Obligation*. Ithaca, N.Y.: Cornell University Press.

Hodgson, Dennis

1983 Demography as Social Science and Policy Science. *Population and Development Review* 9(1):1–34.

1988 Orthodoxy and Revisionism in American Demography. *Population and Development Review* 14(4):541–569.

Hodgson, Dennis, and Susan Watkins

1997 Feminists and Neo-Malthusians: Past and Present Alliances. *Population and Development Review* 23(3):469–523.

Hopkins, Nicholas

1983   The Social Impact of Mechanization. In *Migration, Mechanization, and Agricultural Labor Markets in Egypt,* eds. Alan Richards and Philip Martin. Boulder, Colo.: Westview.

1987   *Agrarian Transformation in Egypt.* Boulder, Colo.: Westview.

Horn, David

1994   *Social Bodies.* Princeton, N.J.: Princeton University Press.

Huntington, Dale

1997   *Abortion in Egypt.* Paper presented at the IUSSP (International Union for the Scientific Study of Population) Seminar on Cultural Perspectives on Reproductive Health. Rustenberg, South Africa, 16–19 June.

Ibrahim, Saad Eddin

1995   State, Women, and Civil Society: An Evaluation of Egypt's Population Policy. In *Family, Gender, and Population in the Middle East,* ed. Carla Makhlouf Obermeyer, 59–79. Cairo: American University in Cairo Press.

Idris, Yusuf

1990   You Are Everything to Me. In *Cheapest Nights,* trans. Wadida Wassef, 6–17. Cairo: American University in Cairo Press.

Ikram, Khalid

1980   *Egypt: Economic Management in Periods of Transition: The Report of a Mission Sent to the Arab Republic of Egypt by the World Bank.* Baltimore and London: Johns Hopkins University Press for the World Bank.

Inhorn, Marcia

1994a   *Quest For Conception.* Philadelphia: University of Pennsylvania Press.

1994b   Kabsa (aka Mushahara) and Threatened Fertility in Egypt. *Social Science and Medicine* 39(4):487–506.

International Planned Parenthood Federation (IPPF)

1993   *Meeting Challenges, Promoting Choices: A Report on the Fortieth Anniversary.* New Delhi, India: International Planned Parenthood Federation.

Isaacs, Stephen, and Lynn Freedman

1992   "Reproductive Health/Reproductive Rights: Legal, Policy and Ethical Issues." Manuscript prepared for Ford Foundation Reproductive Health Program Officers meeting.

Ismail, Abd Al-Rahman

1882   *Tibb-al-Rukka.* Translated by John Walker as *Folk Medicine in Modern Egypt* (1934). London: Luzac.

Ivy, Marilyn

1995   *Discourses of the Vanishing: Modernity, Phantasm, Japan.* Chicago: University of Chicago Press.

Jameson, Frederic

1986   The World Literature in the Era of Multinational Capital. *Social Text* (fall):55–88.

1998   Notes on Globalization as a Philosophical Issue. In *The Cultures of Global-*

ization, eds. Frederic Jameson and Masao Miyoshi, 54–80. Durham, N.C.: Duke University Press.

Jejeebhoy, Shireen J., and Sumati Kulkarni

1989 Reproductive Motivation: A Comparison of Wives and Husbands in Maharashtra, India. *Studies in Family Planning* 20(5):264–272.

Joseph, Suad

1983 Working Class Women's Network in a Sectarian State: A Political Paradox. *American Ethnologist* 10:1–22.

El-Kadi, Galila

1988 Market Mechanism and Spontaneous Urbanization in Egypt. *International Journal of Urban and Regional Research* 12(1):22–37.

El-Kady, Adel, Sarah Loza, Nahla Abdel-Tawab, and Linda Potter

1989 *Dayas' Practices and Maternal Mortality in Giza, Egypt.* Cairo: Social Planning and Analysis Administration Consultants.

Kandiyoti, Deniz

1988 Bargaining with Patriarchy. *Gender and Society* 2(3):274–290.

n.d. *Gendering the Modern: Refashioning Masculine and Feminine Identities.* Paper presented at the Social Science Research Council Conference on Questions of Modernity in Cairo, May 1993.

1994 The Paradoxes of Masculinity: Some Thoughts on Segregated Societies. In *Dislocating Masculinities,* eds. Andrea Cornwall and Nancy Lindisfarne, 197–213. London: Routledge.

1997 Gendering the Modern: On Missing Dimensions in the Study of Turkish Modernity. In *Rethinking Modernity and National Identity in Turkey,* eds. Sibel Bodogan and Resat Kasaba, 113–132. Seattle: University of Washington Press.

1998 Afterword: Some Awkward Questions on Women and Modernity in Turkey. In *Remaking Women,* ed. Lila Abu-Lughod, 270–288. Princeton, N.J.: Princeton University Press.

Keddie, Nikki

1979 Problems in the Study of Middle Eastern Women. *International Journal of Middle East Studies* 10:225–240.

Khafagy, F.

1984 Women and Labor Migration: One Village in Egypt. *Middle East Report* 124.

Khalifa, Mona A.

1988 Attitudes of Urban Sudanese Men towards Family Planning. *Studies in Family Planning* 19(4):236–243.

Khan, Ali M.

1994 "Population and Economic Development." Unpublished manuscript.

Khattab, Hind

1992 *The Silent Endurance: Social Conditions of Women's Reproductive Health in Rural Egypt.* Amman: UNICEF, and Cairo: Population Council.

Khattab, Hind, Abou Seoud, and Syada Greiss El Daeif
1982   *Impact of Male Labor Migration on the Structure of the Family and the Roles of Women*. Regional Papers of the Population Council. Middle East Awards. Cairo: Population Council.

Knodel, J., and Etienne van de Walle
1979   Lessons from the Past: Policy Implications of Historical Fertility Studies. *Population and Development Review* (5)2:217–245.

Korayem, Karima
1993   *Structural Adjustment and Reform Policies in Egypt: Economic and Social Implications*. Amman, Jordan: United Nations Economic and Social Council, Economic and Social Commission for Western Asia.

Krieger, Laurie, et al.
1990   "Patterns and Perceptions of Family Planning Methods: Focus Group Discussion Findings from Egypt." Unpublished manuscript. Cairo: USAID.

Kuhnke, LaVerne
1990   *Lives at Risk: Public Health in Nineteenth Century Egypt*. Berkeley: University of California Press.

Lacouture, Jean, and Simone Lacouture
1958   *Egypt in Transition*. New York: Criterion Books.

Lambek, Michael
1980   Spirits and Spouses: Possession as a System of Communication among Malagasy Speakers of Mayotte. In *American Ethnologist* 7(2):318–331.

Lesch, Ann Mosley
1985   "Egyptian Labor Migration: Economic Trends and Government Policies." *UFSI Reports*, no. 38.

Leventhal, Howard, and Linda Cameron
1987   Behavioral Theories and the Problem of Compliance. In *Patient Education and Counselling* 10:117–138.

Lindisfarne, Nancy
1994   Variant Masculinities, Variant Virginities: Rethinking "Honor and Shame." In *Dislocating Masculinities,* eds. Andrea Cornwall and Nancy Lindisfarne, 82–96. London and New York: Routledge.

Lofgren, Hans
1993   *Egypt's Program for Stabilization and Structural Adjustment: An Assessment*. Cairo Papers in Social Science, vol. 16, monograph 3. Cairo: American University in Cairo Press.

Lukes, Steven
1985   Conclusion to *The Category of the Person,* eds. Michael Carrithers et al., 282–301. Cambridge: Cambridge University Press.

Lutfi, Huda
1993   "The Mulid of Sayyida 'Aisha." Unpublished manuscript.

Macleod, Arlene Elowe
1991   *Accommodating Protest*. New York: Columbia University Press.

Mahmood, Saba

1995 *Feminism and Religious Difference.* Paper presented at the Conference on Gender and the Indigenization of Knowledge, 10–14 April, Amman, Jordan.

Mahmud, Simeen, and Anne Johnston

1994 Women's Status, Empowerment and Reproductive Outcomes. In *Population Policies Reconsidered,* eds. Gita Sen et al., 151–158. Harvard Series in Population and International Health. Cambridge: Harvard School of Public Health.

Mahran, Mehr

1993 Can Population Topics Form the Subject of Educational Action. In *International Review of Education* 39:15–19.

Makat, J. F.

1987 *Child Spacing in Lesotho.* Working Paper in Demography no. 9. Lesotho: National University in Lesotho, Department of Statistics DemographyUnit.

Malkki, Lisa

1998 Things to Come: Internationalism and Global Solidarities in the Late 1990s. *Public Culture* 10(2):431–442.

Mallon, Florencia

1994 The Promise and Dilemma of Subaltern Studies: Perspectives from Latin American History. *American Historical Review* 99(5):1491–1515.

Martin, Emily

1987 *The Woman in the Body.* Boston: Beacon.

1992 Body Narratives, Body Boundaries. In *Cultural Studies,* eds. Lawrence Grossberg et al., 409–419. New York: Routledge.

1994 *Flexible Bodies.* Boston: Beacon.

1996 Meeting Polemics with Irenics in the Science Wars. In *Science Wars,* ed. Andrew Ross, 61–79. Durham, N.C.: Duke University Press.

Marx, Karl

1967 *Capital.* 3 vols. New York: International Publishers.

Mbizvo, Michael T., and Donald J. Adamchak

1991 Family Planning Knowledge, Attitudes, and Practices of Men in Zimbabwe. *Studies in Family Planning* 22(1):31–38.

McCarthy, Justin A.

1976 Nineteenth-Century Egyptian Population. In *Middle Eastern Studies* 3(3): 1–39.

McCoan, J. C.

1877 *Egypt As It Is.* London: Cassell Petter and Galpin.

McNicoll, Geoffrey

1995 On Population Growth and Revisionism: Further Questions. *Population and Development Review* 21(2):307–341.

Mehanna, Sohair, Nicholas Hopkins, and Bahgat Abdel Maksoud

1994 *Farmers and Merchants: Background to Structural Adjustment in Egypt.* Cairo

Papers in Social Science, vol. 17, no. 2. Cairo: American University in Cairo Press.

Mehta, Uday

1992   *The Anxiety of Freedom.* Ithaca, N.Y.: Cornell University Press.

Mernissi, Fatima

1982   Women and the Impact of Capitalist Development in Morocco. *Feminist Issues* (2):69–104.

1987   *Beyond the Veil.* Bloomington: Indiana University Press.

Meyer, Gunter

1986   Migration and Economic Development in the Old and Newer Quarters of Sanaa and Cairo. In BRISMES, *Proceedings of the 1986 International Conference on Middle East Studies,* 385–394. London.

1989   Problems of Industrial Development in the New Desert Cities of Egypt. In *Applied Geography and Development,* eds. Jurgen H. Honholz et al., 90–105. Institute Fur Wissenschaftliche Zusammenarbeit, FDG.

Meyers, Diana T., ed.

1997   *Feminists Rethink the Self.* Boulder, Colo.: Westview.

El-Miniawy, Ahmed, and Esmail Gamal El-Din

1989   "The Egyptian Rice Market: Expected Impact of Policy Reform." Unofficial working paper of USAID and the Ministry of Agriculture, Government of Egypt.

Ministry of Development and New Communities, Government of Egypt

1979   "The Population Problem and Establishment of New Towns in the Arab Republic of Egypt." Unpublished report.

Ministry of Health, Government of Egypt

1980   National Strategy Framework of Population, Human Resource Development and the Family Planning Program.

1981   National Strategy Framework of Population, Human Resource Development and the Family Planning Program.

Ministry of Waqfs and Ministry of Information, Government of Egypt

1994   *Islam's Attitude towards Family Planning.* Cairo.

Mintz, Sidney

1971   Men, Women, and Trade. *Comparative Studies in Society and History* 13(3): 247–269.

Mitchell, Timothy

1988   *Colonising Egypt.* Cambridge: Cambridge University Press.

1995   The Object of Development: America's Egypt. In *Power of Development,* ed. Jonathan Crush. London: Routledge.

1996   *The Space of Property and the Formation of the Nation.* Paper presented at symposium, *Questions of Modernity,* 19–20 April, New York University.

1999   DreamLand: The Neoliberalism of Your Desire. *Middle East Report,* no. 210.

Miyoshi, Masao

1996   A Borderless World? From Colonialism To Transnationalism and the Decline of the Nation-State. In *Global Local,* eds. Rob Wilson and Wimal Dissanayake, 78–106. Durham, N.C.: Duke University Press.

Morsy, Soheir

1978   Sex Roles, Power, and Illness in an Egyptian Village. *American Ethnologist* 5(1):137–150.

1986   U.S. Aid to Egypt: An Illustration and Account of U.S. Foreign Assistance Policy. *Arab Studies Quarterly* 8(4):358–389.

1988   Islamic Clinics in Egypt: The Cultural Elaboration of Biomedical Hegemony. *Medical Anthropology Quarterly* 2(4):355–369.

1990   Rural Women, Work, and Gender Ideology: A Study in Egyptian Political Economic Transformation. In *Women in Arab Society,* eds. Seteney Shami et al., 87–159. Oxford and Paris: Berg (UNESCO).

1991   "Maternal Mortality in Egypt: Selective Health Strategy and the Medicalization of Population Control." Paper prepared for conference, *The Politics of Reproduction,* sponsored by Wenner Gren Foundation, in Terespolis, Brazil.

1993a   *Gender, Sickness, and Healing in Rural Egypt.* Boulder, Colo.: Westview.

1993b   Bodies of Choice: Norplant Experimental Trials on Egyptian Women. In *Norplant under the Skin,* eds. Barbara Mintzes, Anita Hardon, and Jannemieke Hanhart, 89–114. Amsterdam: Eburon.

1995   Deadly Reproduction among Egyptian Women: Maternal Mortality and the Medicalization of Population Control. In *Conceiving the New World Order,* eds. Faye Ginsburg and Rayna Rapp, 162–176. Berkeley: University of California Press.

Mott, Frank L., and Susan H. Mott

1985   Household Fertility Decisions in West Africa: A Comparison of Male and Female Survey Results. *Studies in Family Planning* 16(2):88–99.

Muslim Brotherhood

1994   "Statement on the International Conference on Population and Development." Cairo: Islamic Center for Studies and Research.

Mussalam, Basim

1982   *Sex and Society in Islam.* Cambridge: Cambridge University Press.

Mustafa, M. A.

1982   *Male Attitudes towards Family Planning in Sudan.* Khartoum: Sudan Fertility Control Association.

Myers, Norman

1994   Population and the Environment: The Vital Linkages. In *Population, Environment, and Development.* Proceedings of the United Nations Expert Group Meeting on Population, Environment, and Development, Jan. 1992, United Nations, New York.

Naguib, Nora Guhl, and Cynthia Lloyd
1994   *Gender Inequalities and Demographic Behavior: The Case of Egypt.* Occasional Paper. New York: Population Council.
Najmabadi, Afsaneh
1993   Veiled Discourses—Unveiled Bodies. *Feminist Studies* 19(3):487–518.
Nassar, Heba
1992   "The Impact of Adjustment Policies on Nutrition in Egypt." Unpublished paper, prepared for the Twenty-ninth European Association of Agricultural Economists Seminar on Food and Agricultural Policies under Structural Adjustment, in Stuttgart, Germany.
National Population Council (NPC)
1992   *The Population Component in the Five Year Plan, Arab Republic of Egypt, 1992–1997.* Cairo.
Nawar, Laila, Cynthia Lloyd, and Barbara Ibrahim
1995   Women's Autonomy and Gender Roles in Egyptian Families. In *Family, Gender, and Population in the Middle East,* ed. Carla Makhlouf Obermeyer, 147–177.
Nelson, C.
1974   Public and Private: Women in the Middle Eastern World. *American Ethnologist* 1:551–563.
1996   *Doria Shafik, Egyptian Feminist.* Gainesville: University Press of Florida.
Obermeyer, Carla Makhlouf, ed.
1995   *Family, Gender, and Population in the Middle East.* Cairo: American University Press.
O'Hanlon, R., and D. Washbrook
1992   After Orientalism: Culture, Criticism, and Politics in the Third World. *Comparative Studies in Society and History* 34, no. 1.
Omran, Abdel Rahim
1992   Family Planning in the Legacy of Islam. London: Routledge (United Nations Population Fund).
Ong, Aihwa
1988   The Production of Possession: Spirits and the Multinational Corporations in Malaysia. *American Ethnologist* 15(1):28–42.
1995   State versus Islam: Malay Families, Women's Bodies, and the Body Politic in Malaysia. In *Bewitching Women, Pious Men: Gender and Body Politics in Southeast Asia,* eds. Aihwa Ong and Michael Peletz, 159–194. Berkeley: University of California Press.
Owen, Roger
1965   The Influence of Lord Cromer's Indian Experience on British Policy in Egypt, 1883–1907. In *St. Anthony Papers on Middle East Affairs,* no. 17, ed. Albert Hourani. London: Oxford University Press.
1969   *Cotton and the Egyptian Economy, 1820–1914.* London: Oxford University Press.
1987   *The Middle East in the World Economy, 1800–1914.* New York: Methuen.

1996   The Population Census of 1917 and Its Relationship to Egypt's Three Nineteenth Century Statistical Regimes. *Journal of Historical Sociology* 9(4): 457–472.

Pandolfo, Stephania
2000   The Thin Line in Modernity: Some Moroccan Debates on Subjectivity. In *Questions of Modernity*, ed. Timothy Mitchell, 115–147. Minneapolis: University of Minnesota Press.

Panzac, Daniel
1987   The Population of Egypt in the Nineteenth Century. *Asian and African Studies* 21:11–32.

Pateman, Carole
1988   *The Sexual Contract*. Palo Alto, Calif.: Stanford University Press.
1989   *The Disorder of Women*. Cambridge, England: Polity Press.

Petchesky, Rosalind
1995   The Body as Property: A Feminist Re-Vision. In *Conceiving the New World Order*, eds. Faye Ginsburg and Rayna Rapp, 387–406. Berkeley: University of California Press.

Peteet, Julie
1994   Male Gender and Rituals of Resistance in the Palestinian Intifada: A Cultural Politics of Violence. *American Ethnologist* 21(1):31–49.

Peters, Pauline
1983   Gender, Developmental Cycles, and Historical Process: A Critique of Recent Research on Women in Botswana. *Journal of South African Studies* 10(1): 100–122.

Pfeifer, Karen
1999   How Tunisia, Morocco, Jordan, and Even Egypt Became IMF "Success Stories" in the 1990s. *Middle East Report*, no. 210.

Pigg, Stacy L.
1997   "Found in Most Traditional Societies": Traditional Medical Practitioners between Culture and Development. In *International Development and Social Sciences*, eds. Frederick Cooper and Randall Packard, 259–290. Berkeley: University of California Press.

Pool, Robert
1994   On the Creation and Dissolution of Ethnomedical Systems in the Medical Ethnography of Africa. *Africa* 64(1):1–20.

Poovey, Mary
1992   The Abortion Question and the Death of Man. In *Feminists Theorize the Political*, eds. Judith Butler and Joan Scott, 239–256. London: Routledge.
1995   *Making a Social Body*. Chicago: University of Chicago Press.

Population Council
1992   *The Copper T380 Intrauterine Device: A Summary of Scientific Data*. New York: Population Council.
1994   *Population Growth and Our Caring Capacity*. Issue Paper. New York: Population Council.

Population Reports

1987a *Family Planning Programs: Counselling Makes a Difference.* Series 1, no. 35.

1987b *Why Counseling Counts.* Series 1, no. 36.

Prakash, Gyan

1992 Can the "Subaltern" Ride? A Reply to O'Hanlon and Washbrook. *Comparative Studies in Society and History* 34(1):168–185.

Preston, Samuel

1994 *Population and the Environment from Rio to Cairo.* Liège, Belgium: International Union for the Scientific Study of Population.

Radwan, Samir, and Eddy Lee

1986 *Agrarian Change in Egypt.* London: Croom Helm.

Rageb, Ahmed

1995 "Abortion Decision Making in an Illegal Context: A Case Study from Rural Egypt." Ph.D. thesis, University of Exeter, England.

Rapp, Rayna

1988 Chromosomes and Communication: The Discourse of Genetic Counselling. In *Medical Anthropology Quarterly* 2(2):143–157.

Rassam, Amal

1984 Toward a Theoretical Framework for the Study of Women in the Arab World. In *Social Science Research and Women in the Arab World,* ed. Amal Rassam, 122–138. London: Frances Pinter (UNESCO).

Richard, Alan

1982 *Egypt's Agricultural Development, 1800–1980.* Boulder, Colo.: Westview.

Riedmann, Agnes

1993 *Science That Colonizes: A Critique of Fertility Studies in Africa.* Philadelphia: Temple University Press.

Rieker, Martina

1996 "The Sa'idi in the City." Unpublished Ph.D. diss., Department of History, Temple University, Philadelphia.

n.d. "The Stories of Ahmad at-Tayyib and Others." Unpublished manuscript.

Roter, Debra

1995 Advancing the Physician's Contribution to Enhancing Compliance. In *Advancing Prescription Medicine Compliance.* Binghamton, N.Y.: Haworth Press.

Ruddick, Sara

1989 *Maternal Thinking: Towards a Politics of Peace.* Boston: Beacon.

Rugh, A.

1984 *Family in Contemporary Egypt.* Syracuse, N.Y.: Syracuse University Press.

Saab, Gabriel

1967 *The Egyptian Agrarian Reform, 1952–1962.* London: Oxford University Press.

Saad, Reem

1988 *Social History of an Agrarian Reform Community in Egypt.* Cairo Papers in Social Science, vol. 11, monograph 4. Cairo: American University in Cairo Press.

Saunders, Lucie Wood, and Sohair Mehanna

1988   Smallholders in a Changing Economy: An Egyptian Case. *Peasant Studies* 16(1):5–29.

Sayed, H.

1989   Population Policy in Egypt. In *Population Policies in the Third World: Issues and Practice.* Twenty-Fifth Commemorative Conference, 1988. Cairo: Cairo Demographic Center.

Al-Sayyid Marsot, Afaf Lutfi

1984   *Egypt in the Reign of Muhammad Ali.* Cambridge: Cambridge University Press.

Schneider, Jane, and Peter Schneider

1991   Sex and Respectability in an Age of Fertility Decline: A Sicilian Case Study. *Social Science and Medicine* 33(8): 885–895.

1995   High Fertility and Poverty in Sicily: Beyond the Culture vs. Rationality Debate. In *Situating Fertility,* ed. Susan Greenhalgh, 179–201. Cambridge: Cambridge University Press.

Schulze, Richard

1991   Colonization and Resistance: The Egyptian Peasant Rebellion, 1919. In *Peasants and Politics in the Modern Middle East,* eds. Farhad Kazemi and John Waterbury, 171–202. Miami: Florida International University Press.

Scott, David

1995   Colonial Governmentality. *Social Text* 43:191–220.

1999   *Refashioning Futures.* Princeton, N.J.: Princeton University Press.

Seif El-Dawla, Aida, Amal Abdel Hadi, and Nadia Abdel Wahab

1998   Women's Wit over Men. In *Negotiating Reproductive Rights,* eds. Rosalind Petchesky and Karen Judd, 69–107. London: Zed Books.

Sen, Amartya

1994   Population: Delusion and Reality. In *New York Review of Books* 41:15 (22 September).

Sen, Gita, Adrienne Germaine, and Lincoln C. Chen

1994   *Population Policies Reconsidered.* Harvard Series on Population and International Health. Cambridge: Harvard University Press.

Shakry, Omnia

1998   Schooled Mothers and Structured Play: Child Rearing in Turn-of-the-Century Egypt. In *Remaking Women,* ed. Lila Abu-Lughod, 126–170. Princeton, N.J.: Princeton University Press.

Sobhy, Gorgy

1904   Customs and Superstitions of the Modern Egyptians. *Records of the Egyptian Government School of Medicine,* vol. 2, 101–120.

Social Planning and Analysis and Administration Consultants (SPAAC)

1990   *Qualitative Study of Oral Contraceptive Use in Egypt: Interviews with OC Users and Providers.* Cairo: National Population Council.

Spivak, Gayatri Chakravorty

1995   Empowering Women. *Environment* 37(1):2–3.

1996a Diasporas Old and New: Women in the Transnational World. *Textual Practice* 10(2):245–269.

1996b Woman as Theatre. *Radical Philosophy* 75:2–4.

Springborg, Robert

1990a Agrarian Bourgeoisie, Semiproletarians, and the Egyptian State: Lessons for Liberalization. *International Journal of Middle East Studies* 22:447–472.

1990b Rolling Back Egypt's Agrarian Reform. *Middle East Report,* 166:28–30, 38.

St. John, Bayle

1973 (1852) *Village Life in Egypt.* New York: Arno.

Stacey, Judith

1996 *In the Name of the Family.* Boston: Beacon.

Strathern, Marilyn

1988 *The Gender of the Gift.* Berkeley: University of California Press.

Sullivan, Denis

1994 *Private Voluntary Organizations in Egypt.* Gainesville: University Press of Florida.

Tamari, Salim

1992 Soul of the Nation: The Fallah in the Eyes of the Urban Intelligentsia. *Review of Middle East Studies* 5:74–83.

Tantawi, Mohammed Sayed

1988 *Birth Planning and the Religious Point of View.* Cairo: Al-Azhar University.

Taussig, Michael

1980 Reification and the Consciousness of the Patient. *Social Science in Medicine* 14B:3–13.

Tekce, Belgin, Linda Oldham, and Frederic Shorter

1994 *A Place to Live.* Cairo: American University in Cairo Press.

Thompson, Warren

1929 Population. *American Journal of Sociology* 34(6):959–975.

Toth, James

1991 Pride, Purdah, or Paychecks: What Maintains the Gender Division of Labor in Rural Egypt. In *International Journal of Middle East Studies* 23:213–236.

Toubia, Nahid, and Abdullahi An-Na'im

n.d. "Legal Dimensions of the Health of Women in Arab and Muslim Countries." Unpublished working manuscript for the Population Council and Ford Foundation.

Trouillot, Michel-Rolph

1991 Anthropology and the Savage Slot. In *Recapturing Anthropology,* ed. Richard Fox, 17–44. Santa Fe, N.M.: School of American Research Press.

1995 *Silencing the Past.* Boston: Beacon.

2001 The Anthropology of the State in the Age of Globalization. *Current Anthropology* 42(1):125–138.

Tsing, Anna L.

1993 *In the Realm of the Diamond Queen.* Princeton, N.J.: Princeton University Press.

1997   Transitions and Translations. In *Transitions, Environments, Translations,* eds. Joan Scott, Cora Kaplan, and Debra Keates, 253–272. New York: Routledge.

Tucker, Judith

1985   *Women in Nineteenth Century Egypt.* Cambridge: Cambridge University Press.

1993   The Arab Family in History. In *The Arab Family in Egypt,* ed. Judith Tucker, 195–207. Bloomington: Indiana University Press.

United Nations

1990   *Population Growth and Policies in Mega-Cities, Cairo.* Population Policy Paper, no. 34. New York: Dept. of International Economic and Social Affairs.

United Nations Development Programme

1992   *Strategies for Sustainable Development in Egypt.* Cairo.

1994   "Human Development Report." Unpublished report. Cairo.

United States Embassy in Cairo

1992   *Foreign Economic Trends and Their Implications for the United States.* Report for the Arab Republic of Egypt.

1993   *Foreign Economic Trends and Their Implications for the United States.* Report for the Arab Republic of Egypt.

USAID

1982   *Egypt Population Sector Assessment.* Washington, D.C.: American Public Health Association.

1982   *Informal Housing in Egypt.* USAID Documents. Cairo: ABT Associates.

1987   *Population Program in Egypt.* Cairo.

1992   *USAID Status Report: United States Economic Assistance to Egypt.*

Vaughan, Megan

1991   *Curing Their Ills.* Stanford, Calif.: Stanford University Press.

Visweswaran, Kamala

1994   Betrayal: An Analysis in Three Acts. In *Scattered Hegemonies,* eds. Inderpal Grewal and Caren Kaplan, 90–109. Minneapolis: University of Minnesota Press.

1996   Small Speeches, Subaltern Gender: Nationalist Ideology and Its Historiography. In *Subaltern Studies 9,* eds. Shahid Amin and Dipesh Chakrabarty. Delhi: Oxford University Press.

Wahba, Mourad Magdi

1993   The Nationalization of the IMF: The Nature and Evolution of the Official Discourse on Economic Reform in Egypt (1987–1991). In *The Economics and Politics of Structural Adjustment, Third Annual Symposium.* Cairo Papers in Social Science 16(3):51–62. Cairo: American University in Cairo Press.

Walker, John

1934   *Folk Medicine in Modern Egypt.* London: Luzac and Co.

Watkins, Susan Cotts

1986   Conclusions. In *The Decline in Fertility in Europe,* eds. Ansley Coale and Susan Watkins, 420–449. Princeton, N.J.: Princeton University Press.

1993   If All We Knew about Women Was What We Read in Demography, What Would We Know? *Demography* 30(4):551–577.

Weiss, Linda

1997   Globalization and the Myth of the Powerless State. *New Left Review,* no. 225, 3–27.

Wilson, Ella M.

1934   Zagazig: A Cotton Market. *The Geographic Review,* no. 24.

World Bank

1984   *Status Report on Population Problems and Programs of Egypt.* (Sept.). Washington, D.C.

Younis, Nabil, Hind Khattab, Huda Zurayk, M. El-Mouelhy, M. Fadle Amin, and A.M. Farag

1993   A Community Study of Gynecological and Related Morbidities in Rural Egypt. *Studies in Family Planning* 24(3):175–186.

Zalouk, Malak

1990   *Women, Preliminary Data for Labour Information System Project.* Cairo: CAPMAS.

Zurayk, Huda, Nabil Younis, and Hind Khattab

1994   *Rethinking Family Planning Policy in Light of Reproductive Health Research.* Cairo: Population Council.

1995   Comparing Women's Report with Medical Diagnoses of Reproductive Morbidity Conditions in Rural Egypt. *Studies in Family Planning* 26(1): 14–21.

SURVEYS

Central Agency for Public Mobilization and Statistics (CAPMAS)

1986   Census of Population, Housing, and Establishments. Cairo.

Egyptian Demographic and Health Survey (DHS)

1988   National Population Council. Macro International Inc. Cairo and Columbia, Md.

Egypt Demographic and Health Survey (DHS)

1992   National Population Council (Egypt) and Macro International (USA). Cairo and Calverton, Md.

Egypt Demographic and Health Survey (DHS)

1996   National Population Council (Egypt) and Macro International (USA). Cairo and Calverton, Md.

Egypt Male Survey (1991)

1992   Cairo Demographic Center. Macro International Inc. Cairo and Columbia, Md.

Role of Egyptian Women in the Family (ROWIF)

1991   CAPMAS (Central Agency for Public Mobilization and Statistics). Cairo.

NEWSPAPERS AND PERIODICALS

Al-Ahram Weekly, 21–27 April 1994.
Al-Mussawer, 26 November 1993 (Arabic).
Al-Shaʿb, 24 June 1994 (Arabic).
Sabah el-Kheir, 13 January 1994 (Arabic).
Egyptian Gazette, 25 June 1952, 17 July 1993, 1 July 1994.

Index

194n.20; reproductive-tract diseases of, 145–146; and sexual relationships and sexual pleasure, 80–83, 130–131, 132, 155; side effects of contraceptives on, 34, 52–58, 102, 110, 112–114, 129, 145, 148, 176n.23, 176n.25–26, 189–190nn.16–17; as target of family planning program, 5. *See also* women

feminism, 6, 14, 30, 60, 99–100, 139, 144, 147, 149–152, 193n.15, 193n.17, 194n.19, 194n.27, 196n.5

Ferguson, James, 171n.16

Fernandez-Kelly, Patricia, 104

fertility, 88–90, 91, 93, 110, 119, 127, 128, 185n.9, 189n.13

fertility control. *See* contraception; family planning; population control

fertility rates, 26–31, 33, 169n.4, 173n.27, 174n.10, 176n.21

fitna (disorder), 131, 191n.10

focus groups, 7, 40, 80–85, 152, 184n.2

food and nutrition, 3, 4, 65, 77–78, 79, 102, 113, 114, 131–132, 135, 143, 170n.7, 182n.17, 189n.16. *See also* agriculture

Ford Foundation, 17, 144

Foucault, Michel, 14, 83, 123, 167, 171n.18, 173n.28, 197n.4

Fraser, Gertrude, 185n.5

free subjects and free will, 48, 54, 59

free trade, 5, 172n.22

Freedman, Lynn, 70

freedom, 13, 33. *See also* individual choice

fright (*khadda*), 95–96, 187n.19

funerals, 92

Futures Group, 38

gamaya (saving schemes), 76

Gambia, 189n.10

GATHER acronym, 52

GDP, 3, 170n.7

gender relations: in *aila* (larger family/clan), 108, 189n.9; and domestic realm in Egyptian colonial period, 140–143, 153–154; in Egypt and Egyptian families, 35, 41–46, 121, 122, 124–129, 131, 133–135, 140–143, 153–154, 157–158, 167, 178n.3, 188n.2; and empowerment of women, 33, 103, 146; and Islam, 157–158; in Middle East generally, 6, 37; and "patriarchal bargain," 135, 191n.11; reason-as-to-male versus passion-as-to-female ideology, 96, 117–118, 190n.19; self and gendered norms, 99; and social change, 131–134; struggles over, in modern state, 15; in *usra* (immediate family), 108; and wages, 182n.18. *See also* men; women

genetic counseling, 179n.13

gharbal (sieve-like structure), 185n.8

gharbiyya, 66

Giza, 183n.24

Giza Study, 145–149, 194n.22

globalization, 4, 4–5, 13, 166, 168

God's will. *See* fatalism and God's will

government, 14, 59–60, 171n.18, 179n.12. *See also* citizenship; state

Gramsci, Antonio, 140, 163, 173n.26, 197n.4

Great Britain. *See* Britain

Greenhalgh, Susan, 44

Guha, Ranajit, 140

El-Guindi, Fadwa, 183n.20

Gulf War, 3, 68

Gupta, Akhil, 169n.2

Hacking, Ian, 178n.5

Haiti, 30

hakimas (midwives), 142, 185n.4, 193n.13

Harb, Talat, 195n.1

Harriman Foundation, 28

Hashim, Labiba, 193n.9

health: as civic responsibility, 13; and culture, 7–8; and Islam, 158, 159, 196n.7; Muhammad Ali's program on, 174n.3; payer-supported health delivery system in Egypt, 190n.18; USAID initiatives on, 35; women's health issues, 37, 47, 54–55, 114–116, 127, 145–146, 179n.14. *See also* contraception; diseases; doctors; family planning

Health and Insurance Organization, 176n.18

hegemony, 140

Helwan, 70

hijab (veil), 183n.20

Hofriyati villagers, 91

Hopkins, Nicholas, 180n.6, 182n.14

Horn, David, 173n.27

housing, 66–67, 71–77, 132, 143, 167, 183n.23, 183–184n.25, 184n.27

human rights, 37, 147, 149, 151, 194n.22, 197n.2. *See also* reproductive rights; women's rights

humidity (*ratuba*), 90, 186n.10

Ibrahim, Saad Eddin, 37–38, 177n.30

ICPD (International Conference on Population and Development), 30, 144, 149, 155, 197n.3

identity politics, 194n.21

Idris, 68, 69

Idris, Yusuf, 127

IEC (Information, Education, and Communication) programs, 30, 40–41, 46

imams, 26

IMF. *See* International Monetary Fund (IMF)

impotence, 127, 129, 130, 131, 133, 135

income, 3, 14, 68–69, 77–78, 115, 132, 143, 170n.7. *See also* poverty